A KID FROM PITTSBURGH

A baptism of fire from reform school to World War II

By
Marion Rosen

With
Morris Rosen

Copyright © 2009 by Marion Rosen

All rights reserved. No part of this book shall be reproduced or transmitted in any form or by any means, electronic, mechanical, magnetic, photographic including photocopying, recording or by any information storage and retrieval system, without prior written permission of the publisher. No patent liability is assumed with respect to the use of the information contained herein. Although every precaution has been taken in the preparation of this book, the publisher and author assume no responsibility for errors or omissions. Neither is any liability assumed for damages resulting from the use of the information contained herein.

ISBN 0-7414-5374-6

Published by:

INFINITY
PUBLISHING.COM

1094 New DeHaven Street, Suite 100
West Conshohocken, PA 19428-2713
Info@buybooksontheweb.com
www.buybooksontheweb.com
Toll-free (877) BUY BOOK
Local Phone (610) 941-9999
Fax (610) 941-9959

Printed in the United States of America
Published May 2009

Author's Note

Morris Rosen faced more experiences that seem almost beyond belief before he reached the age of 21 than most people encounter in a lifetime. This book is my husband's story, but writing it evolved into my responsibility and pleasure. I am proud to relate his story not from the viewpoint of a general or other high official, but from that of a private who inadvertently landed the dangerous job of forward observer. This assignment required him to cautiously edge into enemy territory in order to radio back the co-ordinates necessary for directing artillery fire.

All the events in this story are true. Many names you will recognize. Some names my husband never knew or couldn't remember. In these cases I refer to a person simply by rank such as lieutenant or colonel. In a few cases, I changed the name for reasons of sensitivity or provided a "nickname" for the individual.

Surprisingly, my husband remembered many significant dialogues spoken so many years ago. I added a few responses to the words actually spoken to maintain continuity in conversations. My intent was to make this biography read more like a novel than a military treatise.

Even though all events in this story actually happened this is not meant to be a reference book. It is simply a history based on the greenest of many green recruits sent from U.S. towns, cities, and farms to lands completely foreign. They fought in a world war that even some of the generals in charge did not fully understand. It wasn't until the end of the war when Morris Rosen participated in the liberation of the concentration camp at Dachau, Germany that the rationale for the war became fully evident to him.

This book is dedicated to Morris "Morrie" Rosen and all the men who made it home from the carnage and heartbreak of World War II and especially to those who didn't.

Marion Rosen

A Kid from Pittsburgh

Morris Rosen, age 18

Chapter 1

Stark, white light glaring from the relentless North African sun nearly blinded him, but Private Morris Rosen charged toward the waiting train at a run. Sweat ran down his neck. It was hot, but at least it wasn't summer, not yet anyway. He heaved forty pounds of gear and his Springfield rifle over his head before he shinned up the side of the railroad car.

Close to Rosen's ear one of the other soldiers complained at full volume, "Holy, Jesus. It smells like cow shit in here."

Rosen looked up at the guy, but the guy wasn't talking to him, just grumbling to anyone who happened to be in earshot.

And it did smell. Wait a minute. God, it *was* cow shit. They were transporting the artillerymen of the U.S. Ninth Infantry Division in filthy old cattle cars. The animals were gone, but bits of cow or maybe sheep droppings remained imbedded deep within the cracks in the floor. He kicked at a tell-tale clump of straw and manure that stuck tenaciously to one of the wide planks.

"Move it," Sergeant Miller yelled. "This ain't no goddamn Boy Scout picnic. Move."

Miller was thick set with wide shoulders hunched up so high it looked as if he didn't have a neck. From the way Sergeant Miller's face sagged, Rosen figured he'd been in the army a very long time.

Endless columns of soldiers hustled toward the train and pulled themselves aboard until twenty or more guys had wedged into each car. They sat on their packs or stretched out and used their gear as mulish, uncomfortable pillows. Rosen positioned himself next to one of the two open doors so he could breathe easier.

The other men settled down and continued mumbling to no one in particular. They were all brand new recruits. They had yet to learn just how bad things could get in the army. Some were still thinking like civilians and believed it was only natural to feel incensed about the crowded, smelly railroad car. Others complained to fill the void, perhaps to convince themselves they'd signed up for a noble cause even as they were being hauled off to war in a cattle car. Then there were those who simply complained about everything.

"Man, you're breaking my goddamn foot."

"So get your goddamn foot out of my way."

"I gotta have air. It stinks like a sewer in this fucking train."

"So, it reminds you of your first date?"

Rosen laughed along with the others, but he didn't join into the conversation. He knew how easy a volley like this could turn on a guy. Next thing he knew, someone would make a crack about him being "The Kid" in the outfit. Or if things got nasty, someone would end up calling him "Jew Boy." He'd gotten into enough fights to know when to keep his mouth shut, at least most of the time.

Rosen just wanted to arrive at their destination in Algeria or Tunisia or wherever the Americans were pitted against the German Army east of Casablanca and see some action. He'd finished radio school back in Ft. Meade and was shipped out to the Atlantic coast of French Morocco shortly after his eighteenth birthday. The army had conveniently managed to overlook the fact that he'd signed on at seventeen. By 1942, the army recruiters had probably figured that Uncle Sam would need hundreds of thousands of men—of any age—to crush Hitler.

Rosen still hadn't been issued his radio, but he was ready for action, any kind of action. Like the rest of the guys in his division, he'd volunteered to join the army, and now he wanted to see what this war was all about. He wanted the Germans to know who they were up against. Give them a taste of their own medicine. He'd volunteered to travel thousands of miles from home to battle those aggressive Nazi Krauts, but Rosen was trying not to clash with his fellow soldiers. It would be smarter to keep his fists to himself and stay out of trouble no matter how often they goaded him to fight.

The artillerymen continued to gripe about the lingering smell of manure and shoved as close to the two sliding doors as they could. As the railroad car grew warmer, the men gradually stopped grousing. It didn't do a bit of good anyway since Sergeant Miller paid no attention to the men or their torrent of complaints. A few men tried to sleep; others sipped water from their canteens and spit out onto the parched, barren land.

In true army tradition, the men had hurried to board the train that would transport them out of Casablanca only to sit and wait and wait for it to pull out. The other railroad cars had been loaded with men and gear. The big artillery guns would go by truck. The cars coupled to the train stretched along the track as far as Rosen could see. It didn't seem possible that a single steam locomotive could pull this colossal weight, but gradually the wheels began to groan and screech, plunging forward in struggling, jerky leaps. The train was finally moving.

Carlyle worked his way over from his spot by the door on the opposite side of the car and squeezed in next to Rosen.

"Hey, Kid, looks like we're finally going to get into it."

Rosen grinned. Carlyle had been his tent mate while they'd briefly bivouacked in Casablanca, waiting for orders. But he'd first connected with Carlyle at Ft. Meade and again when his troop ship had landed at Safi in French Morocco. From there they'd moved on to Port Lyaute where they'd spent two weeks training in the Moroccan National Cork Forest. Those two weeks of training in the African sun had given Rosen and Carlyle dark, evenly tanned faces and arms.

Carlyle seemed like an all right guy, not a total wise ass like some of the others. He had one of those smiles that you couldn't remove with a chisel. And he smiled all the time, showing off his perfectly aligned white teeth. Rosen had good teeth, too, but he wasn't used to being all friendly and outgoing, not like Carlyle.

"Yeah," Rosen answered. "Finally. So where're we headed?"

"Shit if I know. Some godforsaken hole called Oran is what I heard."

"How far's that?"

"I heard 800, maybe 1000 miles."

Rosen's eyes grew wide. "Shit. At the rate we're traveling, it'll take us a week to get there."

"Yeah."

"Just where is this Oran?"

Carlyle shrugged. "Out there somewhere."

They both gazed toward the horizon. The late morning sun imparted a silvery sheen to the sand. The cloudless sky was clear blue, like a robin's egg. Rosen marveled at how his vision had improved since the army had issued him his first pair of eye glasses back at Fort Meade. He'd never had money for glasses back home. In fact he'd never had an eye exam before he'd joined the army.

Carlyle said, "Don't know why folks would want to live in a dried-up desert. I like trees and grass, you know, like we have at home."

Rosen watched Carlyle spit out through the door. His face was flecked with at least two days worth of stubby whiskers. He hadn't bothered to shave before they were told to march to today's point of departure, but then Rosen hadn't shaved either.

Rosen stood only five-ten, but he was all muscle. Being built like a Roman fortress helped to overshadow his smooth, youthful features surrounded by tawny natural curls. His beard was slow in coming in, but he went through the motions of shaving once a week just so the guys wouldn't start up with him. Usually some joker would start up anyway.

"Hey, Kid, how many whiskers you got now?"

"He's up to three," someone else would chime in.

"Aw, he's got a baby face."

"Smooth as a baby's ass."

The guys found every quip to be uproariously funny. It didn't take more than a tired one-liner to set them off. Everything sent them into hoots of laughter. Sometimes nothing at all sent them into outright hysterics leaving them helplessly doubled over. But Rosen was slowly learning to take a little bit more flak from the other guys. He didn't immediately get his hackles up the way he used to when he was a kid back home in Pittsburgh, back on the streets where he'd gotten his first hands-on training for battle.

Carlyle spit again. Rosen spit, too. Their spittle disappeared the moment it hit the ground, instantly absorbed into the hot sand.

Just then a guy everyone called Dago pushed between them and jumped down from the train.

"Hey, you dumb Dago," someone yelled. "Where the fuck you going?"

"For a walk." Dago frequently put on a show of acting like he wasn't quite right in the head. Maybe it wasn't an act.

"Get back on the train."

Dago laughed. "Look, I'm going as fast as the train. And it smells better out here."

It was true. The train lumbered along so slowly, Dago was keeping up without breaking a sweat.

"Come on, you mugs. Don't you want to stay in shape? How you gonna whup those Krauts if you don't stay in shape?" Dago did a little jig, ran a few paces then jumped into a march.

Sergeant Miller was the only non-com in their car. He glanced at Dago trotting along next to the train but didn't seem concerned. Dago wasn't about to get lost; nobody was shooting at him. He ignored Dago just like he ignored the rest of the men. The sarge paid attention only when absolutely necessary.

Dago continued his antics, cavorting along next to the train. His Italian lineage showed in his black eyes and his thick, dark hair. Rosen had grown up in an Italian neighborhood, and the kids he'd known were always clowning around. When they weren't acting goofy, their Latin tempers could explode into tirades of outrage. Sometimes the Italians seemed even more impossible to understand than the Jews.

The others soon took turns jumping off the train and walking or running for a while. Rosen stretched his legs and ran along with the others, happy to have something to do. It released the boredom of just sitting and staring out into the bleak landscape of eastern Morocco.

Eventually the guys opened tins of C rations and ate the lukewarm hash or meat and beans more out of habit than hunger. The air buzzed with flies and gnats. Even the cigarette smoke didn't deter the insect population from checking into those tins. They tossed empty tins out into the desert, even though some of the men knew it was wrong to dump their garbage along the train tracks. Most didn't think or care about that. Rosen threw away his empty tins just to get rid of the flies. He'd never seen so many flies in one place, and he wondered how the flies had so quickly detected food out here in the middle of nowhere.

The sun was sinking, pulling the sky down to the sands they'd just crossed in the west. The train ground to a stop and the whistle sounded. Up ahead, the engineer was waving and calling to a ragged band of Arabs. The Arabs in turn were nonchalantly swatting at a herd of burros loaded down with large pottery water jars precariously strapped to their backs. The Arabs cried out orders to the burros, or maybe they were simply cussing at them, but they shouted without putting a whole lot of energy into their words. The Arabs seemed to do everything in slow motion.

Sergeant Miller said they had ten minutes while the train took on coal and water. The men scrambled off the train in search of a place to dig a quick latrine. They didn't have a whole lot of choices. Any little berm of sand or a pile of dirt was good enough. The niceties of life in America had not followed the troops to North Africa. The ten minutes stretched into 30 before the train started up again.

Night came on suddenly, dark and deep, enclosing the long, slowly-moving train in purple-blue edges. Rosen remained in his spot by the door even though some had moved closer to the center of the car. Maybe they feared they'd roll in their sleep and fall off the train. Rosen didn't care why they'd moved. He now had a bit more room to stretch out, and that felt great. He was still getting used to the strange newness of army life, men packed into tight surroundings, all the orders, the uncertainty of what would happen next.

Someone said, "This goddamn place is blacker than Satan's soul." It sounded like Dago's voice.

"Damn straight."

"Fucking A."

"Go to sleep," another voice growled.

Rosen slipped his glasses into his breast pocket. He then settled against his pack, punching down something sharp. It wasn't much of a pillow, but he had gradually learned to adapt to all the inconveniences the army provided at no extra charge. Not much worse than the harsh reality of the life he'd known as a boy in Pittsburgh.

A few cigarette tips flared here and there in the car. The men had mostly stopped talking. Even Dago had grown quiet. Rosen thought about his mother, his brothers and his little sister. He hoped they had enough to eat. He refused to let any thoughts or visions of his father enter his mind.

Hundreds of stars winked in the cloudless sky. Rosen searched for the moon, but he couldn't spot it. It was probably low on the horizon, lazing somewhere behind the train. He finally gave in to sleep as the train rattled monotonously on and on into the night.

Chapter 2

Rosen's second day of travel in the ancient cattle car wasn't much different from the first. Pathetic little stands of dusty, stunted palm trees now appeared at wider intervals, miraculously sprouting through the desert sands, but otherwise the tedious Moroccan landscape hadn't changed since the train had pulled away from the railway station at Casablanca. No matter which direction Rosen looked, the sky and the sand radiated the same undulating blur of heat. An oppressive hot breeze seemed to emanate from somewhere near the sun, pushing down on them, shifting the top layer of sand first one way, then another.

At least he'd had some adventure before they'd boarded the train. Following their training session, Rosen's outfit had spent a few weeks stationed at a camp just outside of Casablanca. Visiting Casablanca, with its narrow streets snaking between the low mud-colored stucco structures, had seemed unbelievable, nothing like anything Rosen had ever encountered in Pennsylvania. He'd even had the thrill of seeing the president of the United States, Franklin Delano Roosevelt and Prime Minister Winston Churchill of Great Britain up close, no more than 20 feet away from where he stood.

    Rosen had been walking next to a long row of tents at the Casablanca campsite when the sound of approaching motorcycles ripped through the morning air. He hurried closer to the road to get a better look at what was going on. He spotted a black command car followed by an open jeep traveling away from the city. The jeep was flanked by two shiny British motorcycles. FDR and the prime minister sat side by side in the back seat of the jeep, right out in the open. They looked exactly like their pictures in the newspapers, except they weren't smiling. The prime minister puffed on a fat cigar, his eyes lowered as he listened attentively to the American president.

    Rosen waved frantically, but the president seemed deep in conversation and didn't wave back. They must be headed for a briefing with all the generals, Rosen thought, but maybe FDR and the prime minister also wanted to see how the Allied troops were doing in North Africa. He waved again as the convoy drove past. He was still waving at the tail end of the jeep as it disappeared from view.

    Yeah, Casablanca had been an exciting experience for a teenage kid from Pittsburgh. Rosen had been intrigued by all the activity, the unusual sounds, even the overpowering aromas of exotic spices. The crowd pulsated; far too many people jostled each other for space in the open areas, especially in the marketplaces that were loosely tossed together along street after street.

In the markets, the repetitive daily exchange of a few coins for food escalated to an astonishingly raucous bedlam. The hawkers selling their wares couldn't seem to conduct business without a lengthy harangue of bargaining and quarreling. The women selected items they wanted to buy, setting off a pandemonium of barter, haggling over every egg, every wedge of flattened bread, or small gunny sacks of grain.

Rosen found it hard to believe that so many people could actually make a living by selling those round flat breads, but apparently they did. He wanted to buy a cup of coffee from a one-eyed Arab vendor who spoke no English, but Rosen had only some loose American change in his pocket. He handed the vendor one thin dime. The Arab bit into it and when satisfied that it was real silver, Rosen got a taste of the thickest, strongest coffee he'd ever sampled. The coffee, in fact, set off a buzz in his head.

Rosen was also fascinated by the guttural din of unfamiliar languages that penetrated the colorful marketplaces and the gaudy, smoke-filled cafes. Rosen spoke English he'd learned in school, Yiddish he'd learned from his parents, and Italian he'd learned from the kids in his neighborhood, but he also wanted to understand the men shouting in

Arabic and French or a jumble of both. The Moroccans seemed to enjoy a need to out-shout one another, and Rosen would've liked to join in, to understand what the shouting was all about. He wanted to absorb everything.

He'd even become interested in learning about the solar hot water heaters he'd seen on the rooftops of the European homes in Casablanca. His buddy, Carlyle had pointed them out to him. The Europeans, mostly French, enjoyed more conveniences than the Arabs, but life was still primitive. Even compared to Rosen's run-down neighborhood in Pittsburgh, Casablanca lagged centuries behind the progress that had made America such an attraction to people from all over the world.

But the best part about their stay in Casablanca had been Rosen's first visit to a bar. Rosen and Carlyle had finished training maneuvers for the day and had the evening off. They decided to explore the wreckage of a ship that had been scuttled on the narrow beach outside of the city. Rosen was intrigued simply by the prospect of investigating a shipwreck, but Carlyle soon dragged Rosen away from the wreck and into a little tavern he'd noticed nearby.

"C'mon," Carlyle said. "I'll buy you a drink."

Rosen was still a kid. His previous experience with alcohol hadn't gone beyond the few sips of kosher wine that accompanied the Jewish celebrations and holidays such as Passover. Besides, he'd never had money for anything like a drink in a bar.

"I don't know," he answered.

"C'mon, we'll be shipped out of here soon. They probably won't have any booze at all where we're going. What can it hurt?"

Rosen finally agreed and Carlyle ordered a bottle of red wine. Rosen sipped it slowly at first, but he quickly got into the spirit of things. The two of them drained the bottle. Carlyle ordered a second bottle and topped off Rosen's glass. Then Carlyle began singing:

> *There was a little bird, no bigger than a turd,*
> *Sitting on a telephone pole.*
> *He pulled in his neck and shit about a peck*
> *And puckered up his little asshole.*

Rosen joined in and the two of them got drunk. Actually they got very drunk. They finally staggered back to camp, arm in arm, still merrily singing about the little bird.

Time passed slowly as the train labored between its frequent stops. The men in the Ninth Division again ate C rations from tins and took slow, measured sips of water from their canteens. The terrain was still mostly desert, but occasionally they'd pass a windswept field of grain, scrawny herds of cattle, or stacks of hay bound in loose bales sitting along the railroad tracks, all signs that they were approaching an Arab village.

"Hot damn," Dago shouted, "I see a bunch of cows up ahead."

"That's a mirage," one guy said.

Another guy laughed. "You crazy bastard. Next you'll be seeing cow girls roping those heifers."

"No," Dago said. "Look for yourselves. If they got fucking cows, they got farmers. If they got farmers, they got daughters."

Now they were all at the door, straining to see up ahead. The men who were running along next to the train, jumped back on board.

"Ooh, la, la, bring on the girls." Dago began to half-sing, half-whistle his "girlie show" music. He was compact but muscular for someone so short. When he went into his version of "The Dance of the Seven Veils," his wiry motions caught everyone's attention. He had a twisting, sinewy way of moving his hips, almost like a woman.

"Jesus, Dago, if you had tits I'd go for you."

"Aw, don't hurt the girlie's feelings."

"Guys like Dago ain't got no feelings."

The guys started hooting, urging him on. It didn't take much to get Dago and some of the others cranked up to a near frenzy. Johnson, who was married and usually more circumspect, started dancing with Dago.

Tucker, or Friar Tuck as they now called him, chimed in with his harmonica. Rosen and Carlyle joined the guys who were clapping, goading on the craziness because they had nothing better to do.

"Hey, Dago, how much time you need to fuck one of those A-Rab beauties?"

"Not much."

The laughter grew louder, drowning out the tedious clacking of the train's wheels.

"I'm gonna get me some," Dago cried.

"Hey, I thought you was Cat-o-lic. Ain't fucking A-Rabs against your religion?"

"Not my religion."

"Yeah," one of the guys chimed in, "he goes to Our Lady of Perpetual Poontang."

The sound level shot ever higher. They'd reached the cattle that Dago had spotted earlier, and now a few of the drowsy, dull animals looked up.

"Hey, there's something you can fuck!"

"No," Dago insisted, "them cows look too much like your mother."

The whistle sounded. The train stopped next to an enormous pile of twigs. An old man was methodically tying the twigs—two or three at a time—onto the back of a donkey. He looked up for a moment then nonchalantly went back to his twigs. The American Army with their rowdy soldiers held no interest for him.

It was a tiny village with only a few crumbling stucco houses. Lean-to-style tents near the houses shaded burros, larger donkeys, and a horse or two. Rosen watched as the seemingly lifeless houses began to disgorge people who scurried toward the train. A boy, who looked to be no more than 12, pulled a little girl by the wrist toward the tracks.

"Fique, figue. My seester figue. One dollar."

The boy pushed the younger girl ahead of him, shoving her right up to the train. She was seven or eight at the most, and she looked terrified. She was covered with nothing more than a long skirt, a dirty length of cloth fashioned haphazardly around her waist. Her flat, undeveloped chest was completely exposed.

Dago stepped forward. "What's he saying?"

"What? Are you stupid?" Johnson said. "He's selling his sister."

Friar Tuck called out, "Hey, let's all chip in and give Dago a buck."

Dago was crowing and flapping his arms like a chicken. He seemed ready to go along with anything the other guys suggested.

Rosen thought of his sister Molly as he watched the fear in the little girl's face intensify. He remembered guys like Dago from back home; they grabbed at women, even young girls, like they owned them before they even knew their names. Rosen jumped off the train and decided right then and there that he would beat the crap out of any guy who touched this child.

Of course, Dago had no idea what Rosen had on his mind, but it didn't really matter, for Sergeant Miller had begun to stir. He'd lain in his corner of the railroad car, supposedly ignoring all that was going on. The guys had almost forgotten he was there.

Miller sat up and came to life like a grizzly awakening from hibernation. His face was puffy, the puffiness partially hiding his eyes. A little pocket of spit had accumulated in one corner of his mouth.

Something about Sergeant Miller suggested a strut when he wasn't even moving. He spoke slowly; his fiery eyes glared at Dago. "Dago, you set one foot off this fucking train and I'll put your sorry ass on report for the rest of this goddamn war."

Dago and the others froze. No one paid any attention to Rosen who stood with his back to the girl and her brother like her own personal bodyguard. The boy continued to shout around him, hawking his sister to the men. Rosen pulled two chocolate squares out of his shirt pocket. He turned and handed a chocolate to the boy and one to the girl.

"Take this and get out of here."

Confusion clouded their eyes, but they understood chocolate.

"Beat it." Rosen yelled. He waved his arms, swatting at the air to let them know he was dead serious. "Get out of here. Go home."

The kids raced back to their hovel, thrilled that they'd made such a huge profit with so little effort. Rosen hoped the boy wouldn't snatch the chocolate away from his sister, but then he noticed that she'd already stuffed her share into her mouth.

Someone muttered, "Goddamn Jew Boy's gone soft in the head."

"Did you see that? Jew Boy just up and gave them chocolate."

"Maybe Jew Boy wants the kid for himself?"

Miller said, "Shut up. All of you. Just shut the hell up."

The men went back to their games of dice and cards. Johnson got off the train and walked over to Rosen.

"So why'd you give them the chocolate?" Johnson asked. Somewhere in his early twenties, Johnson was a good-looking man in a cold, hard sort of way. Something about his eyes resembled the color of ice on a frozen pond, but so far he'd been friendly enough to Rosen.

"I don't know," Rosen answered. "It was just something I wanted to do. Dago's out of his mind. She's only a little kid."

They paced a few steps away from the car. "Yeah, I know. I guess it ain't easy for kids in this miserable hell hole. What a way to live."

Rosen kicked at a stone. "Yeah."

"You climbing back on?"

"Nah, I think I'll stay out here for a while."

"Don't let these guys get to you."

"Pisses me off when they call me Jew Boy."

"I know. They're stupid, but I think a lot of their fun and games is pure bullshit. They're scared to death, wondering if they're gonna catch a bullet in the gut during the course of this war."

"Sure," Rosen said. "We all think about that."

"Yeah, I know. Just don't write off all these guys. We're heading into some rough territory. Who knows what the hell we're gonna face. You might need one of these knucklehead bums to watch your back."

"Okay, I get it." Rosen picked up another stone and threw it off into the distance. "So, do you know where this train is going?"

"No one knows. The brass ain't talking. Just as well with all the big mouths we got on board."

The whistle sounded. The train was ready to move. Johnson climbed back into the train, but Rosen headed for the exterior iron ladder fastened near the front of the car. He placed his foot on the bottom rung and mounted one step at a time until he reached the roof. The train rammed into a gut-dropping lurch. Rosen grabbed hold of one of the fittings for balance. Once again they were creaking forward.

He sat down, cross-legged, and surveyed the desolate surroundings from this higher vantage point. Standing like sentinels along the railroad tracks, concrete telephone poles supported drooping wires. He'd learned that in the desert utility poles had to be constructed out of concrete because trees were so scarce. He couldn't imagine a place without trees, but here he was. The treeless landscape seemed liquefied by the heat, like everything had melted together, yet it wasn't all that hot. Except for the train tracks and the thick concrete poles, dreary, bone-dry, sandy nothingness seemed to stretch forever.

He looked back, somewhat astounded at the lengthy extent of the train. He couldn't even count how many cars followed his. He knew two were ahead, just behind the coal cars and the locomotive. Several guys were sitting on the roof of car number seven or eight and they waved to get his attention. Rosen smiled and waved back, but then he turned to face forward. He liked the heat of the pleasantly warm, fresh air pressing against his face.

The smoke from the steam engine sometimes shifted toward him, but the smoke didn't bother him either. Back home he'd learned to endure the extremely hot temperature of an iron-worker's forge while he hammered white hot iron into tools or other useful gadgets. Working and sweating long days in the heat of the forge now seemed like a foggy memory. He'd just turned 18, yet he felt as if the three years he'd worked before he'd enlisted in the army had taken place a very long time ago.

Sitting alone high on the roof of the train suited him just fine. He didn't mind being alone. He'd spent countless hours all by himself while he was growing up. Because his youthful exuberance had always been stifled by his father, anger, rebellion, and unhappiness instead had shaped his actions. He'd joined a street gang, actually did almost anything he could to get out of the house and away from his fanatically religious father and his unbending, abrasive rule.

His father. The tension had always quivered between Rosen and his father as if it were a living, breathing organism. Rosen's father displayed an anger that bordered on rage whenever his son displeased him, and that seemed to be almost constantly. His father's belt had taught him not to talk back, so as Rosen had grown older, he'd learned to hold his tongue. The beatings became less frequent. Father and son would then reach a livid stand-off, staring each other down in hot silence.

Rosen listened to the steady clanking of the train's wheels against the track. It had a hypnotic effect: clickety-clack, clickety-clack. Over and over.

He thought back to the last semester he'd attended school in Pittsburgh. He'd been 13 that year, in the eighth grade, five years or perhaps several lifetimes ago.

Chapter 3

At 13 Rosen had been a strong-willed tough kid, hanging out with a grungy gang of boys who'd looked up to him more or less as their leader. Except for Rosen, they were all Italian, and they stalked the dingy, cobblestone streets of their Pittsburgh neighborhood acting like they owned the world. They stayed out late at night, ignoring pleas and orders from parents. They never worried about following rules set in place by adults. They made their own rules.

As much as they roamed the streets at night, they did make an effort to attend school during the day. Some of the boys feared getting nabbed by the truant officer, but Rosen had his own reasons for showing up at school every day. He actually enjoyed learning. He was curious about everything. He often tried to teach his mother the highlights of what he'd learned in school each day, especially words in English. He wanted to teach her to read and write, something that had been denied her as a young girl in Russia.

One winter night in early March, Rosen had been feeling especially discontented. His father had groused at him and chased him out of the bedroom he shared with his two brothers because—according to his father—Rosen was wasting electricity. He was told to do his homework by the light of the single naked bulb that hung from a cord in the kitchen. Why was it that his father never listened to him? Rather than trying to explain that he didn't have enough room to work, or that it was too chaotic in the kitchen to really concentrate, Rosen stormed out of the house with his homework unfinished.

He rounded up several members of his gang, and they headed out to have some fun. They'd hoped to find a kid they could bully or a drunk who'd dropped a nickel, but the streets had just about emptied out for the night owing to the bitter cold and the late hour. The other boys were a sullen lot, but then Rosen thought all Italians had a mysterious, sulky look about them. But, as tough as they acted, their egos bruised easily.

Rosen usually didn't worry much about the cold night air, but the wind was starting to surge right through his thin cotton jacket. He guessed it was just about time to give up their bad boy routine and go home when a kid named Fredo tugged at his sleeve.

"Hey, Moach, look at that." Fredo pointed to a small appliance and electrical goods store directly across the street.

In those days Rosen responded to the name Moach, something the kids had picked up from Rosen's parents who spoke to him only in Yiddish, calling him Moishe. Behind his back and sometimes even to his face the kids called Rosen "Moach the Roach." He didn't mind his nickname; it gave him a kind of status with the gang.

Rosen stepped off the curb and crossed the street; the others followed.

"Lookit, Moach, sumbody threw a brick right through the window!"

"Hey, yeah," another kid cried out. "The brick's still in there."

They moved right up to the shattered store window. Broken glass lay everywhere.

"They didn't even take nuthin'. They just busted the window."

Rosen pointed to the merchandise lying right there within easy reach. "Anybody need a big cook pot?"

They all laughed, but Fredo reached inside and grabbed the large, shiny soup pot. "Heck, yeah, my mom can use this."

The others sidled up closer and decided what they wanted to pilfer from the broken display. Rosen knew right from wrong, but he also knew what it was to do without. In his family, hard times were all he'd ever known. He'd grown up in a home where poverty was simply a matter of fact. He slowly scanned the scene, looking for something he could sell, until he spotted the toaster.

Naturally, his mother didn't have an electric toaster; she possessed only a few dented pots and pans, mostly second-hand. But there was something about the smell of toasting bread that appealed to him. He'd often inhaled that marvelous aroma at the little restaurant on the corner. The restaurant was one of his regular stops when he was out selling his daily allotment of newspapers. The memory of that deliciously, warm aroma made it easy for him to decide. Rosen elbowed a large shard of glass out of the way, swiped the brand new toaster, and clutched it to his side.

In less than a minute each boy had grabbed what he thought his mother could use. No one stole more than one item. They weren't greedy, just dirt poor. The boys eyed each other and Rosen noted the petrified looks on some of their faces. No wonder they looked to him as their leader. He grinned, gave them a nod, and they scurried away like cockroaches when the light has been turned on.

The next morning, Rosen placed the toaster on the kitchen table. He felt proud of himself. He'd made a worthy contribution to the family, and it looked spectacular sitting there on their old but well-scrubbed wooden table. Like the other rooms in their tiny row house, the kitchen was worn and shabby. The walls had been papered so many years ago that the design had since disappeared, faded to an unpleasant lackluster brown. The only window in the kitchen was covered with a blistered window shade that no longer rolled up and down. In its perpetual down position, the shade dimmed all hope of the morning sunlight ever entering into their daily routine.

The toaster was new and shiny, out of place next to the cracked crockery that served as their cereal bowls. The toaster had two little doors that dropped down on each side of an upright electrical element. Two slices of bread could be toasted at once which made him even prouder of his clever selection from the vandalized store.

Breakfast was ready, a thin, soupy oatmeal. As usual, Pauline Rosen worked her magic at stretching a morsel of food into a meal for the six of them. Then his father's gaunt, tubercular-looking frame seemed to suddenly materialize out of the darkness of the hallway.

Samuel Rosen wore a beard, but it didn't hide the deep lines scored in his face nor the purple bag of flesh he carried under each eye. Every day he wore the same trampled dark suit that had been repeatedly patched and mended by Rosen's mother.

Samuel Rosen spotted the toaster. He cast a judgmental gaze at his son and pointed a knobby finger. He spoke in Yiddish, his tone abrasive. "What is this?"

His father's eyes possessed a disturbing power, but Rosen wasn't afraid. He did, however, feel a flush spread from his ears down to his throat.

"It's a toaster. Electric. To toast bread." Rosen spoke Yiddish, his first language, as easily as he spoke English. He was also fluent in the Italian he'd picked up from the kids in the neighborhood.

His father stood as if rooted to the spot. He was just barely controlling his rage. "So where did you get a toaster? Electric."

"I found it."

"You stole it." The old man insisted, glaring at his son with those eyes that harbored contempt, maybe even hatred.

Rosen had a hard time finding anything likeable about his father. He'd given up trying. He just wanted the old man to leave him alone.

Rosen shook his head violently. "No, it's not the same as stealing. It was just sitting out in the open. Anybody could've picked it up. You don't understand. Someone else would've taken it home."

"No."

His father's face was wooden, but Rosen could feel the tremor in that one word. His father worked himself into a near frenzy over minor disagreements with his second son on a regular basis. This was nothing new.

Rosen's chest tightened. He tried to explain. "It wasn't my fault. I didn't break the window. The window was already broken."

"You smashed it."

"No, I swear; I didn't. The window was smashed before we got there."

"Why did you steal?"

"All the kids took just one thing to help out their families. The toaster was waiting there for us, like it was meant to be."

Surely his father could see that his mother cooked their meager meals with her old, worn pots. She clearly had nothing in her nearly-bare kitchen that could compare with this remarkable find. Imagine warm toasted bread. It would taste wonderful on a cold morning, even though they had no butter or jam. He'd read in his school's library books about people—even people in faraway lands—who sometimes spread butter and honey or a thick, sweet homemade jam on their bread.

A protruding blue vein throbbed in the center of his father's forehead. The firm set of his mouth and the flare of his nostrils usually meant his father was ready to reach for his belt, his father's solution to every problem.

Only Rosen had grown taller and much stronger than his father. At times, Samuel Rosen had actually seemed afraid of his rebellious second son. Moishe, the defiant one, he called him. Rosen had been standing up to his father's belt for almost two years now, refusing to cry when his father whipped him. No matter how angry and wounded he felt, he refused to cave in to the total submission and obedience his father demanded. Except this time his father didn't reach for his belt.

Rosen thought at the very least he'd be ordered to return the toaster to the store. But his father simply bundled up the toaster and its cord and carried it to the front door.

"This goes to the police," he said. "Stolen property."

Samuel Rosen walked to the neighborhood police station and turned the toaster over to police custody. He later told his family that he'd informed the police about the way the toaster had been stolen in the night by his son. He'd even insisted that the police should write down his son's name. He'd wanted the police to be aware of Morris Rosen. He would pray for his son, but the matter was now out of his hands. End of discussion.

Rosen's father had nothing more to say, and he never mentioned the toaster again. He glared at his son with the infuriating air of someone who was certain he'd eventually be proven right. A kind of uncharacteristic quiet fell over the household.

Rosen spent the next few days waiting for one of the Irish cops that patrolled the neighborhood to grab him by the neck. When a cop strolled in his direction, the hairs on his forearms rose in anticipation. But the cops left him alone, and none of the other boys had been apprehended or in any way punished for what they had done. Their mothers used and enjoyed the gifts their sons had quietly brought home. The source of the impressive new devices was never questioned.

Rosen went to school and did well on every test in spite of the fact that he rarely studied. He sold his newspapers after school each day and shined shoes on street corners every weekend.

The few coins that he earned went directly to his mother for food. There was never enough to eat. They ate whatever his mother cooked, but every night they still went to bed hungry.

Pauline Rosen did her best to hold the family together. Rosen remembered his mother had once been remarkably beautiful. Well, actually his memory of the mother of his childhood was vague, but he'd seen a photograph of her that had been taken when he was only four. It was a time before the Great Depression, before Sidney, Rosen's younger brother, had been born. She stood next to her husband, the three children seated in the foreground. Sadly, she no longer resembled that elegant, smiling woman in the photo, with youthful smooth skin and dark shiny hair.

Ever since the depression had squeezed the life out of his family, his poor mother had roamed the streets of their neighborhood collecting junk and cardboard for salvage. The local movie theater saved empty boxes for her. They even baled old movie posters to make the load easier for her to carry. She collected newspapers, scrap metal, anything that could be exchanged for a few pennies to buy food.

After Rosen and his older brother, Hyman or simply "Hy," had finished selling their newspapers each day, they delivered their mother's last load of salvage to the junkyard. Once they'd relieved her, she was able to return home to cook the family's evening meal. His mother never complained but Rosen wasn't stupid. He knew that she cried when she thought she was alone in the house, not that her tears did any good.

All the years his mother scrounged in the gutters retrieving junk, his father stayed home and prayed for God to rescue his beleaguered family. The elder Rosen wore his religion like a coat; prayer was his only occupation. He'd given up on the idea of the American way when a bank failure had left him penniless. He never worked another day in his life.

A knot thickened deep in his gut every time Rosen laid eyes on his tyrant of a father. In those days his father ruled. No other choices were available to his mother. She simply had to endure a life of shame in order to survive. His father's sole contribution to his mother's humiliating daily drudgery had been to build her a small wagon. She used it to haul her scraps of metal and cardboard to the junkyard.

Whenever Rosen saw his poor mother dragging that pathetic, crooked wagon through the streets of the neighborhood, his heart died a little.

Chapter 4

By the time school concluded in June, Rosen had almost forgotten about the toaster. He walked directly home, bursting with pride because he'd graduated from the eighth grade with exceptional marks. He'd scored much higher on their final tests than most of the other kids. He carried his report card like a badge of honor.

When he entered the house his mother didn't say hello. Her wire-thin shoulders slumped forward; it looked as if she'd been crying. Her eyes were watery, reddened. She sat with her hands in her lap, threading and unthreading her fingers, her mouth set in a grim line. She didn't even react to the good news about Rosen's success in school. Usually she was proud of his outstanding reports and his passion for learning.

His father stood rigid, staring out the front window with the bearing of a military general reviewing his troops. A diabolical fire lit his eyes, but he said nothing.

Moments later, a sharp knock rattled the front door. His mother ran to open it, her eyes swimming in tears. She let the door swing inward, but she immediately turned away from their visitors, tears now streaming down her face. She grabbed Rosen's sister Molly and his younger brother Sidney by their wrists. Without a word, she abruptly yanked the two children out of the room. Rosen had to look away from her deep anguish. He stood perfectly still, waiting with every nerve on edge.

Two Irish cops Rosen recognized from the neighborhood stood at the door.

One tipped his hat, "Afternoon. We've come for your boy."

Samuel Rosen didn't say a word. He simply pointed to his son. This was not a coincidence. His father had somehow orchestrated the well-timed arrival of the policemen on the very day school let out for the summer.

For an eternity, Rosen stood still, hardly breathing, eyes fixed on the cops. His mind raced, but he saw no way of escape. The policemen, one on each side, took him in tow and pulled him outside. A police paddy wagon stood in front of the house. The words Pittsburgh Police Department had been carefully painted in impressive gold lettering on the side of the highly-polished black vehicle.

It was a warm, sunny day; the whole neighborhood had surrounded the paddy wagon waiting to see what would happen next. The air pulsated with growing excitement as if the circus had come to town. The crowd seemed to be expanding at the edges; little children were pushed forward so the others could see. More distant gawkers kept an anxious eye on the policemen and their young prisoner from the other side of the street. They whispered and gestured to each other as the uniformed men led Rosen up the back steps of the police vehicle. A few shook their heads in sadness.

Rosen swallowed over the lump in his throat. He was close to tears, but he held his chin high. No, he wouldn't cry. He wouldn't cry in front of all these people. He felt the eyes in the crowd boring into him, accusing him of heinous crimes he hadn't committed.

Once inside the windowless van, Rosen was ordered to sit and be quiet. The van was dim and empty except for two wooden benches, one on each side. Rosen sat on the bench to the left.

One cop jumped onto the bottom step at the open rear door of the wagon. He stood tall with a firm grip on the two brass rails that flanked the doorway. The other cop went around to the front and climbed into the driver's seat.

The wagon bumped along the cobblestone streets that were hardly wider than an alley until it reached the Boulevard of the Allies. They drove away from the familiar sights of Rosen's dismal neighborhood where tight, narrow houses sat like books on a shelf. They passed fancy stores and palatial mansions. He couldn't get a really good view because the cop on guard stood in the way, but he knew he was entering a world far different from anything he had ever seen in his thirteen years.

They traveled the streets of Pittsburgh for nearly a half-hour before the wagon finally drew to a stop.

"Okay, Laddie, this is it. Dinwiddie Street Police Station," the guard said. "Follow me."

"Where are you taking me? What are you going to do?"

"Teach you to keep your bloody hands to yourself. A bit of time in reform school just might shed some light on what's right and what's wrong."

Reform school! He'd heard of the place, but a reform school locked away hardened criminal-type kids who'd killed someone. He'd taken a toaster, nothing more than a toaster. Besides, the store had gotten it back thanks to his over-zealous father.

The police did not hold a hearing or conduct a trial. They didn't even ask Rosen if he pleaded guilty. In fact, his offense wasn't even mentioned. His guilt was assumed because his own father had turned him in. Rosen was simply led to a cell, thrown into a cage like a runaway dog ensnared by the city dog-catcher.

A series of shivers swept over him as he sat in the drafty cell for what seemed like a very long time. He bit his lip, but he didn't cry. He continued to tell himself that no matter what, he wouldn't cry.

The clock on the wall at the far end of the corridor ticked loudly, its pendulum marking each second Rosen had to wait. The police officers talked among themselves, apparently discussing the information they had written on numerous forms. Suddenly, as if someone had finally remembered he was there, a guard came to open the door.

"This way, Boy. Be quick about it."

"Where are you taking me?"

"Not far. You're going to our cozy little reform school, your new home."

Chapter 5

The Pittsburgh Reform School sat like a solemn fortress adjacent to the Dinwiddie Street Police Station. The buildings that housed this penal colony for wayward young people were surrounded by a vast yard with thin patches of scruffy grass doing their best to poke through the hard-packed earth. A high chain-link fence, topped with twisted coils of barbed wire, enclosed the yard. Rosen had never seen anything like this ancient citadel, except in pictures. He remembered seeing ominous-looking castles that had been built to ward off enemy attack in his history books. But this was America. The reform school could have been a foreign country unto itself.

The guard led him up a well-worn path to the main entrance. His keys jingled pleasantly against one another on a big ring, but nothing else about this place seemed pleasant. Rosen tried to lag behind, but the guard had a firm grip on his upper arm and roughly shoved him along. The guard used one of the keys to open the door.

The interior hallway was cool and dim and smelled of something that had long ago turned moldy. The guard's footsteps echoed loudly, like the ice man's horse clomping on cobble-stoned streets. The stark stone two-story building had tiny slits for windows as if they anticipated riotous teenage attempts at escape.

Rosen heard a steady thumping. It took a moment before he realized that the sound in his ears was actually his own heart pounding away like a hammer in his chest. Just looking at this place had turned him into a ball of nerves. He wouldn't cry, though. He kept telling himself, no matter what they did to him, he wouldn't cry.

"In here, boy."

The guard punctuated each word with a poke or a slight push against Rosen's shoulder as he ushered him into a room that was set up like an office. The guard was going soft with the big belly of a heavy drinker, but he probably felt that his job required him to act tough. Had one of the kids in the neighborhood slapped Rosen around like this, the kid would already be lying on the floor with blood running out of his mouth, and he'd be spitting out teeth. But Rosen was no fool; he'd also noticed that the guard carried a short padded night stick on his belt, like the cops on the street. The kids called these heavy padded weapons a sap. The guard's sap was no longer brand new, like he'd pounded some poor kid with it at least once a day every day for years.

Inside the room, a second guard sat at a desk. He eyed Rosen up and down before he stood and walked over to a wide row of shelves. He grabbed a set of folded clothing, a pair of high-top gym shoes, and a paper bag. The first guard stood off to the side, glancing at the wads of paperwork he held scrunched together in his hands.

The second guard sat down at his desk again. "Go into the changing room," he said, gesturing which way with a sideways jerk of his head. "Take off all your clothes and shoes. Put everything in the bag. Get dressed in your school issue clothing and report back to this desk. And make it snappy."

Rosen entered a room no bigger than a closet. He'd been given short-sleeved brown coveralls that buttoned all the way up the front. The clothes were not new, but they'd been washed and ironed. The coveralls felt stiff and smelled like the disinfectant they used to clean the lavatories at his school. His new gym shoes may have been worn briefly by someone else, but even so they were in much better shape than his own shoes. They hadn't given him socks and his shoes had no laces.

Looking like his over-sized coveralls had swallowed him alive, Rosen handed his bag of clothing to the guard at the desk.

The guard glanced at Rosen and wrote something on one of the papers. "Everything fits," he said.

"Yeah," Rosen answered. "It's okay, but you forgot socks."

The guard looked up with an odd sort of detachment. "You don't need socks."

The first guard, the fat one, said, "I think this one's kosher."

The second sighed. By the look of him, he must have gone through this before. "Just our luck. Well, I guess we can give him something plain like oatmeal for his meals."

Oatmeal. Three times a day. The very thought made Rosen's teeth clench. "No, you're wrong," he piped up. "I'm not kosher."

"Says here, your father said you was."

"Not me. My father and mother, yes. But I'm done with that stuff. I eat regular food."

So it was at that very moment that Rosen broke with his family's tradition of eating strictly kosher food, or at least what they could get of it during these hard times. The guard crossed out the word kosher, and Rosen felt pleased that his father hadn't managed to sentence him to endless bowls of oatmeal in addition to his imprisonment in reform school.

The fat guard led him through a maze of corridors that connected the many long, narrow, blocklike buildings that comprised the facility. They went outside and crossed over squares of blacktop apparently used for outdoor games, except no games were in progress at the moment. The young prisoners were probably all indoors figuring out how they might scale the wobbly chain-link and barbed wire fence in a breakout to freedom.

"I have to assign you to your work area. What can you do?"

Rosen gave him a blank stare. "I can do lots of stuff. I have a paper route; I shine shoes. I can fix things that break." Then some rational part of his mind forced him to remember that he no longer had a paper route. They'd give it to some other kid the moment he didn't show up to collect his papers tomorrow morning. He no longer had anything.

The fat guard made some more notes in his paper work. "Okay, I'll assign you to the janitor. He'll find some job you can do."

Something else finally hit Rosen square between the eyes like a blunt instrument. He would no longer be able to help his mother at home. He'd always managed to add several dollars to her food budget each month. Now, until Sidney grew a little older, his brother Hy would have to do it all. His guilt settled high in his chest like a bad case of heartburn. Dammit, this was his father's fault. Hatred roiled inside him until he actually felt beads of sweat accumulate on his upper lip.

The fat guard jabbed his shoulder, pressing him into a building marked Dormitory #3. The dormitory held 12 cots, six on each side of the narrow room. The guard pointed to the second cot on the right.

"This one's yours. You have to make your own bed each morning. You'll take the bedding to the laundry on the first Monday of the month. You forget, O'Malley won't like it."

"Who's O'Malley?"

The haggard look on the guard's face mellowed into something that was almost a smile. "O'Malley's in charge of #3. He'll tuck you in each night and kick your butt if you don't do everything he says."

"Oh."

"The janitor's name is Ben. Find him first thing in the morning."

"Where?"

"Where what?"

"Where will I find him? Ben, the janitor?"

"How the hell would I know? Ask someone. You'll see him sweeping floors mostly. Look for him."

The fat guard left him alone in dorm #3. Rosen sat on the cot that had been assigned to him. The bed wasn't too bad, maybe a little lumpy, but the room itself smelled funny. He thought he identified that same heavy pine-scented odor from his coveralls overpowering other weaker and less definable smells. He stretched out on the cot and thought he might as well take a nap. This had been some day, and it was still light outside.

The door flew open, making a sharp slap against the inner wall. About six boys bolted into the room. They all wore the same brown coveralls.

"Hey, who's this?" a tall boy with buck teeth said. He walked right up to the foot of Rosen's cot.

Rosen jumped to his feet, ready to pummel this guy into dust. The guy seemed to sense that Rosen was not someone who would shrink from a fight, so he backed off a few inches.

"So what's your name?" Buck Teeth said.

"Who wants to know?"

The other kids all laughed at that. They moved in closer. Rosen wondered if it was worth his trouble to organize this bunch into a gang as he'd done at home. He'd have to beat up each and every one of them, and that might make this guy named O'Malley unhappy. He figured it would serve no purpose to be a troublemaker in reform school. After all, they obviously wanted him to reform, and he didn't want to spend his entire life in some reform school or jail doing it.

"I want to know. I'm Jake. I'm the oldest in #3. What are you in for?"

"I'm Morris Rosen. You can call me Rosen or Moach."

"Moach? What kind of a name is that?"

"Just a nickname, from my neighborhood."

"What'd you do?"

"I stole something."

"What? What'd you steal?"

No way was he going to tell them it was only a toaster. They'd all laugh themselves silly. "I stole a car," he lied. "Drove it to the Ohio line."

"Hey, that's all right. Most of us are just runaways."

Rosen said, "Ever think about running away from this place?"

Jake laughed. "We think about it every day, but it ain't easy to bust out of here. The guards are old, but they watch us like hawks."

A much smaller boy spoke just above a whisper. "I decided I don't want to run away. I want to stay right here until they let me out."

"Why?" Rosen asked.

"Because I get more to eat here than I did at home."

"That's stupid," Jake said. "We all get more to eat, but that don't make this place any better. It's still a stinking jail."

The door slammed open again. The other boys quickly scattered to their own bunks and stood at attention like uncombed, bedraggled soldiers. A big meaty guy with a sour expression on his face marched in. He wasn't fat so much as lumpy, mean and lumpy like the old mattresses on the cots in Dormitory #3.

"Okay, where's the new kid," he said just as he spotted Rosen.

Rosen took a half step forward. "I'm new here."

"I'm Mr. O'Malley. You come to me if you have a problem, but I don't like problems, you hear?"

"Yes, Mister. I hear."

"Okay, you mutts get yourselves down to the chow line. Supper's in ten minutes."

Rosen simply followed the other boys to the dining room, only they called it the mess hall. Wonderful smells of cooked meat and grease hung in the air. Dozens of tables with benches for about eight or ten stood in very straight rows across the enormous room. It wasn't all that noisy, but every sound bounced off the cavernous walls like an echo chamber.

One corner of the room near the windows was already occupied with about 50 girls seated closely together. The girls didn't move, but their eyes drifted up from their half-eaten food and fastened onto the boys as they sauntered into the room. A swirl of color rose on some of their cheeks.

It seemed to be understood that the boys and girls were not to communicate with each other, but the boys were clearly showing off their stuff as they walked up to the cafeteria-style steam tables. Rosen swaggered along behind the other boys and smiled at the group of straight-faced girls.

But Rosen lost all interest in the girls as soon as he reached the steam table piled high with food. Mountains of creamy white mashed potatoes were served with something the boys called mystery meat loaf. He'd never tasted meat loaf. Maybe it wasn't kosher, but he no longer cared. He'd given up that way of life. He remembered the last supper he'd had at home.

His mother had concocted a watered-down soup by boiling a handful of chicken feet she'd gotten free from the butcher. Otherwise the butcher would've thrown away the usually undesirable feet. His mother added a turnip and some onion and anything else she could find in the ice box to the nearly transparent broth. His family had learned to make do with anything that eased their hunger.

Rosen settled into the routine of reform school as soon as he stumbled across Ben, the janitor, the following morning. Like the guard had said, he spotted the janitor sweeping.

"I was told you would find some work for me," he said to the tall fellow with stilt-like legs.

"Sure, always plenty to do around here."

Rosen learned the layout of the campus very quickly because he was sent to sweep or scrub everywhere except the girls' dormitories and bathrooms. The girls cleaned their own quarters. He didn't mind working as the janitor's helper, but old Ben quickly sensed that Rosen could do more than clean.

One day he said to Rosen, "I saw you fixed the base of that lamp in #2. I've been meaning to get to that myself."

"It was just a loose screw."

"So you've fixed things before?"

"Sure, I used to fix everything at home. My father . . . well, he never fixed anything. Of course he fixed me pretty good by turning me in to the cops."

"Your father, huh?"

"Yeah, he hates me, I guess."

"So what did you fix at home?"

"Anything that broke. I took apart the wringer on my mother's washing machine and put it back together. Had a stripped gear. I put in a new one."

"Where'd you get a new gear?"

"Junk yard. The wringer works okay now." He didn't mention that he'd picked up the gear in exchange for junk his mother had gathered from the neighborhood streets and alleys.

Ben said, "I'll bet you're itching to learn a trade, something you'd be able to work at after you get out of here, ain't you?"

Rosen looked up from the faucet he was polishing. "Yes, Mister, I'd like that."

"They don't teach many worthwhile trades here, but they do have a decent machine shop. Measures up to the real shops in and around Pittsburgh."

So Ben sent him to the school's machine shop where Rosen promptly caught on to the process of threading pipe, turning bolts on a lathe, and working at the forge. His strong arms seemed perfectly suited to the job of hammering a hot piece of metal into a useful tool. He tailor-made strong hooks for the kitchen staff to hang pots on the wall. In less than three weeks, Rosen was teaching the other boys these same skills.

Every now and then one of the boys would remember that Rosen was the only Jew in the school. Shouts of "Hey, here comes the Jew Boy!" always erupted into a fight, and Rosen always held his own, especially after he'd "borrowed" a wrench from the machine shop. It was small enough to fit in his coverall pocket, and he carried it everywhere, even to the shower.

After he'd clipped Jake on the side of his head with the wrench, Jake became his only friend, except Rosen really wasn't interested in collecting friends. He'd learned to appreciate his freedom in the machine shop. He even felt as if he were working on his own when he helped Ben with the sweeping, taking his time but doing a good job.

He figured keeping to himself and minding his own business would be smart. Even though he was in a jail of sorts, his father was not here to criticize him, so, in a way an enormous weight had been lifted from his shoulders. Strangely enough, he was actually happier than he'd been in a long time. He worked effortlessly, enjoying this set up for a month or so.

One Friday after he'd spent several hours in the machine shop repairing a broken pick-axe, O'Malley approached him at the forge.

"Hey, Rosen. I hear you ain't going to school."

Rosen looked up. He didn't like being interrupted as he worked. "What school? It's summertime."

"We have schooling all year long. No summer vacations here."

"Well, nobody told me to go anywhere except this machine shop. I've learned plenty right here."

O'Malley's hard, brown eyes smoldered. "Good, for you, but now you're going to learn some reading, 'riting, and 'rithmetic."

Rosen stood up straight. "I can read and write, and I'm real good at math."

Color blotched O'Malley's face from the neck up. "Now ain't that nice? Well, you're going to report to Mrs. Adams first thing Monday morning and see if you can learn a little bit more."

Chapter 6

Rosen joined Mrs. Adams's classroom Monday morning. The only available seat was in the first row, right next to the teacher's desk. He sat down, feeling squeezed. The furniture was much too small for him. Forty or more other boys were in the room, also sagging uncomfortably in the grade school-sized chairs. No girls attended this class. He looked around and saw Jake and some of the other kids from #3, but he didn't know most of the boys, at least not by name.

"Now children," Mrs. Adams said, "I want you to turn to page 89 in your arithmetic books."

Children? Rosen hadn't bothered to make many friends, but he did know that the reform school population consisted of teenagers ranging from 13 to 17 or 18. And, judging by their defiant attitudes, most of these kids would no longer be considered children by any standards. It seemed as if Mrs. Adams had wandered away from an elementary school and ended up here by some wildly humorous mistake, but Rosen wasn't laughing.

He noticed the others searching through the shallow, inconvenient shelves located directly under their desktops. He slid his chair back a few inches and bumped into the desk directly behind him.

"Hey, watch it," the boy behind him said.

Rosen shrugged at the kid and began to pull out the items stored under his own desk. A few books and wrinkled work sheets belonging to former students had been shoved forward into a corner. The math work sheets were the kind of problems he'd done in second grade. When he located the battered math book titled ARITHMETIC ON PARADE he knew for certain he didn't belong in this class. A great big numeral "3" smiled back at him from the lower right hand corner of the cover. Mrs. Adams was teaching teenagers third grade math.

Mrs. Adams pranced across the front of the room, passing out clean sheets of newsprint paper. "Now, class, I want you to solve the problems at the top of page 89. Now these are word problems, so you'll have to read very carefully before you begin." She'd dragged out the words "very carefully," emphasizing how tough the problems would be.

A collective moan ballooned across the room. Mrs. Adams tapped her ruler sharply against her desk. Quiet gradually resumed as the boys retrieved their pencils from a little groove cut right into the desk top to prevent the pencil's escape. Rosen felt stuck in a groove of his own. They lifted the pencils to writing position as if each pencil weighed hundreds of pounds.

Rosen read the first problem: "Mary has two yards of cloth; Alice has three. They need six yards of cloth to make napkins for a school party. How many more yards of cloth do they need?"

Mrs. Adams, with little wire-rimmed glasses balanced on the tip of her nose, was a regular hummingbird of a woman, flitting between the rows of desks from one student to the next. She tried to encourage her pupils to figure out the problems for themselves, but mostly she simply told them the answers. At least this way she created the illusion that the pupils were actually doing the problems, learning something. Maybe illusion was all that mattered in this school.

The teacher stopped at Rosen's desk. "You must be the new boy. What's your name?"

"Rosen, Ma'am. Morris Rosen."

"Welcome to our class." She picked up his paper. "I see you finished very quickly. Did you read the problems carefully?"

"Yes, Ma'am. This is easy stuff. I graduated from the eighth grade."

She cast him a suspicious glance, but she looked over each and every problem. "Why, my goodness. Your answers are all correct, and you remembered to show your work. You must have had excellent teachers."

"Yes, Ma'am."

She was about to dart off again when she spun around and returned to Rosen's desk. He picked up the odor of something sweet on her, something like honeysuckle blooming in the spring.

She spoke barely above a whisper. "Since you've finished with the assignment, would you like to help some of the other boys? You see they don't all have your understanding of word problems. That is if you don't mind."

"No, Ma'am, I don't mind."

And so, just as he had become the instructor's assistant in machine shop, he became Mrs. Adams's assistant in the classroom, only by now in his mind, he thought of her as Mrs. Hummingbird. At first the boys poked fun at him for being the teacher's pet, but they soon stopped taunting him.

"Hey, I get it," one of the boys said to Rosen. "You make this 'rithmetic stuff easy."

"It is easy."

"How come the teacher didn't tell us to figure it this way?"

Rosen was proud that he could teach math so easily, and he soon had the kids coming to his desk, actually waiting in line to ask him questions. Mrs. Hummingbird now spent part of each class sitting at her desk, smiling at how clever she'd been to delegate some of her teaching responsibilities to Rosen.

After math class, he helped the others with reading and social studies as well. Most of the boys came directly to Rosen for help as if Mrs. Hummingbird were not in the room. Rosen had been serving as the teacher's helper for about three weeks when one day Mrs. Hummingbird approached him as the class was leaving for lunch.

"Morris, could you please remain after class for just a moment?" she asked. She fluttered her hummingbird feathers from the desk toward the door, clearly in a highly agitated state.

"Sure," Rosen answered.

"Oh, dear, I don't know what to do."

"What's wrong?" he ventured.

"Oh, nothing wrong, it's actually very good, a godsend you might say, but it's more than I can manage myself. I wonder if you might want to assist, to help me. I can excuse you from class if you're willing to help."

"Help with what, Ma'am?"

"Oh, silly me. Here I am going on and on, and I didn't even explain what I want you to do, now did I?"

"No, Ma'am, you didn't."

"Come let me show you."

With that she was out the door, flittering down the hallway. Rosen trailed after her.

They entered a sizeable room that had always been dark and unoccupied when Rosen had passed by the door. He'd never swept in here because Ben said no one ever used this room. It smelled musty, almost airless. The stale air even had a strange yellow cast to it.

Mrs. Hummingbird flicked on a whole series of overhead chandeliers. Some of the bulbs had burned out, but even so the dim space was instantly transformed into a lovely though dusty room. The walls were lined with magnificent wood paneling that formed a dramatic background for row after row of shelves. In the center of the room, a gigantic pile of cardboard boxes reached literally to the ceiling.

"This is our library," she began, "but we had so few books that, well, we just haven't bothered. But now," she gestured toward the boxes, "all of these boxes, filled with wonderful new books, have been kindly donated to us by a very wealthy benefactor."

Rosen could tell she was dying to talk about this wealthy benefactor, but she'd probably been told to keep the details to herself. He decided not to ask questions; wealthy folks had nothing to do with him.

"I don't know why I was nominated to organize the library." She sniffed indignantly. "The other teachers could help, but no, they insist that I have adequate time to do it by myself. Imagine, doing a job of this enormity, all by myself."

"What do you have to do to organize the library?" Rosen asked.

"Do you know the difference between fiction and non-fiction?"

"Sure. We had a library at my school."

Her whole body seemed to quiver in relief. "Well, then you can separate the books, place fiction perhaps over there." She pointed. "And non-fiction over there."

"Oh, so then I just have to put the books in alphabetical order."

"Yes," she drew out the word, urging him to offer more.

"I know you would alphabetize by the author's last name for fiction and by subject for nonfiction."

"Yes, yes, that would be wonderful. And do you suppose you could dust the shelves, too?"

"Sure, I can get polish from the janitor and make everything look real nice."

"Oh, you are a treasure."

Rosen smiled. "And you're sure it's okay if I set up the library instead of helping the other kids with their school work?"

"Oh, my yes. Take as much time as you need."

She'd said the magic words. Although he didn't actually mind helping the other boys, the third-grade level work had become monotonous. He was more than willing to organize the library books in order to get out of the classroom. He was anxious to do something else, and this seemed like a perfect escape.

From then on, each day after breakfast, Rosen reported to the library. He unpacked hundreds of books and sorted them, creating stacks of categories all over the floor. Everyone was happy to see the library developing, and Rosen was thrilled with his good fortune.

He'd come across dozens of books that he wanted to read, so he arranged a little reading corner for himself. He piled up empty boxes like a wall along one of the windows. He'd created a perfect hideaway for reading, but he hardly knew where to begin. So many books called to him, and soon some of the characters in the stories he'd read were like old friends. His hunger for books out-stripped his hunger for food. He usually skipped lunch so he could spend more time reading.

He sat on the floor behind the boxes and read one book after another. No one could see into his corner, and when he heard a noise, he simply emerged from behind his wall of boxes and walked around to the center of the room.

But most days no one disturbed his reading. After noticing how well the project was coming along, Mrs. Hummingbird didn't even bother to check in to see if Rosen was actually doing his job. He was always at his post early and remained long after she'd gone home for the day. After a few days it was as if she'd forgotten all about him, and Rosen thanked his lucky stars for the privacy.

Each day throughout the month of August, he started out by arranging books on the shelves, but he would soon retire to his corner. He was fascinated with adventure stories, especially those dealing with Native Americans and cowboys on the prairies.

The Altsheller series about Native American Indians in the Rocky Mountains became his favorite. In one story, a white boy and his Indian friend became trapped in the mountains, so they had to use their wits to survive the winter. Rosen was intrigued with their resourceful methods of snaring animals and building fires. They fashioned weapons out of sticks and bits of twine they'd woven from strands of grass. He paid close attention to the way the Indian boy cut his long hair and interlaced the strands together to make a bow string.

One day Rosen got so caught up in SWISS FAMILY ROBINSON that he skipped his evening meal. He finally finished the book and turned off the single light he'd used for reading. It was after midnight, so he quietly crept through the halls and slipped into his bed. O'Malley was in an adjacent room, snoring loudly as usual. Probably drunk as a deacon, O'Malley had descended too far into his boozy dreams to be aroused by Rosen's quiet footsteps. O'Malley apparently hadn't even noticed that Rosen was missing from Dormitory #3 at their 10 PM lights out.

Gradually Rosen organized all the books, but he always kept a few random stacks piled on the floor near the doorway. He made certain the job always appeared unfinished so he could continue his reading.

"Hey, anybody in here?" a voice called out late one afternoon.

Rosen jumped to his feet and hurried around his makeshift wall of boxes. It was one of the girls, a raw-boned little thing with corn-yellow hair that looked like a storm blown over.

"Nobody in here but me," he said. "I'm setting up the new library."

She rubbed at her skinny arms. Her elbows were purple with black and blue marks on top of healing scabs. "Yeah. My teacher said we have a library now. She said you might have some books I could read 'cause I'm sick to death of sewing every single day." She spoke to the floor, avoiding any direct eye contact with Rosen.

"Do you like mysteries?" he asked.

"I don't know. I never read one."

"They're kind of like a puzzle. Fun to read."

"Oh. So, what's your name?"

"Rosen."

"I'm Stella. We're not supposed to talk to the boys." Her voice sounded pinched, too high-pitched and kind of squeaky.

"I know, but I'm the one in charge of the books if you want something to read."

"Oh."

"I think you might like Nancy Drew. We have a whole set of them."

He didn't admit that he'd read a few books in the Nancy Drew series in spite of the fact that they seemed to be intended for girls. He liked the way the teenage detective solved the crimes even though she was a girl. He'd read all of the Hardy Boys stories as well. Those were more for boys.

"Okay." She began picking at one of the sores on her arm.

"So you want Nancy Drew?"

"I guess."

He walked over to the fiction section and grabbed the first book in the Nancy Drew series from the shelf. He dusted the spine of the book against the leg of his coverall pants and held it out to her.

"Bring it back when you're finished, and I'll give you another one."

Her eyes looked tired, somewhat fragile, but she almost smiled. "Thanks."

Two days later, he was again reading in his private space when a scraping sound broke through the quiet. He hurried to the door. Stella stood there, her watery eyes blinked. She didn't look quite as dirty as before, and her cheeks now glowed a little pink, even rosy.

"Here." She held out the book. "I liked it. The sewing teacher lets me read in class instead of doing her damned Swedish embroidery."

Rosen returned the book to its spot on the shelf and brought her another. She made no effort to take the book but, instead, began to walk around the room. She studied the colorful spines of the books but didn't touch any of them.

"So how come you're in charge of the books?" she asked.

"It was just a job the teacher gave me."

"Did you ever have to scrub toilets?"

"Yeah, when I first came here."

"So, what did you do?"

"When?"

"You know, before. I was a runaway." He noticed a deep ocean of sadness in her eyes.

"Oh, that. I stole. . ." he was about to say a car. "I stole a toaster."

"You mean for bread?"

"Yeah."

"They put you in here for stealing a toaster?"

"Yeah."

"Jeez."

"Why'd you run away?"

Her shoulders drooped; she looked down at the floor. "My mom's a drunk. She beat me all the time, so I ran away. Five times."

By now Stella had made the full circle of the room and she headed for his wall of boxes.

"No books back there."

She went into his reading corner anyway and promptly plopped down on the floor. "It's nice here. No one can see you."

He joined her on the floor. "I know. I read back here sometimes."

"Yeah, this is a really nice place."

"I know. Private."

She scooted closer to him. "Did you ever do it?"

"Do what?"

"You know, for Pete's sake. What boys and girls 'do' to each other."

God, she was talking about sex, the thing he bragged about to the other guys, but just had never actually gotten around to trying. "Oh, yeah, I didn't know what you meant at first."

"So have you?"

"Oh, sure, I have. Plenty of times, but not since I came to reform school. No contact with the opposite sex, remember."

"So, you wanna do it with me?"

Rosen felt his cheeks grow warm. "Hey, yeah. We can do it right here. No one can see us."

He'd been so flabbergasted by her unexpected offer to "do it" with him, at the way this had just kind of fallen into his lap that he couldn't seem to fumble fast enough to get to her. He started undoing the buttons on his coveralls.

Stella leaned back on her elbows, silent for a moment as she watched him grope awkwardly with the buttons. Finally she said, "You know they'll probably shoot both of us if they catch us."

But by now, Rosen had shrugged out of his coveralls and wrenched up her skirt. He'd never felt more clumsy in his entire life. She helped him remove her panties. He didn't care if they did shoot him. It was September, one month before his fourteenth birthday, and he was about to experience his first sexual encounter.

He thought he knew what to do. Lord knows the guys talked about it enough, but he'd never been this close to a girl before. He took it slowly at first. Then he worked himself faster, his breath coming in ragged gasps. They finally seemed to moan in unison and he collapsed on top of her. After a few moments she'd become so quiet, he was afraid he'd smothered her. Rosen rolled to one side until they'd separated. He lay there on his back, still breathing hard.

A stupid grin crinkled the corners of his mouth. So that's what sex was all about. He'd been dying to find out. Not bad. A guy could get used to letting off a little steam like that every now and then. Not bad at all.

Stella rolled away from him and put her clothing back in order. She stood up and tugged her skirt into place. Finally she smiled down at him.

"I think I'll take the next book now."

Chapter 7

The long days dragged into weeks. Summer was over and a dank autumn chill seeped into every corner. It looked as if the reform school wasn't going to bother much with heat during the winter; drafts blew in from cracks around the narrow windows and creaky old doors.

One day Ben came along and flattened all the boxes that formed the wall around Rosen's private reading corner, and a few boys and girls had started to meander into the library in the late afternoon. So Rosen had to give up his private hideaway in the library and find time to read on his bunk or even in the machine shop. Most of the other boys had yet to discover the pleasures of reading while Rosen had made up his mind to devour every book in the library.

Almost four months had passed since he'd been sent to the reform school back in June. Rosen helped Ben sweep and clean every morning before he sneaked away to find a nice, quiet spot to read. He often finished a book in a single day. No one said anything about attending classes with Mrs. Hummingbird, so he didn't bother to go. Off and on he'd help out in the machine shop, but the shop teacher never insisted on a rigid schedule of work there either.

He'd learned that the guards wouldn't hassle him if he stayed out of fights and didn't bother anyone. The kids who avoided trouble were pretty much ignored by the over-worked staff. The guards concentrated on rehabilitating the handful of "problem" students. Except for being confined to a county institution, life actually wasn't too bad.

The boys played dodge ball; the girls assembled into a thin-voiced chorus that performed for the entire school on Saturday evenings after supper. When Rosen watched the girls sing, he tried to catch Stella's eye, but she always seemed to be gazing somewhere above his head, staring into some faraway place that only Stella could see.

Rosen was getting dressed one morning when O'Malley barged into #3. He shoved a wrinkled brown paper bag at Rosen.

"Here. This is your stuff. Wear this instead of the coveralls. You're going to see the judge. Report to the front desk in ten minutes."

"Now?"

"Yes, now. What's the matter, you didn't get a fancy engraved invitation?"

"Will I be coming back here?"

"Hell, no. You'll be going off to Troy Hill until you're 21 unless the judge goes soft on you and gives you probation."

O'Malley laughed his crude jackass laugh and stomped out of the dorm. He didn't care that he'd announced Rosen's business to all the other boys.

O'Malley's words stabbed at his heart. Troy Hill until he was 21. He'd heard about Troy Hill, but it was a regular prison, hard time for men and teenage boys who'd killed somebody, not for a kid who'd stolen nothing more than a stupid toaster. His mind flashed on Stella, the machine shop, and even the hundreds of books he had yet to read. Prison wasn't going to be as easy as reform school.

The bag contained the clothing that Rosen had worn the day they'd taken him away from home in the paddy wagon. A musty odor rose from the bag; no one had bothered to wash his things. He now wished he'd taken time to fold his shirt before he'd stuffed it into the bag.

A guard escorted him out of the school building to the juvenile hall located in the basement of the police station. Rosen remembered it well especially the holding cell where he'd languished that first day. He sure didn't want to return to that miserable hole.

They walked down a stairway and entered an ominous-looking corridor with ornate light fixtures suspended from the ceiling. Even with the fancy lights, the basement hallway seemed dark and gloomy. The floors were cold, bare marble. They approached two elaborate doors set into a recessed doorway.

"Sit here." The guard pointed to a wooden bench along the opposite wall. "Don't move from this spot; a bailiff will come for you when the judge is ready."

Rosen sat down. No one else appeared in the hallway; in fact the entire floor seemed vacant. He shifted his weight and tried to get comfortable on the exceedingly uncomfortable bench. He stretched out his legs then crossed them again. It was hard to sit still. He thought about bolting out of this place and running far away. He knew he could run impossibly fast, far into the night. He'd run and run and he wouldn't stop until he simply couldn't run any more.

But he didn't run. Instead he waited. And waited. The seconds droned into minutes. Nothing happened. No one came for him. They had some nerve. Were they planning to make him sit on this bench forever? He leaned back against the wall and started to whistle a happy little tune the girls' chorus had performed last weekend. When he'd finished, he wasn't sure if he'd gotten it right so he whistled it again.

The bailiff suddenly appeared. "Follow me. In here. Go right in." The bailiff walked to the intricately carved double doors directly across the corridor and yanked open the one on the right.

Rosen walked ahead of the bailiff into a room that was shrouded in complete darkness. Maybe he'd gone the wrong way. He turned to look for the bailiff and saw instead a window in the wall directly behind him. The window framed a perfect view of the hard bench where Rosen had suffered for almost a half hour. He hadn't even noticed that he'd been facing a darkened window the entire time he sat alone in that dimly-lit corridor.

The bailiff hurried past Rosen and reached for switches that flooded the room with stark, overhead lights. Rosen blinked as his eyes adjusted to the sudden brightness. Two men sat in front of him at a narrow table. He felt confused, wondering why they'd been sitting there in the dark. One was a distinguished-looking old man wearing a long black robe. He must be the judge. Rosen's gaze hastened away from the judge to the other man.

Rosen panicked inwardly. Sitting next to the judge, with eyes narrowed and jaw muscles tensed, was Rosen's father.

He swallowed hard; a chill swept down his back. The silence in the room was louder than any sound he'd ever heard.

The bailiff tapped Rosen on his shoulder. "Straighten up. Stand respectfully. This is Judge Nathan. State your name."

"Rosen. Morris Rosen."

Judge Nathan gave him a long, unwelcoming stare. "What is the nature of your offense?"

Rosen stood there, dumbstruck.

"Let me rephrase that. Why were you arrested?"

"I took a toaster from a smashed store window, but I didn't smash it. It was already broken when we . . . when I discovered it. It was only a toaster."

"And have you learned your lesson?" the judge asked.

"Oh, yes, sir, Mister Judge. I sure have learned my lesson."

Judge Nathan slowly folded his hands on the table in front of him. He seemed very tall even though he remained seated.

"I'm afraid I don't believe you. I don't think you've learned anything at all. You see we were watching you through one-way glass the entire time you waited in the corridor. You didn't look one bit sorry about anything. You whistled a tune as if you're still just as smug and arrogant as ever."

With his heart tripping and his mind racing out of control, Rosen looked the judge square in the eye.

"Oh, no, Mister, I knew if I didn't whistle, I would cry, and I didn't want to cry, not here, not before an important judge."

As the words escaped his mouth, Rosen marveled at how he'd come up with such an instantaneous explanation for his whistling. Perhaps it was something he'd picked up from one of those library books he'd read. Now that he thought about it, he'd done a pretty good rendition of Tom Sawyer or Huck Finn talking his way out of a tight situation.

The judge was taken aback with Rosen's straightforward explanation. He stroked his chin for a moment before he spoke. "Well, that certainly sheds a different light on your behavior. And we have had favorable reports from your teachers and the staff."

For the first time, Samuel Rosen moved slightly in his chair. He seemed to be boiling with outrage or maybe it was shame, but he said nothing. Rosen couldn't see his father's hands under the table, but somehow he knew that his father's fists had clenched in his lap.

"All right, young man," the judge continued, "I will release you to the custody of your father. You will be on court probation, and you will be assigned a probation officer."

Rosen and his father rode home on the street car in silence. His father's face appeared somber and dark except for his severely white forehead jutting out from beneath the brim of his black hat. Samuel Rosen held onto the seat in front of them, his hands square and callus-free.

Did his father realize that he was blatantly showing the world the hands of a man who never worked? Just thinking about how his father's smooth fingers compared to the painfully raw and bruised hands of his hard-working mother turned his stomach into chaos. He wanted to fling curses at his father. He wanted to scream his resentment. He said nothing.

Rosen shared a tearful reunion with his mother and his sister and brothers. Molly and Sid both seemed taller. Hy looked about the same, and he definitely seemed happy to have his brother home once again. They exchanged wordless grins and hugs. No one asked questions about the reform school.

Then his father flatly stated that Rosen would not be allowed to attend high school or even a trade school.

"But in reform school I worked in the machine shop. I was good at it. The teacher said I could get a job as a machinist's apprentice. I can work a lathe. I'm good with my hands."

His father said, "You're good with your mouth as well. Enough talk. I've already decided what's to be done with you. You will go to work for your mother's brother, in Jack's fruit and vegetable shop. He can use some help right now."

"But . . ."

"Enough I said."

The discussion had ended.

His father exiled Rosen to his uncle's produce shop. Uncle Jack was relaxed and giving with his own two children, but he ruled his nephew without compassion. Jack had obviously been convinced that it was now his duty to make Rosen learn responsibility and the value of a hard day's work. Rosen had no doubt that his father had pleaded with Jack to do the job that he as the boy's father had failed to do himself.

Uncle Jack had fought in World War I, and his face bore a cruel, vulgar scar, carved from his right ear to his chin by a German bayonet. He strutted around his Squirrel Hill store issuing orders as if he were still in the military.

According to his father and his Uncle Jack, Rosen's stubborn will simply had to be broken. If anyone could turn Rosen into a respectful, obedient son, Jack was the man who could do it.

Chapter 8

So early each morning, Rosen rode his bike to his Uncle Jack's fruit and vegetable shop. Before he'd been sent away to reform school, Rosen had bought the bike for 50 cents from one of his old gang members. At the time, he'd known that the kid had stolen the bike, but even at 12 he'd been plenty street wise. He immediately filed off the serial number printed on the bike. No one could read those numbers now.

He pedaled three miles across town to Squirrel Hill. Six days a week he worked from early morning until Uncle Jack closed up shop about six in the evening. He usually ate only an apple or a banana as he worked because he had no lunch or even a lunch break. He was young and strong and hard work never bothered him. Uncle Jack was his only real annoyance.

Jack's commands never stopped.

"Moishe, carry this watermelon home for Mrs. Abrams."

"Unload the sacks of potatoes from the truck."

"Pick out the biggest and best potatoes to save for the restaurants. They pay me more when I send them the big ones."

"Moishe, sweep the floor."

"Deliver this order to the lady on the corner. Third floor, 3A."

Rosen hauled 50 pound sacks of potatoes and set up towering displays of apples. He sorted out the rotten fruit, but he spotted his uncle slipping an occasional rotten item into a customer's bag when no one was looking and he thought he could get away with it. Women seldom walked the extra blocks back to the store to return just one piece of rotted fruit.

He kept the shop clean, sweeping every moment he had no other task at hand. The shop still had a disagreeable somewhat sweetish odor that no amount of sweeping could remove. Rosen could detect a rotted item just by its smell. The worst was a spoiled potato than had slipped into a corner in the back of the shop where Jack had the big sacks stored.

Rosen returned home late one evening and found his father sitting in the parlor with a stranger, drinking tea. The stranger turned out to be Rosen's probation officer, but the man seemed more interested in telling Rosen's father about the sad state of all that was wrong with today's young people.

Bone-tired, Rosen sipped a bowl of his mother's thin, watery soup and went directly to bed. He never saw the probation officer again.

After he'd worked a full month at his uncle's fruit and vegetable shop, Rosen eagerly anticipated his first pay. His father made a special trip, traveling to Squirrel Hill on the street car to be there with him for this event. Rosen rode his bike as usual so he wouldn't have to listen to his father complain about the pennies it cost to ride the street car.

"Here," Uncle Jack said. He handed Rosen a crumpled five-dollar bill.

"Five dollars? Six days a week for a whole month. That's less than 25 cents a day!" His math skills were still pretty sharp.

"It's not very much," Samuel Rosen agreed.

Jack shrugged. "He ate too much fruit. He eats so much, I lose money. Times are hard; people don't buy as much as they used to. I have to make a living and five dollars is all he deserves."

Rosen glared at the money still in his uncle's hand. "You can keep your lousy five bucks."

His father quickly grabbed the money from Jack. "Such a hot head, this boy. I'll take his pay for him, and I thank you. I'm sorry he ate so much fruit." His voice choked with shame.

That evening Rosen pedaled his bike home twice as fast as usual. He'd had enough of living under his father's thumb. He was still only 14, but he'd grown strong, his arms rippled with muscle. He could easily pass for 17 if no one noticed the lack of whiskers on his face.

Early the next morning, he wrapped his few threadbare articles of clothing into a tight bundle and took off on his bike. But he didn't head for the fruit shop. He was finished with potatoes and onions and especially with his Uncle Jack. He pedaled hard and didn't stop until he'd covered the thirty-five or forty miles from Pittsburgh to East McKeesport. His father wouldn't come looking for him here. He probably would be so relieved to be rid of him that he wouldn't look for him anywhere.

Rosen set out to find work. But of course, in 1938 everyone was looking for work, and jobs were scarce. He asked at dozens of places and finally found his way to Latham's Tool and Die Company. Mr. Latham spoke English with a German accent. Rosen guessed he was close to 50, a big man at about six feet of solid muscle. His hair, wild and bushy, was the same color as that of a buffalo he'd once seen pictured on the cover of a Wild West story in the reform school library.

"I'm looking for work," he said to Mr. Latham.

"What kind of work?"

"Any kind. I'll do anything. I learned how to shape metal at a forge. I know how to turn a lathe. I can sweep the floor, anything."

Latham gave him a look that would've shattered granite, but the sorry plea in Rosen's eyes must have convinced Latham to help this pathetic scrounge of a kid. "Well, I do have a new government contract to make gauges, so we'll be mighty busy tooling up for that. I guess I could use a new boy if he's a hard worker."

"I'll work very hard."

"No slacking off?"

"No, sir."

"Okay, then."

"You'll pay me?"

A smile cracked across Latham's wide face. "*Ja*, I'll pay a buck a day for starters."

"Thank you, Mister."

"Hey Kid, you from around here?"

He hesitated for a brief second. "No. My family's having trouble right now, so I had to leave home, to find work."

"*Ja*, I know, I know. What's your name?"

"Rosen, Mister."

"Okay, Rosen. You've got the job. You have a place to sleep?"

"Well, no. Not yet."

"I got a little spot behind the forge. You could sweep up the shavings from the floor. And I have a couple of old blankets you can use."

"Gee, thanks, Mister." A job *and* a place to sleep was more than he could've hoped for.

Latham grabbed a big metal lunch pail from a shelf. "Here. The wife gives me too much food. You eat something then I'll show you what to do."

He couldn't find the words to express his thanks. It was as if the man understood the panic and trepidation swimming through Rosen's mind. He ate one sandwich and an apple, leaving another sandwich, a wedge of cheese, and apple pie in the pail for Latham. Rosen then followed Latham through the entire machine shop, taking mental notes about every piece of equipment and every shop procedure.

Latham said he was willing to teach Rosen how to be a master machinist. How lucky he'd been to land in Latham's shop. He worked hard, but he was learning so much that he didn't mind a hard day's work. And he was actually grateful that he had a place to sleep on the hard concrete floor behind the forge.

By day the forge was fiery hot. The constant, deafening clang of hammers against steel anvils reverberated through Rosen's head until the sound became so commonplace that he no longer heard it. At night the concrete floor maintained residual heat from the forge. His bed was warm enough, but it was still a hard concrete floor. But Rosen slept like a baby behind the forge. He was miles away from his father and his Uncle Jack. He was relieved; he was even happy.

He didn't know how he'd managed to be given a second chance at life, but that's exactly how he felt. He remembered his months of incarceration in reform school, and the terrible month he'd worked for his uncle, but only dimly. His memory of being ripped from his home at the tender age of 13 was not one he wanted to safeguard. As far as he was concerned, all of that had happened many, many years ago.

He was finished with Pittsburgh and his father, but he mailed money to his mother each and every month. He vowed he would never forget her. His father might take the money away from her the first time he sent it, but even though she was uneducated, his mother wasn't stupid. She'd learn to look for the postman and hide the money from her husband. Maybe Rosen could make his mother's life a little easier. She was a good woman and she deserved better than she got.

But in order to set aside money to send to his mother, he had to live a very frugal existence. He slept behind the forge for six months before he'd saved enough to pay a deposit for a tiny room in a boarding house. He continued to work for Latham for a year and a half, but then it seemed his luck had run out. All of a sudden Latham's machine shop swarmed with official-looking men in suits who certainly were not machinists.

"Who are those guys?" Rosen asked the man who worked next to him.

The other worker gave him a curious look, as if Rosen hadn't been paying attention to something important. He set aside the tool he'd been working on.

"Inspectors," his co-worker said, "from Rock Island Arsenal. After they inspect the shop, they're planning to run background checks on all of us."

"Background checks? No kidding? Are you sure?"

"Well, of course I'm sure. Now that Latham landed himself two big government contracts, they have to check out everything we do here."

"You mean because of the gauges for the army?"

"Yeah, sure. Rock Island wants to know what kind of guys we got working on rifle parts." He laughed. "Hey, what's the matter, Kid? You some kind of German spy?"

Rosen gave a hollow laugh. "Nah, not me."

Britain and Germany were at war in Europe. The men at the shop said the United States was silently gearing up for war, but Rosen had his own fears. He wasn't certain how far a background check would go. After he'd run away, he'd never reported back to his probation officer in Pittsburgh. Were they still looking for him? If his background check went far enough, they might somehow connect with the fact that he'd skipped probation. If this violation of probation caught up with him, would they send him to jail at Troy Hill after all?

He made a flimsy excuse to Mr. Latham and quit. He got a job running a lathe at another machine shop, one that didn't have any government contracts. But after a while, he decided to move out of the area altogether. His mother had his address, and if his father discovered it, he might find some sort of perverse pleasure in sending Rosen back to prison.

Rosen hitched rides across the state and eventually found machine shop work at a bar-bell factory in Lancaster, Pennsylvania. He knurled the ends of iron bars to create a precise fit into the heavy weights. Weight lifters from all over the world hefted bar bells that Rosen had worked on. But this was a back-breaking job, and by now he'd decided that he wanted to be a mechanic, or more precisely an airplane mechanic. He believed he could find that opportunity in the army. He was only seventeen when he walked into an army recruitment office and asked about the prospect of becoming an airplane mechanic.

The man behind the desk got up and walked around it to shake hands. He wore a crisp uniform and the shiniest shoes Rosen had ever seen. "Yes, certainly we will need airplane mechanics. We need workers in many technical categories, but yes, we plan to train airplane mechanics."

"You'll teach me what to do?"

"Yes, of course."

"Then that's what I want to do."

"How old are you?"

"Eighteen."

"Good. You'll have to sign papers and submit to a physical exam."

Assured that the army needed workers in so many interesting jobs, Rosen had lied his age and enlisted.

As the train trudged across the Moroccan desert with Rosen sitting on the roof of the third car, all of these memories had come painfully alive once again. He forced himself to put aside his father's hate and focus instead on the rest of his family, especially his poor mother. He'd managed to take care of his mother starting at age 14, and thanks to the United States Army, he was still supporting her.

The army paid Rosen $21 a month. He kept five dollars for himself and $16 went directly to his mother. His father remained unemployed, praying when he could have been working, but in the army's eyes, this made Rosen the head of his parents' household. The army matched Rosen's $16 and then added an additional stipend to support his sister and younger brother.

He hoped the money provided by the government was enough to put an end to his mother's wretched existence, scraping for crumbs and free chicken feet, gathering cardboard and scrap metal like a vagrant in the streets. He felt shame, even now, whenever he remembered his mother pulling her dreadful little wagon through the neighborhood. He hoped she'd been able to hurl the damned thing into the junkyard along with her last load of junk.

Chapter 9

The third and fourth days out of Casablanca on the Ninth Division troop train again played out the same as the first two. The men were bored; the scenery hadn't changed. They were in the middle of nowhere, facing miles and miles of sun-baked, treeless desert, stretched out in all directions as far as the eye could see. Like the waterless landscape, the men had taken on a parched and ruined look.

They saw nothing like the well-remembered scenes from back home. Even though he'd never owned a car, Rosen missed the familiar sights of Texaco and Sunoco filling stations. He rarely spent his hard-earned money on anything as extravagant as eating out, but still he longed for the sight of a Howard Johnson's blue-roofed restaurant. Morocco didn't know about Kroeger or A & P Markets or Reich's ice cream. The Moroccan landscape displayed no billboards, no smiling faces of attractive, energetic young women sipping iced Tetley tea or a

Coca-Cola soft drink. Comfortable places like drug stores with a shiny chrome soda fountain had become simply a fond memory.

Back in reform school, Rosen had learned about the remote, painfully inaccessible American scrubland featured in some of his Wild West stories. But the desert wasteland that occupied most of Morocco was even worse, almost merciless.

The glaring sand was interrupted only by an occasional Arab village or small town. At one village Rosen had observed a man riding on the rump of a donkey poised behind a considerable load of twigs. The man had burdened the donkey with so many twigs that he couldn't possibly see over his cargo, but the donkey seemed to know the way. A woman carrying an equally huge batch of twigs inexplicably balanced on the top of her head walked directly behind the man on the loaded donkey.

Rosen felt sorry for the woman who was treated no better than the donkey, but in all probability this was the only way of life she'd ever known. Perhaps the woman had resigned herself to following behind her husband like a beast of burden long before she'd ever married him. But not knowing another way of life, of course, still did not make her circumstances acceptable. Rosen thought of his mother and her little wagon over-loaded with junk. He sent up a silent prayer, hoping that his mother's life had become more dignified or at least more tolerable.

The sight of a sun-scorched field of wheat generated excitement among the men because it meant they were approaching a village. The villages offered a brief respite from the boredom of their incredibly slow journey. Crowds of scrawny, dark-eyed children would quickly gather around the train. Stringy, long-legged men and women with savagely pock-marked skin would soon join the children, their grins revealing wide gaps of missing teeth.

The engineer would take the opportunity to replenish the train's coal and water supplies; the men would fill their canteens even if the water they extracted from deep, rock-lined wells looked questionable. They'd gone through weeks of dysentery when they'd first landed in Morocco, but by now their systems had acclimated to the strange foreign bacterium that infested the well waters in North Africa.

Day four was so crystal clear that Rosen could see every rock and clump of scrub brush along the rails. He watched the waves of heat rising from the sand. They passed a wheat field then a few camels that stood chewing near a palm tree.

Finally the train screeched into a town that seemed far larger than any of the other villages they'd passed through since leaving Casablanca. Visiting any sort of civilization would be a welcome change after all that sand, and getting off the train for 30 minutes was like a three-day pass. The soldiers of the Ninth were immediately surrounded by men and women shouting in Arabic sprinkled with a few American phrases. Arms flailing, they beckoned the soldiers to come closer, to buy their wares.

"Hey, G.I., you buy?"

The women held up hand-woven items, perhaps shirts, shawls, or blankets. Rosen couldn't tell one from another. The designs were colorful, but he didn't want to lug around Arab shirts in his pack.

Dago and Friar Tuck both traded chocolate and biscuits from their C rations for striped woven shirts that pulled over the head. The hand-stitched shirts were long enough to be worn as a dress.

"Hey," Rosen asked, "what are you going to do with those?"

Dago held up the shirt in front of him. "Mine's for my sweet mother. Pretty, no?"

Friar Tuck laughed. "A crazy bastard like you probably ain't even got a mother."

Dago flipped him the finger.

A girl walked by balancing a pottery water jug on her head. She gave them a shy, sideways glance, but only for a moment.

"I'll bet that's heavy," Friar Tuck said.

"You carry it for her, she'll give you plenty. Plenty of clap." As usual, Dago doubled over laughing at his own joke.

The crowd pushed closer to the train. Burros and cows quietly nosed in between the Arabs as if they were also interested in seeing what these American troops might have to offer. Chickens flapped their wings and squawked loudly when people or the larger animals got in their way. The noise level escalated.

Women and children from the town were still tumbling out of the stucco-covered stone houses.

Except most of the stucco had fallen away from the structures over the years and now lay on the ground in broken little heaps. No one had bothered to remove the rubble; it had simply become an added ingredient to the face of the town. Outer walls of some of the houses had partially collapsed. No one seemed worried about repairs. Rosen couldn't even begin to guess how old this place must be.

"Egg, G.I. Buy egg?"

Rosen turned around and saw a skinny, brittle-looking woman holding a pottery bowl containing six eggs. Her hands and fingernails looked as if she worked doing manual labor other than gathering eggs.

"How much?"

"Buy egg?"

"Yeah, sure." He held up two fingers and the young woman didn't just smile, her intense dark eyes seemed to glow with happiness and gratitude. Two eggs would constitute one-third of her inventory.

Rosen patted down the pockets of his shirt and pants, searching for tins from his C rations to trade for the eggs. All the men crammed their pockets with any chocolate, coffee, biscuits, or cigarettes they hadn't consumed. In Morocco, American G.I. odds and ends were the going medium of exchange.

"I guess you like chocolate, but I'm low on that. Ah, here's coffee and a pack of cigarettes. Okay?"

She tucked the small tin of ground coffee and the package of Lucky Strikes inside one of the many folds of her dress. Still smiling, she approached Friar Tuck.

"Egg, G.I.?"

"What the hell am I going to do with eggs? Make an omelet?"

Rosen said, "You just suck it out of the shell, raw. It's good for you. Pure protein, at least I think it's called protein."

Rosen had already poked a hole in the end of one of his eggs and demonstrated. The raw yellow yolk ran down his chin. "Aw, that's the best thing I've eaten since we landed in Africa."

"Man, you're one sorry son-of-a-bitch if that's the best thing you've had. How do you know that egg ain't rotten?"

"Tastes fresh. Buy one and try it."

"Hey," Dago said, pushing between Rosen and Friar Tuck, "I remember sucking eggs. We did that back home in Jersey."

Dago traded a chocolate bar for an egg, and Friar Tuck turned over two tins of biscuits for his.

The noise level had reached a fever pitch, almost deafening. The air was thick with acrid fumes from animal dung. It reminded Rosen of the East McKeesport Fair he'd attended once while he lived there. He'd eaten a non-kosher hot dog for the first time at that fair. Thick with mustard, the hot dog seemed more like a forbidden fruit, but he enjoyed every bite.

At the fair, he'd also watched with increasing apprehension as a cow gave birth to a slippery new calf. Rosen had been so totally mesmerized by what he was witnessing that he couldn't take his eyes off the emerging newborn. Wouldn't it be great, he thought, to become a doctor and learn about things like the miracle of birth? He'd held more interest in that blessed event than the new bovine mother.

The carnival-like atmosphere at this stop had lightened everyone's spirits. The egg-sucking craze had traveled the length of the train, and the town's fresh egg supply was soon exhausted. Chickens scampered out of the way, clucking with righteous indignation over the sad fate of their eggs. The town folks smiled and waved goodbye when the train jerked back into action, and the artillery men whooped and waved back.

Underway once again, the men told their egg-sucking tales on and on.

"You guys all got fucking egg on your faces."

"Look at Dago."

"Hey, The Kid started it," Dago protested.

Rosen said, "You sucked eggs back in Jersey, remember?"

"That's not all he sucked," someone else piped up. "They'll suck anything in Jersey."

"The bums from Jersey are all a bunch of fuckin' egg suckers," another guy said.

Dago shot back, "You should talk. I saw you whanking your willy while you sucked yours!"

The laughter all but shook the train. The guys took longer to settle down into their usual card games and dice rolling tonight. With most of his army pay going home to his mother, Rosen never joined in on the gambling. He really had no interest in their penny-ante games anyway. He kept the few dollars he had saved from his last pay safely hidden deep in his shirt pocket.

He sank into his favorite spot by the door and watched the sky and the ever-changing slopes of sand gradually change colors. The landscape was bleak and completely foreign, but the hypnosis of travel had actually become pleasant for him.

The train now seemed to be heading directly north after days of a north-easterly direction. Rosen thought he saw mountains looming in the distance, but perhaps it was a mirage. So far the deserts of Africa had offered no elevation higher than a sand dune, so an actual mountain range would surprise him.

One of the guys said he'd heard a rumor that had come from the rear of the train. They were supposed to reach their destination tomorrow. Rosen was ready. It would feel great to finally get off this train and do what they were sent here to do. On the other hand, reaching their destination would bring them right into the war. Rosen recalled their training maneuvers near Casablanca. They were all such greenhorns; none of them knew anything about actual combat.

The air felt cooler as night fell. Gradually, the sun was lost, consumed by the night sky. A great, shining moon took its place.

Chapter 10

A rosy light began to color the sky as a dazzling sun edged up from behind soaring, craggy mountains perhaps a hundred miles to the east. So Rosen actually had spotted a mountain range off in the distance last night. The wheels of the train clattered against the track just as slowly as before. It was as if they'd traveled halfway around the world at little more than a snail's pace inching toward their destination a speck at a time.

Eventually they crossed the border into Algeria. Grinding past drab farms and tattered houses on the outskirts of Oran, the train now barely moved. The chunky concrete telephone poles that Rosen had observed along the path of the railroad tracks soon branched out and followed narrow dirt roads on into Oran. Slowly, ponderously, their train drew nearer to the town.

The Ninth Division entered a wide valley east of Oran and eventually pulled into a flat, gray plain crisscrossed with train tracks. Other trains—some only a single unencumbered locomotive without the usual assemblage of connected railroad cars—puffed and shunted back and forth through the yard.

It was barely daybreak, but men and burros were already going about their work for the day. Sitting astride their burros, the railroad workers meandered between the slow-moving trains, hollering instructions. Things got done in North Africa only if the task was accompanied by endless rounds of bickering and shouting.

Along the perimeter of the yard, a few Arabs hauling supplies urged decrepit trucks over and between the tracks. The trucks were dented, fenders lost, and each one had been sand-blasted free of any traces of its original paint. The ruthless lashing of persistent sandstorms took a toll on everything and probably everyone.

The sun was not yet high in the sky, but the artillerymen in Rosen's division were still sitting on the train, and they were all complaining about the heat.

"Jesus, Mary," cried Dago. "Let me out of here."

"These railroad cars are fucking ovens."

"Shut up. Your hot air just makes it hotter."

"Who're you telling to shut up?"

Rosen's shirt was already soaked through with sweat. He dripped warm water from his canteen down the front of his shirt, but it didn't cool him. It was just plain hot. The train clunked to a full stop at the far end of the rail-covered yard.

Sergeant Miller came to life and jumped from the train. After he'd conferred at length with a group of officers, he returned to car three.

Sergeant Miller announced that a full infantry division had arrived on an earlier train. The infantry and a host of army trucks were waiting to join up with the Ninth Division Artillery. Twenty-four trucks had been fitted with 105-mm howitzers, but the portentous presence of an additional twelve enormous 155-mm howitzers indicated that they were gearing up for something big. No question they were through with their hurried round of training maneuvers; all that had been left behind in Morocco. Rosen and the other inexperienced and untested soldiers of the Ninth Division were heading into their first actual battle of World War II.

"Okay, get your gear and load onto those trucks. Move it."

Like robots, they followed orders. The men appeared rumpled and sooty from the long train ride. Their sallow faces, thickly stubbled and unwashed, had hardened with their weariness. Rosen ran his hand over his chin, searching for some stubble of his own. He probably could go another week before he actually needed to shave. They all smelled of cow dung, a smell they now accepted as the norm.

A guy named Creasy spoke up. "How're we gonna fit in those trucks? They're already full of guys." As an afterthought he added, "Sir."

Sergeant Miller turned to him. "We ain't got enough trucks, Creasy. We'll move ahead and the trucks will come back for the infantry. We gotta transfer men and gear to Tebessa in relays."

Creasy seemed nervous. He fell back and walked with Rosen. "Where the hell is Tebessa?"

"Algeria, but it's close to the border with Tunisia, I think."

Carlyle caught up. "I heard Tebessa is General Eisenhower's headquarters."

Rosen said, "We're going up into those mountains, aren't we?"

"Yeah, Tebessa is at the foot of the Atlas Mountains in the west. Rommel is kicking the shit out of us on the other side, in the east."

"So," Creasy said, "now we're gonna let the lousy Krauts kick the shit out of us?"

Carlyle smiled. "Hey, not the Ninth Artillery. You're forgetting about fucking Sergeant Blimp at training camp. Didn't you hear him telling us how tough we are? That we eat sauer-'Krauts' for breakfast."

Rosen remembered. Back at the Moroccan Cork Forest where they'd trained, a regiment of British had joined the Americans in maneuvers. The Brits called any pompous officer "Blimp," after a character named Colonel Blimp in a British cartoon strip. Rosen had never seen the British cartoon, but once the Americans understood the underlying insult of the name, they adopted it as their own.

The trucks were loaded with artillery men and equipment. Hundreds of infantry soldiers had to bed down and camp in a field adjacent to the railroad yard to wait for the trucks to return for them. They complained, but no one listened. The trucks moved out.

Rosen couldn't find enough room to stretch out his legs. His throat felt raw and dry, but his canteen was buried somewhere in his pack. His pack was under his left leg, but it seemed like far too much trouble to reposition it and search for his water. He'd have to strap the canteen over his shoulder or clip it to his belt like the other guys did. There was so much to remember, and he was still getting used to the idea of carrying every item he could possibly require wherever he went, strapped on his back or his belt.

The truck transport was even more uncomfortable than the train. Not that the train's old cattle cars had been anything special, but once Rosen had gotten used to the stink of manure, he'd actually appreciated the opportunity to watch the seemingly endless sandy expanse of Morocco slide by. Before joining the army, Rosen had never been anywhere outside of Pennsylvania, but he imagined that the territory in Northern Africa must resemble the rudimentary surface of the moon.

The column of trucks stopped occasionally, but mostly they just pushed on, covering about 50 miles before they came to rest for the night. The men unloaded the trucks and detached the howitzers before setting up camp. The empty trucks turned around and went back to pick up infantrymen who had marched most of the day. Once they met up with the trucks, the infantry got a welcome lift to the camp.

The drivers didn't stop to sleep or take a break; they took turns driving and catching a few winks on the road. Poor bastards had to be feeling even worse than Rosen felt. Why was the army ordering the artillery into such an urgent push? He had a feeling it wouldn't be long before he would know the answer.

Rosen studied the sun-blistered land that extended out from their camp site for what had to be miles and miles. It was interesting how the heat gave a curious watery quality to the desert sands. The merciless sun was dipping lower in the western sky, but the hot, dry wind was oppressing, much hotter than any air he'd ever breathed back home in Pennsylvania. He remembered reading about winds in Africa blowing in off the Serengeti, winds so hot they almost sucked the life out of a person.

"Hey," he said to a guy they called Stringer, "is this what you call a Serengeti?"

"A what?"

"A Serengeti. It's a kind of wind, I think."

"Who the fuck gives names to the wind?"

"I once read something about a hot wind coming off the Serengeti."

"Where'd you read that?"

Rosen hesitated, not wanting to give Stringer too much information. Stringer was a big guy who'd dropped out of school at the end of the fifth grade to help his father run their farm. He'd go back to that same farm in Kentucky after the war. "In a book," Rosen finally said. "A library book."

"I ain't read no lie-berry books since grammar school. Ain't you got nothing better to do?"

Rosen thought about the many hours he'd spent in the reform school library hidden behind his wall of cardboard boxes. "Back when I was reading, no. I guess I had nothing better to do."

Stringer shook his head and walked away. Rosen had many particles of information stored in his head that were not yet properly connected. Maybe, if he survived the war, he'd be able to finish high school, actually make something of himself. If only his father had permitted him to attend high school back in Pittsburgh. He knew Pittsburgh had excellent schools. But there was no use thinking about Pittsburgh or his mean-spirited father. He'd get an education on his own. Perhaps a few years in high school could help him weave all his random bits of information into a sensible order.

He'd become a top-notch machinist thanks to Mr. Latham, and he didn't mind a hard day's work. He'd learned Morse code and how to lay wire for radio communications in radio school back in Fort Meade. He was a radio operator who would be sent forward into German territory to observe the enemy and make decisions about where the artillery's gunfire should be directed. He was heading out to an unknown destination to do his incredibly dangerous job for the very first time.

But now he realized the world was filled with things he wanted to experience and understand. He wanted to learn all that he could.

God help him, if only he could somehow manage to survive this war.

Chapter 11

The men sat around eating from their tins of C rations. Rosen opened a tin of meat and beans, probably his favorite of the few choices they had. Some of them slept, using their packs as a pillow; many just sat and smoked. Friar Tuck found an audience for his harmonica, and he gently wound out several slow, tender songs that reminded everyone of home. Finally the men who'd traveled in the railroad cars toward the end of the train began to mingle with the men who'd traveled in the third car with Rosen. A whole group of them approached the spot where they sat.

One of them spotted Rosen and let out a yell. "Holy Christ, look who's here!"

Rosen cringed. He hadn't run into Kaminski since his first day in the army back at Fort Meade.

Kaminski pointed at Rosen and continued to holler. "Jesus, will you look at this, the Kid is here. Marcus, Tony, look at this! Get the hell over here."

Kaminski bounced from one foot to the other trying to get the words out. "Holy Christ, we was sure you'd been shot. I thought you'd been sent up before a firing squad." He slapped his knee and continued jumping around like he'd gotten a wasp stuck in his underwear. "Goddammit, Kid, how come they didn't shoot you?"

Marcus and Tony, two other guys he hadn't seen since boot camp, ran over to Rosen and began pounding him on the back.

Tony shouted, "You sonuvabitch! How come you wasn't shot?"

Friar Tuck stopped playing his harmonica. Guys were moving in closer to Kaminski and Rosen, knowing there was a story to be told. Listening to any kind of story—true or otherwise—would be better than the monotony of sitting around with nothing to do except watching the sun set over the shifting sand dunes.

Rosen's friend Carlyle, who always had something to smile about, was now grinning like the cat who'd swallowed the canary. "Go ahead, Rosen. You may as well tell them what happened before Kaminski delivers up a whole pack of lies."

Kaminski looked offended. "Me? I don't have to tell no lies. I was standing right there, not ten feet away when this crazy bastard and the general . . ." Kaminski was laughing so hard he'd lost his voice. He fell to the ground, next to Rosen, holding his sides and roaring with laughter.

"It's not that funny," Rosen insisted.

"Not that funny? It's fuckin' hysterical." Marcus said.

"Let me tell it," Tony chimed in. "These guys are gonna piss their pants when they hear what you did to a general."

Dozens of guys got up off the ground and moved in closer to the circle surrounding Rosen. Everyone wanted to hear what the incredibly naïve kid from Pittsburgh had done to a general.

"What general?" someone asked.

"C'mon, tell us."

"Okay, okay, you guys, I'll tell it," Rosen said.

"Tell them about all those tags on your new government issue uniform," Carlyle said.

"Okay. This is what happened. It could have happened to anybody who didn't know the ropes. It was my first day. I was new."

"We was all new in the beginning."

Rosen ignored that remark. He took a deep breath and went into it. He knew of no way to shut up all these guys short of starting a fist fight. But a fight could really get him shot way out here in the desert where the army had no jail. Besides they would eventually hear it anyway, and it was best that they heard his ridiculously implausible story directly from him.

"It was my first day on the base," he began. "I'd signed on at Indian Town Gap and right away they put me in a truck and delivered me to Fort Meade. Seems I was the first new recruit brought in that morning. I got off the truck and the driver told me to go straight to supply. So I went, and they gave me brand new fatigues, new shoes, a hat, the works. The supply sergeant told me to report to the barracks. So I go there and everything is a mess. They were delivering a truckload of mattresses for the bunks, just dumping them on a big heap in the middle of the floor."

"Tell them about the tags," Carlyle repeated.

"Yeah, yeah," Rosen said. "The little tags. You know how they stapled tags on everything, hundreds of little white paper tags all over the pants and shirts, even on the hat."

"Yeah," Kaminski said, grinning. He was already enjoying the story that Rosen had just barely started. Kaminski said, "The rest of us just pulled those tags off, didn't we?"

"Well," Rosen continued, "I didn't have time. Since I was the first enlisted man to arrive, the sergeants were looking for someone to get that base in order so they wouldn't have to do all the dirty work themselves. One sergeant yelled at me to get my ass over to the mess hall and start scrubbing pots and pans. I put on my fatigues and started pulling at the tags, but then another guy started hollering at me to get busy. The first sergeant saw me still standing there, and he got so mad I thought he was going to blow a fuse."

"I can see it all now," Kaminski said with a big, satisfied grin on his face.

Rosen continued, "I ran out of the barracks and found the mess hall, but my uniform was still covered with all those white tags."

Carlyle said, "While Rosen was running around, getting his bearings, another truckload of recruits arrived. I was in that bunch with Kaminski and these other guys. It was just like Rosen said; the whole goddamn base was crawling with sergeants. The base hadn't been used for much of anything since World War I, and they wanted everything ship-shape by fifteen-hundred because the brass was coming to inspect."

Rosen said, "That's right. We were told to get the kitchen in order. There had to be two-hundred pots and pans that needed scrubbing, but before I even got to the sink, the mess sergeant got right in my face and told me to scrub the concrete floor around the old cook stove.

"So I got down on my hands and knees with a strong soap and a stiff wire brush. It looked like nobody had *ever* cleaned the floor around that stove."

"Yeah," Carlyle said, pausing while another ten or fifteen guys walked in closer to hear the rest of the story. "So, there we were, washing windows, sweeping, cleaning just about everything in sight. The enlisted men were doing the real dirty jobs, like Rosen scrubbing that god-awful greasy floor, but I gotta say a bunch of sergeants from the regular army were also doing their share."

Rosen nodded, "I was trying to make that hall spotless; we all were. But then some guy stood up and yelled, 'Attention!' I figured he had something to announce to all of us, so I gave him my full attention and looked up right at him."

"You didn't fuckin' stand up?" one guy asked.

"No, I didn't know I was supposed to. The rest of the guys had stopped working and stood there stiff as boards, like they were taking a break. I was used to hard work and I didn't need a break, so I just kept working, on my hands and knees, scrubbing that floor."

Carlyle said, "Now twenty or thirty guys are standing at attention and a general walks in. We were trying to give Rosen eye signals, to get him to stand up, but he just kept scrubbing. I swear you could've heard a pin drop in that mess hall. The general, he doesn't say nothing, but he spotted Rosen straight away."

Rosen grinned. "I was wondering why that guy was dressed so fancy. He had his necktie tucked into the front of his shirt, and he wore riding breeches and boots like he'd ridden to the base on a horse. Oh, and he had a short leather whip like they use on horses tucked under his arm. Real fancy."

Carlyle said, "Just try to picture this. The general's all decked out in his dress uniform, wearing a tight little mustache and carrying that goddamn riding crop. The general looked us over, but he marched directly up to the stove and glared at Rosen down there on the floor. I thought the general was gonna tear him to shreds, but then he must've noticed all those brand new tags sticking out all over Rosen's clothes. Rosen had on boots so new, the fucking soles didn't even bend."

"I remember. My boots were stiff like that at first," one guy yelled out.

Carlyle nodded. "Right about then, a little smirk kind of spread over the general's face. He knew Rosen was as green as they come, at least as far as army regulations were concerned, and he probably also figured the kid was too young to know his ass from his elbow, so do you know what the general did?"

"What?" about 20 guys said at once.

Carlyle was enjoying this, so Rosen just let him roll with it. "The general dropped down on his knees right next to Rosen. So he says, 'Son, that's no way to scrub a floor. You have to do it in circles.'"

A couple of guys edged into the growing crowd. No one said a word. They all just listened, waiting to hear the outcome.

Carlyle went on. "So, the general takes the brush away from Rosen and shows him the right way. The general dips the brush into Rosen's pail of water, and he starts scrubbing that greasy concrete in nice, neat little circles." All the while he spoke, Carlyle gestured how the general made his circles with the brush.

"Holy shit," someone in the crowd finally murmured.

"So Rosen shrugs and says to the general, 'Okay, Mister. Why don't you finish the floor, and I'll start in on the pots and pans?'"

The men were speechless for a moment, and then they started to howl.

"What did the general do?"

"Well, he dropped the scrub brush back into the pail and he stood up. He looked around, but the rest of us were so frozen in place we weren't even breathing. So the general just spun on his heel and marched on out of there. He didn't hang around for the inspection, and I never laid eyes on him again. Never even learned his name."

Rosen said, "The guys went nuts after the general walked out. They told me the gold star on his collar meant he was a general, and that I'd just shot myself in the ass. Now that general would have to make an example of me, teach me respect for his rank. They said I would be sent before a firing squad, shot at sunrise, on and on. I didn't know how much of it was true, but they sure had me scared."

"Were you punished?"

"No, not unless you count having to scrub half of Fort Meade all by myself. I was scrubbing everything they could find, doing it in neat little circles just like the general taught me, right up until they sent me away to radio school."

The guys gradually walked away and took up their little patches of sand and settled into what had to pass for a comfortable position for the night. Most of them were still laughing about Rosen's first encounter with a general. There was no question they were all green, but Rosen had to be the greenest, raw recruit the army had ever known.

In a way, they weren't making fun of him so much as they were marveling at his innocence. Rosen didn't mind all the attention.

Tonight he actually felt comfortable with his status of being "The Kid" for the first time since he'd joined the army.

Chapter 12

The next morning the trucks returned, each carrying so many soldiers from the infantry division that guys were clinging to the outside of the truck as if it were some sort of carnival ride. Except for a few scattered gripes and groans, the infantry unloaded themselves quickly and almost quietly. Even the level of their complaining seemed less than usual. Rosen could see in their faces just how dog-tired they were after their march across the dessert in the sweltering sun. They'd marched many miles before the trucks had reached them.

Rosen was also gradually getting the sense that the American troops were headed toward a major regimental emergency. He had no idea what sort of confrontation lay ahead of them, but he could see the army was transporting hundreds of men to the front as swiftly as possible. Comfort and ease of conveyance had nothing to do with it. Tension mounted until the atmosphere seemed charged with electricity. The artillerymen checked and rechecked the big howitzers. They made certain everything, especially the shells, were secured for transport. They went about their jobs with mouths set in firm, tight lines.

The infantrymen were so exhausted they wanted to collapse right where they'd jumped down from the trucks, and some of them did. But most of them moved away from the trucks before they sat or fell down. They were a sorry-looking lot, and now they'd have to sleep in the heat of the day while the trucks took the artillerymen on the next leg of their relay across Algeria. After a rest period, the infantry would resume their march.

"Man, what are we planning to do in Tebessa? We ain't all gonna fit into General Eisenhower's tent." Creasy was grumbling to no one in particular, but he was sitting right next to Rosen on the truck.

"They'll tell us what we're going to do when we get there, I guess."

"Fucking army. Why can't they fucking tell us what we're heading into? Why do they always keep us in the dark?"

Rosen had wondered the same thing, but he played Devil's advocate. "I guess the plans are classified. They don't want word about our movements to leak out to the enemy."

"So who am I gonna tell? A fucking camel?"

Creasy had a point. Creasy also wanted to go home. He'd been announcing his dissatisfaction with the army ever since they'd boarded the train in

Casablanca. Everyone had heard him, but Rosen didn't want to butt into Creasy's problems. You ask a guy what's eatin' him, and the next thing you know they've laid it out for you with more details than anyone wants to hear. Everyone had a problem, and sometimes Rosen just didn't want to listen to another sad story. For all he knew, every guy riding in this truck wanted to go home.

There were moments when Rosen wanted to go home as well, but something kept pulling at him. He didn't think it was the sense of honor or even the sense of duty that the sergeants always ranted about. He'd signed on to do a job, and he would do just that. Nobody had ever called him a quitter. But nevertheless, no matter how many times he ran this through his mind, it came up sounding like anything to do with this war in Africa was a bad idea. Except for the British Isles and Switzerland, the Germans had occupied all of Europe and North Africa even before the Americans had arrived and entered into the war.

But at least he was artillery not infantry. Artillery carried only ten or twelve men in each truck. A load of infantrymen was three times the size of a load of artillerymen. With ten or fifteen guys hanging on the outside and double that inside the truck, it made for an exceedingly uncomfortable ride.

Creasy sniffed then blew his nose into a stiff, filthy handkerchief. He stuffed the handkerchief into his hip pocket before he leaned closer to Rosen. "You afraid to die?"

"I don't know. You?"

"Fuck yes. Everybody's afraid to die. Jesus, I don't even know why I signed up for this fuckin' war? Why'd you sign up?"

"I wanted to be an airplane mechanic."

"This ain't no fuckin' airplane."

"Yeah, I know. When I signed up they didn't bother to tell me that the army air force wasn't fully equipped to go into service. So far they don't have more than a couple of piper cubs, so they don't need mechanics. At least not yet."

"Why didn't you just walk away?"

"I'd already signed all the papers, and they weren't gonna let me walk away. I was in the army. They gave me a few tests and said I would be sent to communications school."

"Communications? That the same as radio school?"

"Yeah."

"So what did you learn?"

"All kinds of stuff. My hearing is pretty good, so I could figure out Morse code signals. They had me learning Morse code almost non-stop."

"And you learned about radios? I talked to a guy who went to school to learn how to work those radios the guys take into combat. You'll be doing that?"

"Yeah. I'll be operating the radio from a forward position. I'm gonna be doing a job they call a forward observer."

"Forward observer?"

"Yeah, I'll report back what I see and direct your artillery fire with my radio."

"What are you, fucking nuts? If you're sneaking around up front near the enemy, you'll be the first one to get shot."

Stupid Creasy had made another point. Rosen hadn't thought much about death. He'd just turned 18. He was more interested in life. His life was just beginning, but this war could be an end to life—for all of them.

"Well, forward observer, that's my job."

"Did you know you was gonna be sent out first, to catch the first bullets?"

"Well, they didn't explain it exactly like that."

"You thought it would be just like talking to your pals on the telephone?"

"No, I didn't think that. I knew I'd be stringing telephone wire, working my way forward, ahead of artillery and infantry," Rosen said, suddenly not so thrilled with his job.

"Did you practice stringing wire with live ammo flying all around you?"

"No."

"Jesus, and everybody says *I'm* stupid."

The men were much less talkative on the second night of the relay. They were quietly folding in on themselves, anticipating what would lie on the other side of the mountains. The Atlas Mountains had come closer into view, but they'd need at least another day of shuttling the men in the slowly plodding caravan of trucks for all of them to reach the base of the mountains. Some of the guys were still laughing about Rosen's crazy experience with the general showing him how to scrub the floor back at Fort Meade, but even the humor of that story seemed to be fading.

The Earth had just begun to tilt toward daybreak when the trucks returned with the infantrymen. The artillery division loaded their equipment and the howitzers were once again attached to the tow bars on the rear of each truck. They climbed back into their usual seats and set off on yet another day of tedium as the trucks wobbled toward the mountains.

By late afternoon on the third day, they'd arrived at Tebessa. The trucks pulled into a U.S. Army campsite located on the edge of town. Just as he'd never really seen Oran, it looked as if Rosen wouldn't actually see this city either. The campsite outside of Tebessa was much rockier than the desert they'd just crossed. Hundreds of rocks of every imaginable shape surrounded gigantic boulders, some the size of a small house. But in spite of all the rocks, this bivouac did have one thing going for it, the incredible smell of real food cooking, not spicy Arab stuff, but good old American-style food.

The men were rounded into chow lines by the cook's personnel. A short distance away, open tents housed more brass than Rosen had ever seen in one place. Smartly-dressed generals raised wine glasses to each other and to the other officers in their command. Their voices drifted toward the artillerymen, but most of the men ignored the big shots. They were more interested in getting their hands on a meal that didn't come out of a cold little tin can. Soon the troops were making so much noise that the party of officers had been completely drowned out.

Rosen waited in line until he'd reached the cook's table. He was handed a large, juicy beefsteak surrounded by heaps of potatoes and vegetables. After he'd found a place to sit with the other guys, another kitchen worker came around and handed each of them a beer!

The steak was wonderful. Rosen chewed slowly, completely surprised that the meat almost melted in his mouth. He'd never tasted anything this good. He'd dreamed of lavish meals like this, something he'd never known while living with his parents, in reform school, or even in the boarding houses that provided meals along with his room. He was used to soups and stews where tough cuts of meat could be cooked and cooked until tender.

"Hey," Creasy said to Rosen and the others, "ain't this the kind of chow they give to convicts for their last meal, right before they strap them into the electric chair and pull the switch?"

The others laughed. Rosen didn't think it was all that funny.

Chapter 13

The sun lingered blood red on the western horizon while a delicate bank of scattered clouds slowly rolled in. Up to now clouds had seemed almost non-existent in North Africa, but the men didn't focus on the weather. They were fed and happy. Most of them sat around smoking, still talking about the extraordinary meal the army cooks had served, when someone suddenly ordered them to snap to attention.

Rosen had learned that particular lesson well, and he stood ramrod straight, eyes forward, along with the other men. A voice called out saying a captain was about to speak.

After a moment the same voice echoed, "At ease."

The captain had scaled an enormous boulder that jutted up from the desert floor like a stage. He was in full army dress with leather boots and riding breeches. Like the general at Fort Meade, he was a little man who carried a riding crop. Rosen guessed that the presence of a horseman—even one without a horse—was supposed to impress the troops.

The captain postured confidently on top of the rock, paced the few available steps, turned and paced back. His footsteps issued a harsh, scolding sound. The men stood at ease while the captain paraded before them. The air was still.

Someone whispered the captain's name, but Rosen saw only the pompous demeanor of the British cartoon character, Colonel Blimp. Just as Mrs. Adams, his reform school teacher, had become Mrs. Hummingbird in Rosen's mind, it seemed only natural to name this guy Captain Blimp.

"Men," Captain Blimp began, "you may sit down."

The troops dropped to the ground. Some moved in a bit closer, but the captain's throaty stentorian voice could easily be heard across a wide area. Captain Blimp was a peacock of a man. Rosen imagined his peacock tail fanning to its full flourish as he geared up to speak.

"You may have wondered why we've pushed so hard to move so many men here to Tebessa. We've rounded up every unit we could spare because we are at a crucial point in this war in Africa. Rommel's forces have been winning far too many battles, making fools of the American forces in this god-forsaken desert. Now it's become our job to push the Germans back, move them out of Africa altogether. British troops are in the mountains, holding the Germans at bay, but two of the five mountain passes have already fallen into Axis hands."

A low murmur passed through the twilight.

"Rommel's panzer divisions are fighting their way to Tebessa. The Germans plan to crush us right here where we stand in order to capture General Eisenhower's personal headquarters. They'll take American supplies, our trucks, and our ammo. They desperately need the fuel we've got stockpiled here in Tebessa. We simply can't let them get through to our supply depot. We have to stop their advance. We have to make a show of strength against these bloody Nazis, and I'm confident that if anyone can do it, the Ninth Division can."

Captain Blimp brandished his riding crop and slapped it forcefully across his palm. Rosen thought Captain Blimp was the only person he'd ever encountered who seemed more zealously hell-bent than his father, but he listened closely.

The captain went on. "Now I realize a lot of you are fairly new to this army, but you're Americans, you're Ninth Division, and it's up to you to stop the Germans. Some of us will die, but we have a job to do, and we're in this to win. You have to live up to the reputation of all the brave American soldiers who have gone before you."

He paused to let that sink in. "I know each and every one of you will do your duty. You won't let anything stand in your way. Grab your rifles and mount up. Men of the Ninth, you're finally going into battle, and it will be a courageous battle." He paused again. "Men . . . this is it!"

With that, the troops were dismissed. The men hooked up the howitzers and immediately boarded the trucks. The drivers cranked up the engines and the trucks moved out. They'd been lulled into submission with bellies full of steak and beer. Most of the men had lapped up the captain's pep talk until the level of a renewed spirit of patriotism had reached an astonishing high. They'd become believers. Rosen thought the men were just about ready to believe that Captain Blimp could move those Atlas Mountains.

The skeletal clouds that Rosen had noticed earlier had finally become fast-moving, meshing together to create a murky blackness in every gully. Indistinct shadowy pockets lurked behind every rock. The air felt heavy with moisture as if the sky could drop down on them like a rain-soaked ceiling. Night fell over the desert.

The men had been ordered to cover the lights on each truck. Tiny slits in the covers over the tail lights permitted the truck ahead to be just barely visible to the one following behind. The long column of hundreds of phantom-like trucks slowly headed up into the Atlas Mountains. The trucks hauling the big guns, the 9000 pound 155-mm howitzers, led the way.

Rosen found himself in a truck with Sergeant Miller and some of the guys he'd traveled with in the third railroad car. Dago sat on one side of him, Carlyle on the other. In the deep intensity of the night, the men couldn't see one another unless someone lit a cigarette.

"What about that whole infantry division?" Dago asked. "The trucks didn't go back for them."

Sergeant Miller said, "We needed the trucks to move artillery. Infantry can march."

Dago let out a long whistling breath. "They're 50 fucking miles behind us, plus this trek up the mountain. It'll take them a week."

"Probably."

"We should've waited for them."

"We have our orders, Private," Sergeant Miller said as if that ended it.

Then the clouds broke loose and the rain began. But it wasn't the kind of ordinary rain that Rosen remembered from Pennsylvania. Torrential plumes of water literally teemed down on them. The loosely-fixed canvas covering the truck bed wasn't intended to keep anyone dry in a downpour like this.

"Jesus, I'm soaked," one guy said.

"Shut up, jerkwad. We all are."

The trucks shook and began to teeter on the rise in the center of the road, slipping and swaying side to side. The ancient road they were following was little more than a trail. Deep ditches along both sides of the slick roadbed made it imperative that they keep the trucks on track at dead center, so the howitzers wouldn't get stuck in the mud. The rear end of Rosen's truck fish-tailed and shimmied as the tires lifted off the road and then smacked down again, jarring everyone.

The ground became scarred with deep, black channels where the cumbersome howitzers had gouged tremendous ruts into the road. The road had turned into a treacherous, slippery mess, but the trucks slogged on, barely moving at 10 or 15 miles per hour.

The men were wet. Everything smelled of rot. The rank stink of their unwashed bodies combined with the smell of wet canvas and rope reminded Rosen of wet dogs, except wet dogs didn't usually cram into trucks where they had to sit together hour after hour. The dark, leaden night sky threw him off. Time was never certain in this pitch black place, and even though Rosen was one of the few soldiers who owned a watch, it was too dark to tell the time.

He tried to imagine what lay beyond the darkness. Maybe tiny villages were tucked into little crevices in the mountains? Did the concrete telephone poles follow the road this high to provide phone service? Probably not. He doubted that they even had electricity this high up into the mountains.

He suddenly heard a sound that was different, the tires of the truck rumbling at a different pitch. Then, just as abruptly, it stopped. They must've crossed a bridge.

Perhaps the hills sheltered a secretive forest, filled with exotic animals. More likely the hills concealed German troops, anxious to open fire on the intruding Americans. He wished that they could round a bend and come across a blue-roofed Howard Johnson's Restaurant. He'd even settle for an A&P Supermarket.

The truck wheezed and coughed, winding its way higher and higher into the darkness. Rosen was jerked and jostled from side to side. The guys in his truck had pretty much given up on conversation. They'd all hunkered down into their seats to keep dry, but the cold wind continued to slap a steady stream of even colder rain right into their faces. The heavy damp entered every crevice of the truck and closed around them.

With his glasses tucked safely in his pocket to keep them dry, Rosen closed his eyes. Besides he was dead tired. After so many days of catching just a few minutes of sleep here and there, he felt a searing pain in his forehead; his whole body weighed heavily against the side of the truck. His arms, his back were made of lead. Somehow he'd learned to sleep in bits and pieces, no matter what was going on around him, but this ride up into the mountains was something else. How was a guy supposed to sleep while being hurled back and forth like this?

He thought about how good it would feel to lie down in a bed. His bed in the room he'd shared with his two brothers hadn't been fancy or even very wide. It was actually just an old army surplus cot, but it had always been his private place. He wondered whether his mother was able to stretch out for a nap each day. But no, his father would be after her to bring him a cup of tea or broth. He hoped she was happier now or at least more comfortable after working so hard her entire life.

God, he was beat. He'd even settle for his lonesome spot on the floor behind the forge at Latham's Machine Shop. The machine shop and its forge seemed like something from another lifetime.

Had he really slept on the floor behind a forge? Had he actually landed in reform school at thirteen? For that matter had he told a general to finish scrubbing the floor while he started in on the pots and pans? He was only eighteen and already his young life was filled with impossibilities that had all happened.

He needed to sleep. He felt his teeth chattering, perhaps from the cold, or maybe it was from the relentless tossing of the truck.

Finally, against all odds, he dozed off.

Chapter 14

Rosen awoke with a start. His heart was thumping wildly but he wasn't sure why. The truck was still struggling up the mountainside, so they hadn't been ambushed. He pulled one of the canvas flaps to the side and looked out. A hint of daylight skimmed the horizon to the east. He must've had a bad dream, one that he couldn't remember.

Carlyle said, "Jesus, Kid, how the hell did you manage to sleep with this truck bouncing all night long?"

"I don't know," Rosen answered. "You didn't sleep?"

"Off and on. Mostly off."

The hammering rain had stopped. The column halted for the men to stretch their legs and relieve themselves. Now that the rising sun shed a bit of light, Rosen spotted what looked like a party of men walking toward them along the side of the road. They had to be soldiers, stragglers, but were they Germans? Except for pictures, Rosen had never seen a German soldier. The other men had also spotted the strangers, and most of the men quickly shouldered their rifles, getting ready to fire.

Sergeant Miller yelled, "Hold your fire, they're Americans."

The scattering of bedraggled foot soldiers slowly approached the column of Ninth Division trucks. The first man who'd reached them was a haunted-looking private, his lean, unshaven face giving away his hunger, fatigue, and fear.

"Hey," he said, "you guys are going the wrong way; turn around."

"Who are you with?" Sergeant Miller asked.

"First Armored Division."

"What happened? Who's in command?"

"All dead, I guess. There's a sergeant back there somewhere. Took a machine gun bullet in the face. Looks pretty bad. Lots of wounded. We got a few trucks toward the rear, all crammed full of guys who got hit."

"So your whole unit is retreating?"

"Yes, sir. The fucking Germans are pushing this way. You're heading directly into a massacre. You better turn around. Go back the way you came. Just get the hell out of here before they start firing at you, too."

Rosen studied the terrain surrounding them. It looked as if the trucks carrying his division couldn't turn around even if they wanted to. The sheer, rocky hillsides faced right up to the road.

A second group of men staggered up to them, then another. Now they could see that the line of broken, battle-weary soldiers was strung out over the entire mountain road. Some were from the First Armored, others from the Thirty-fourth Infantry. The sarge stopped asking. They weren't all from the same unit, but they all had the same message. Rosen's division was going the wrong way, heading directly toward an apparently hopeless battle with German-Italian Panzers. Plus they were going in without the infantry. Their artillery unit would be out-numbered by the Germans ten to one.

They learned that the German army boasted seasoned, professional military men while the American troops were nothing more than sadly inexperienced amateurs. Rosen flashed back to his first day in the army and how dim-witted and inept he must've seemed when he told the general to finish scrubbing the floor. He and the rest of the men in his division were still untested as soldiers, now only slightly better indoctrinated into the army than he'd been that first day. He couldn't help thinking that Captain Blimp and the generals had knowingly fed them steak and beer before sending them off on a suicide mission. Stupid Creasy had seen it coming, why hadn't he?

One soldier who was limping said, "It was a fucking slaughter. Wiped out most of us."

Another said, "We was overrun by thousands of fucking Krauts at Kasserine."

"Fucking German tanks are much better than ours. Fuckin' blew up our tanks and us." This guy had a filthy bandage wrapped around his head covering one eye. Blood seeped through the dirt.

"We were ordered to retreat and regroup back at Tebessa."

"Eisenhower don't know how bad it is. The Brits are following right behind us."

"Nobody can hold back those fuckin' panzers. We had to get out of there."

The others nodded in agreement.

Rosen felt sorry for these poor bastards with their hangdog faces. They'd taken a real pounding. The warnings kept coming; the men of the Ninth were undoubtedly advancing toward disaster. The disorderly chaos of the retreating troops was certainly not a morale booster, but the officers soon rounded up the artillerymen and got them back onto the trucks.

Military police ordered the withdrawing men over to the side of the road so the column could pass. As the trucks and a few ambulances caught up with those retreating on foot, they were also forced to wait in the ditches that bordered the road.

They might be heading the "wrong way," but the trucks sped up. The Ninth Division had been ordered to face the enemy no matter how grim the prospects. The trucks pressed forward, leaving behind the undisciplined pandemonium of the troops who'd retreated.

Dago said, "Those poor sons of bitches got their asses kicked."

"Sarge, shouldn't we turn around?" another soldier asked.

"No," Sergeant Miller said, "we've got orders. Brigadier General Irwin himself is in command of this division, bringing up the rear. He ordered us to move out, so we're moving out."

"Ain't right somehow."

"Don't matter. There's no one else to send into this fight except the Ninth, so we're going in." His voice was chilling; the space between the men and the sarge seemed to close up with a charged icy atmosphere. The sarge was an army man through and through. The men in his command would not retreat.

Rosen stared out through the open flap on the back of the truck. The rain had started up again and was fast turning into sleet. They'd come from the hot desert floor up into the coldest cold he'd ever felt. It didn't help that he was sopping wet.

They passed dilapidated mountain villages consisting of a few shabby huts built of rocks, some plastered over with stucco. Crude sheds had been erected using woven reeds that had weathered to a colorless gray. The cruelties of nature had painted entire villages and everything in them this same raw, hapless color. A few donkeys chewed at the shrunken-looking scrub brush surrounding the villages; no tall trees were visible. He couldn't imagine how people survived up here, yet the tiny squeezed-looking settlements nestled firmly between the surrounding rocks and boulders most certainly were centuries old.

Along the road they were now spotting an increasing number of abandoned trucks and equipment. American equipment. They came upon British soldiers, also weary and disheveled, and even picked up a few of them. The British confessed that all the American troops had retreated from the front near the village of Thala in Tunisia. A handful of British had remained, holding the line, trying to prevent the Germans from gaining access to the pass at Thala that would give them direct passage to the American supply depot at Tebessa. The British also confessed that Thala was a lost cause. Those Brits who insisted on retreating were not stopped.

Rosen and the others ate from their cans of rations; they watched it grow dark once again. They had a few forced stops for truck maintenance, and the mechanics somehow kept the overworked and exhausted engines running.

Night was upon them; the men smoked, but didn't speak. The silence was, perhaps, the only thing holding the outfit together. In the distance great flashes of light erupted from time to time. No one asked what these flashes were. They somehow knew it was German artillery fire pounding away at the flimsy detail of British troops who'd remained at Thala as the last line of defense.

The Ninth might not even arrive in time to put up a fight. They were heading into an abysmal situation and they all knew it. If they were able to take a stand, Rosen would have to move forward to find a spot where he could see to direct the artillery fire. Going into his first battle, all he could think of was doing his job well. He'd make his mother proud.

At some point during the night they'd crossed into Tunisia. The steep clay road had turned icy as they descended the eastern side of the Atlas Mountains heading downhill toward Thala. Except for the distant artillery fire, the sky was black, as if a heavy curtain had been stitched all around them.

In their blindness, they finally reached the handful of British troops who were holding the pass.

Chapter 15

One by one the long column of trucks pulled to a stop. Someone said it was ten at night. Someone else said it was midnight. They had until daybreak to get ready. No one had to tell the artillerymen to unload quietly; they knew instinctively that if they were to have any impact on the Germans at all, their arrival had to be a complete surprise.

General Irwin and the other American officers headed for the only lighted area in the encampment, the British command tent. The low-slung tent held a single weak lantern that flickered barely brighter than a firefly. In the glow from the lantern, the American officers joined the few remaining British officers. They hunched together, poring over a map of the area, discussing strategy. They spoke in such completely hushed tones that not one word of it leaked outside the tent.

Rosen didn't remember it ever being this dark in Pittsburgh, but within the stark shadows that swallowed up the hillside, the Americans prepared for battle. They had no idea which way to point their weapons so they relied upon the British for instructions. The Ninth Division set up their artillery using the stars, coordinating the direction of their planned attack with surveying transits. It took hours of meticulous calculations to finally get a fix on the most appropriate positioning of the howitzers. The Americans found themselves preparing to direct their fire over a rounded berm of dirt and rocks. According to the British, the German tanks lay in wait downhill, somewhere on the other side of the berm.

Sergeant Miller approached Rosen. "Here's your radio equipment."

Rosen groped inside the box, fumbling with many more pieces than he expected. "This isn't right," he whispered. "The radios are all busted up. They're not supposed to be in so many pieces like this."

"I guess the bumpy ride was too much for them. A lot of stuff got knocked apart."

"What am I supposed to use?"

"See if the telephones work. You know how to string telephone wire, don't you?"

"Yeah, but it's so dark. There's no moon."

"Just do it, Private. Get Creasy and whoever else you need to help you string the goddamn wire. Report back to me as soon as it's working. You drag your feet, the captain will ream his foot up your ass."

Rosen wasn't interested in seeing any part of Captain Blimp, including his foot, so he went right to work. If only it weren't so goddamned dark. And cold. God it was cold. The only good news was that it had stopped raining and the sleet underfoot had melted somewhat, but that left him plodding through a sea of half-frozen mud. The mud squished under his boots with every step. He was able to identify the approach of another soldier by this same oozing, sucking sound.

He heard someone whisper, "It's colder than a witch's tit."

The voice sounded like Dago, but then a lot of the men sounded like Dago on this pitch black mountainside.

While Rosen searched for Creasy and the telephone wire that he would need, men crept all around him. Hundreds of men moved like fog, doing what had to be done in the dark. They whispered, they cursed, but they worked. Like disembodied spirits, they did their jobs by feel. Rosen heard muffled grunts as heavy shells were lifted, then the sound of metal sliding against metal as the breeches skidded opened and the big guns were loaded.

"I can't see a fucking thing," someone said, as if everyone else didn't already know that.

"I can't see the guy in front of me."

"I can't see my own ass."

A few more men gathered around Rosen. The voices sounded familiar. "Creasy," Rosen whispered into the night, "Creasy, goddamn it, is that you?"

"Where the fuck are you?" Creasy came back.

"Right here." Rosen spoke toward the passing crowd. "I need you to help me string wire. For the telephones."

"Rip!"

The voice came from a spot just outside the command tent. Captain Blimp was whispering a bit too loudly, calling for First Lieutenant William "Rip" Rybka. Rip had been assigned to the captain as his Executive Officer, and he sent Rip running on endless errands. Rip would no sooner dash off in one direction than Captain Blimp would call him back. Rosen was glad that his own detail as a forward observer would take him away from the commotion that surrounded the captain. If a German spy overheard the captain issuing orders to Rip, no doubt a shell would be lobbed right at him.

Rosen and Creasy enlisted the help of a lieutenant and two other guys. They climbed a hill that flanked their position, moving forward toward the Germans. They had to install a field telephone system, no easy matter in the dark, but they managed to lay the wire all the way from the top of the hill back to the command tent, about 300 yards away. For a guy who desperately wanted to go home, Creasy worked steadily, without a single complaint. Like Rosen, Creasy was doing what had to be done. A check showed the phone worked as it was supposed to with just a bit of static.

From this vantage point, Rosen—taking orders from the lieutenant—would advise the commanding officers on the accuracy of their shelling.

The officers would then correct the directional aim of the big shells, ordering the howitzers to be moved a few degrees to the left or right as needed. God, this was a big job. Calculating these urgent, life or death adjustments could make a crucial difference in the outcome of the battle. It hadn't seemed all that tricky in his training sessions back in the states, but now the intensity of his duties loomed terrifying and overwhelming, far more critical than he'd ever realized it would be. He wondered if Creasy and the other guys were as nervous as he was.

It was one hour until daybreak. No one had slept. The men were tired, cold, and hungry, but they were ready. They sat in their positions, waiting. They breathed in the thick, soggy night air filled with the smell of mud and rot. They didn't make a sound.

They waited. And waited.

Chapter 16

The sky had grown light enough to blot out the stars. It was morning. Finally the sun brought forth that faint, silvery-white tone that materializes just before sunrise. The men waited, painfully stretched on tenterhooks, waiting for the ever-increasing breach of daylight to give them a better view of what they were facing.

"Holy shit," came from one of the guys who'd helped Rosen lay the wire. His voice was barely a whisper, but distinguishable enough.

Rosen blinked. He looked down the hillside toward the German line. This couldn't be right. He couldn't believe the staggering scene before him. The Allied troops that were braced behind paltry mounds of earth were just a couple of hundred yards away from what looked like the entire German army, stretched out like an impossibly endless fan below the hill. Tanks, big guns, and trucks were positioned all over the pass, hundreds of them, maybe more. Many of the trucks were American issue, obviously captured by the advancing Germans when the Americans retreated. And soldiers. Scores of German soldiers were bedded down close to their equipment.

The order to fire was given and the American howitzers ripped into the German camp. Shell after shell slammed home; the noise was horrendous. The mind-numbing rapid-fire explosions rattled Rosen to his very core. He tried to use the telephone to contact the command tent, but the noise was simply too intense. They couldn't hear him. Creasy had shrunk way down low, his hands over his ears.

The Allies had taken Rommel and his men by surprise all right, but there the advantage ended. The German army outnumbered the Americans and the handful of British by thousands. The Germans lost very little time before they started returning fire. Soon all the German guns opened up and both sides were now fully engaged.

They fired non-stop, shelling constantly. Rosen ducked as shrapnel rained all around his position. He felt his blood pulse everywhere, even in his fingertips. The panzers were on the move and two American 105-mm guns were taken out. The Germans also lost tanks and men in the barrage, but the firing never stopped, not even for a moment.

Rosen's head pounded, the hideous noise slashing into his brain. The thunderous explosions reverberated in his ears as the artillery on both sides blasted shell after shell into the sky. The ground beneath them shook. Rockets burst overhead like one-hundred 4th of Julys. The sky glared red, smudged with angry smoke.

After several hours of relentless battle, the Germans had finally garnered air support. Stuka dive bombers attacked, shattering American men and equipment. The smoke descended on them, thick like fog. Now the air whistled with the piercing shrieks of the Stuka bombs in addition to the uninterrupted roar of constant shelling from the big German guns.

Then the unthinkable happened. Creasy was hit by one of the Stukas. Rosen saw him go down. He rushed to Creasy's side, not knowing what to do. Instantly, blood colored the mud beneath them. Creasy made only a few wet, choking, thrashing sounds before he went completely still. In seconds, his life had been blown out of him, vaporized just like that.

Creasy had died almost instantly, inches from where Rosen had been crouched trying to get through to the captain on the telephone. Rosen carefully slid Creasy's eyelids shut. He didn't know why that seemed so very necessary; he just couldn't bear having Creasy's dead eyes staring at him in that pleading way. As if Creasy were imploring Rosen to explain what had happened.

Rosen had never witnessed a person dying right before his eyes, let alone a friend being killed so callously, so indiscriminately. Creasy didn't have a moment to say even one good-bye. God help them all, Rosen thought. He hadn't heard any of the other guys actually say the words: suicide mission, but the idea had probably crossed their minds just as it now crossed his. And it looked as if it weren't simply a wild speculation. The Ninth Division artillerymen had been knowingly sent to their deaths. The army could not have expected any of them to come out of this grotesquely uneven battle alive. Rosen felt dragged down, knowing now that he, too, would probably come to his end in this horrible mire of liquefied mud.

The lieutenant was hit next. One of the two remaining men helped Rosen carry the lieutenant down the hill. He wasn't dead, but from the looks of him, he'd been blown to a scrambled mess. Rosen felt certain the lieutenant had been castrated. The horror of the scene pressed against the back of his eyes, straight through to his core.

By now the telephone line that Rosen and the others had laid so carefully had been destroyed by the steady bombardment of German shells. He had to repair the wire, but meanwhile the gunfire never stopped. All day, the Americans fired round after round. At the same time, the German tanks tried to take out the American guns.

The night before the Ninth had arrived at Thala, several British tanks had attempted to steal into the darkness and travel back to the British supply depot. Ammunition stores had been just about exhausted and fuel supplies registered dangerously low. But the Germans had used Arab spies to keep track of British troop movement, and a column of Germans quickly pulled together and pursued the British. The British fired; so did the

Germans. The skirmish left behind a logjam of disabled British and German tanks, completely blocking the narrow road. The ridgeline to the left of their position resembled a junkyard.

Then Rosen spotted a line of German troops creeping toward them along this same ridgeline, partly concealed by the tangled wreckage of tanks that had been put out of action the night before. The Germans were trying to surround their position from the left. If the Germans came around from behind the berm that protected the Americans and British at least somewhat, the Germans would have them hemmed in. From there the Germans would be able to advance directly into the Allied stronghold.

Rosen had to find the captain, fast. Captain Blimp wasn't anywhere near the command tent, but Rosen relayed the information that the Germans were attempting to surround them to anyone he could find. Someone said he'd report the news to General Irwin. Rosen ran back and forth, searching for Captain Blimp, but the captain was nowhere to be found. Then he spotted Rip.

"Where's the captain? The Germans are on the ridge, over there."

"I see them," Rip said. He pointed up the hill, behind the command tent. "I saw the captain head up that way!" he yelled before running into the tent.

Following the captain up the hill looked like a bad idea. He'd probably gone up there to take a crap. German gunfire pounded erratically over the rocks and crevices all around the berm. But it was Rosen's job to inform the captain about any change in the enemy's position. He took his rifle and climbed carefully toward a crevice that looked as if it had been hacked into the rock by a gigantic cleaver. He scaled higher and higher. Smaller crevices jutted off to both sides of the larger one forming an intricate network of passageways through the rock. This was crazy. The captain wouldn't climb this high just to take a dump. He was supposed to be down the hill giving orders, taking charge of the situation.

Rosen was scared. Maybe he should turn back. If just one German sharp-shooter spotted him, he'd be a sitting duck against the backdrop of the rocky slope. But as he was about to retreat, he spotted something, someone lodged into one of the shallow crevices to his left.

"Captain, Captain . . ." Rosen called out. He was about to tell him about the German infiltration when he realized that Captain Blimp, sitting there curled into a fetal position, was not relieving himself. He was hiding and shivering in this out-of-the-way spot for a reason. Captain Blimp had collapsed into a trembling display of cowardice; it had to be shell-shock.

"Oh, shit," Rosen said to himself, but the words echoed out loud.

The captain's whole body, everything about him looked beaten. A numb stillness had somehow drawn his unshaven face into an awkward grimace; his sunken cheeks had paled to a sickly, watery white. Even his lips had drained of color.

The captain's hard, empty eyes met Rosen's. The captain looked at him, his eyes not exactly pleading like Creasy's, but perhaps seeking at least a moment of kindness. Rosen had pegged him as a peacock of a man, but he was simply an officer who was scared like everybody else, in fact, scared shitless. But the men under his command were on the line getting pounded non-stop by the Germans.

Creasy hadn't crawled into a hole. The poor lieutenant, if he lived, probably would never father a child, but he hadn't disgraced himself by hiding for his own protection.

"You poor, sick bastard," Rosen whispered to himself before he turned away and descended the hill.

Chapter 17

Rosen left the captain wallowing in his own cowardice. His job was to get back to the rest of the men in his unit, not to hold the pathetic captain's hand. Rosen's earlier warnings had reached the general, and other officers had stepped in to fill the void created by the missing Captain Blimp.

Off in the distance along the ridgeline, trucks pulled four "C" Battery howitzers up the dirt road toward the approaching Germans. Carlyle ran up to Rosen and they watched the repositioning of the howitzers. The Germans were already moving panzers into position to attack the big American guns.

"They're silhouetted against the sky," Carlyle cried. "They're making themselves fucking targets for the Kraut tanks."

"Those 105s can take them," Rosen said, but he wasn't entirely convinced. "If they can push the howitzers to the top of the hill, they'll be in position to hold off the tanks."

Rosen and Carlyle shouldered their rifles and watched from behind a truck, partially shielded from enemy fire. The Germans immediately began shelling; the screech of metal against metal tortured Rosen's ears. Two of the American howitzers went up in flames followed by an enormous plume of black smoke. But the two other howitzers reached the top of the hill and began rapidly returning fire, one shell after another, blasting and pounding away at the Germans as fast as the men could reload.

"Holy Christ," Carlyle said.

They ducked as the dirt and debris from the shelling spewed all around them. Great clods of mud and stone fell from the sky, but the Americans kept those two howitzers firing.

"I've never seen anything like this," Carlyle shouted over each massively powerful blast.

With each explosion, Rosen hiked his shoulders up to his ears, but his shoulders couldn't prevent the cruelly deafening echoes of the shock waves from screaming through his head. Then, just as suddenly as they'd begun, the Germans stopped shelling. After a few minutes, the howitzers also fell silent.

Rosen watched the scene on the ridgeline as the dust and smoke gradually began to clear. For a moment, he figured the artillerymen had simply run out of shells. Word had passed among the men that American ammo reserves had fallen dangerously low.

More dust cleared and he got a better look. "Holy shit," Rosen shouted. "The Krauts, they stopped firing; they're pulling out!"

"Christ on a mountain," Carlyle added. "They're going back down the hill. They're fucking retreating."

The American and British troops were triumphant. They stood there and watched the German tanks turn around and return to the German line to regroup. German shelling had slowed almost to a complete stop. Both sides were undoubtedly trying to conserve ammunition, but as night approached, the Allies continued to launch their heavy artillery fire. Shells flared over the berm down into the German camp.

By nightfall, British reinforcements had arrived. It was only a small column of tanks, but they'd brought along desperately needed ammo. The Americans and the British fired into the night until their supply of ammo was reduced to little more than a handful of shells for the howitzers. One of the lieutenants spread the word that in the morning they'd be able to fire upon the Germans for no more than 15 minutes before they'd have to stage a full-scale retreat. According to the lieutenant, the Ninth had fired 1,904 rounds from the big guns alone over the last 24 hours.

The next morning the first thin glow of sunlight revealed a cloudless sky. The air was still. The troops prepared to spend what was left of their ammo. Rosen crept up the hill to his forward position. His first quick look over the ridge left him speechless. Sometime during the night, the Germans had left. Their former position was littered with a sea of crushed equipment and the German dead, but the German army and their superior tanks were gone, completely withdrawn. Thala had been given up to the Allied Forces.

The good news spread among the men in seconds. A small unit of British artillery and the American Ninth Division artillery—both without the benefit of infantry support—had miraculously stopped the German advance toward the American headquarters and supply depots at Tebessa in North Africa.

Rosen, at the tender age of 18, had taken part in a suicide mission that had unexpectedly become the first actual land victory in World War II. He scrambled down the hill to join the others. Their surprising victory amazed everyone, even Division Commander, Brigadier General S. Leroy Irwin. Men were smacking each other on the back, smiling and laughing through the layers of grime on their unshaven faces.

But along with the sweet joy of triumph, a grim reality lay all around them. Incredibly, the Ninth had suffered only 45 casualties. Of that number, eight had been killed, including Creasy. The Germans had lost many more men; bodies had been left behind in their haste to stage their retreat under the cover of night.

The battlefield still smoldered. The men of the Ninth dug shallow graves for those who'd lost their lives. Their peeled faces and torn limbs seemed already puffy with death. The crude graves were simply marked with an upturned rifle and the soldier's dog tag. The grim panorama of American graves, dead German soldiers, and broken equipment possessed an eerie, permanent silence.

Rosen retrieved his radio and rolled up the wire that hadn't been completely destroyed. The unit was preparing to move out, on to the next battle. As soon as the trucks were reloaded, the men were about to depart when someone spotted a handful of Arabs digging up Creasy and the other guys they'd just buried. One Arab was frantically pulling the boots off a dead man's feet.

"Look at those fuckers, robbing the dead," Stringer yelled.

Stringer, Dago, Rosen and dozens of others began taking pot shots at the Arabs in order to scare them away. Bastards couldn't even wait until the division had pulled out. Rosen aimed above the head of an Arab who was poking into Creasy's grave. The man went down.

Rosen hadn't tried to kill him—after all they weren't at war with the Arabs— but he wouldn't have cared if he had nailed the Arab. Creasy had been his friend, his friend who had wanted out of this war in the worst way, but not this way.

Dammit, Rosen thought, was there any sense to this war? Was there ever any sense to any war?

Heroes of the Battle of Thala.
Artillerymen of the Ninth Division Infantry Division
Reunion October 2006.
Front row, second from right: First Lieutenant William "Rip"
Rybka. Front row, far right: Morris Rosen.

Chapter 18

Following the same pathway of the retreating Germans, the Ninth Division moved to a rugged, mountainous region southwest of the Kasserine Pass in Tunisia called El Guettar. No longer feeling quite as green as they'd felt before Thala and still gloating over their victory, they geared up to kick a little more German ass.

If the truth be told, however, Rosen and the rest of the men in his artillery division knew that they were still basically amateurs when it came to combat. In spite of their efforts to pull together as they'd done at Thala, they remained a far cry from Germany's well-oiled professional fighting machine.

As the column of trucks pulled into El Guettar, they were caught in the middle of a widespread sand storm. They pulled into line, but with such limited visibility, they couldn't see what they were up against. They'd been told that the Ninth Division

Artillery would be joining forces with the British and other American units already in place under the command of Lieutenant General George S. Patton, Jr. Just days before they'd arrived at El Guettar, General Patton had been assigned to take over the American forces in North Africa.

Rosen draped his jacket over his head to keep the whirling sand out of his eyes. The men in his unit sat huddled together, waiting for the wind to relent. Infantry divisions were in place, firing away at close range, but the artillery divisions on both sides were forced to wait out the sand storm. Naturally, the German artillery was facing zero visibility as well.

"Hey," Friar Tuck said over the roar of the wind, "your eyes look like a Russian roadmap."

"No, shit," Rosen shot back. "You doing any better?"

Friar Tuck shrugged. "I guess we all got sand in our Schlitz."

Rosen tried to eat, but a fine layer of sand peppered each tin of food within seconds after he'd pulled back the lid.

"Goddamn sand. Goddamn desert." Rosen grumbled mostly to himself, but he ate his gritty C rations nonetheless.

Finally, the sand storm died down after almost three days of bruising their eyes and their spirits. Artillery pulled into place and Rosen and two other guys moved forward to observe the action. He hurriedly laid telephone wire as they advanced up a dirt road to a high, rugged peak that looked out over the rocky terrain where the battle raged on.

Rosen was lying flat on his stomach, calling back to the field officers below, when he noticed a procession of three jeeps traveling along the base of the hill toward his position. The first jeep displayed two little American flags fluttering from the front bumper and a license plate bearing three shiny stars. The general's jeep.

General Patton's jeep and the others stopped right below Rosen's observation point. Closely followed by his officers, Patton got out and marched up the hill in long, measured strides. His slick leather riding boots were a bit dusty but not crusted in mud from Thala like everyone else's. His helmet sparkled in the sunlight.

The general noticed the three men lying under cover, but then his glance turned to a piercing glare aimed directly at Rosen. His eyes seemed riveted to Rosen's. General Patton said, "Buckle that chin strap." His tone was curt.

"Yes, sir." Rosen fumbled with the strap on his helmet until it clicked into place. At least he now remembered to address officers as sir, not mister, as he'd done back at Fort Meade.

Patton stood there on the ridge, smooth and important, surveying the battlefield with binoculars. A shiny pearl-handled gun rested in a holster against his hip. Apparently satisfied with what he'd observed, Patton returned to his jeep. Almost on Patton's heels, the other officers hastened back to their own vehicles. They drove back down the hill in a cloud of dust.

No sooner had the dust settled when the Germans fired a few rounds at Rosen's hill. Patton with his binoculars reflecting brightly in the sun had given away Rosen's position.

"Jesus Christ, Rosen," one of the guys said. "Patton got on you for your chin strap. Ain't you ever heard that Patton's a real stickler for chin straps."

"Yeah, I wasn't thinking, but Patton wasn't thinking either. He gave us away, showed the Germans exactly where we are."

"He did kind of stand out up here on the edge of the hill."

"Yeah," the third guy said, "like he was egging on the Krauts, daring them to shoot this way."

Another volley rained down on them. Rosen grabbed his telephone. "Let's get the hell out of here. Roll up the telephone wire. Come on."

The three of them hurried to a safer point on the far side of the plain, overlooking a dry river bed. Rosen had learned that the Arabs called these dry ravines a *wadi*.

Patton quickly reached his goal of seizing the high ground at El Guettar. Orders went out that Patton's army was moving on.

Rosen had gathered up the telephone equipment, and the other guys were salvaging and coiling the wire. He'd been told to report back to unit headquarters, along with his equipment, but the others were already taking care of that. His curiosity had gotten the best of him. He wanted to see what lay beyond the first turn of the twisting trail that led down deep into the *wadi*.

Just as he never tired of exploring new ideas when he read library books back in reform school, this gnarled pathway that sliced into the rock intrigued him. He figured he could look around and see what it was like down there in just a few minutes. He'd get back before anyone missed him. He might even locate some stranded or wounded American soldiers.

Rosen held his rifle close to his body as he descended the rock-strewn river bank. The *wadi* hadn't seen much water lately, but he could see how flash floods over the years had formed this exquisitely unusual setting. Then he rounded a bend and nearly tripped over a wooden crate sitting on the ground. It was filled almost to the top with dazzling brightly-colored, egg-shaped objects. Holy shit. It was a whole box of Italian hand grenades!

Looking more like Easter eggs than the pineapple-shaped brown grenades made in the states, they begged him to stop and investigate. The grenades were different, but they followed the same basic principle of operation.

Rosen picked up a grenade, pulled the pin, and lobbed it down into the *wadi*, just to see how far he could throw it. The blast from the grenade raised a flapping confusion of startled birds. Hot damn. This was more fun than skipping stones. He quickly grabbed another and heaved it with all his might.

The second grenade must have traveled farther, because the explosion sounded more distant, muffled. While the dust rose into a huge white cloud, he reached for a third ornately-painted grenade. Then, through the gradually settling dust, Rosen suddenly spotted a white flag, waving anxiously in his direction.

The bearer of the flag approached slowly. He was a short, stocky fellow followed by one Italian soldier after another, all with their hands and weapons raised high over their heads in surrender.

Rosen had unwittingly captured at least 100 stragglers from Mussolini's army who'd been hiding out in the ravine.

Chapter 19

"Holy shit," was all he could say. Rosen gripped his rifle but held onto the third grenade as well. What the hell had happened?

The string of weary-looking Italians kept trudging toward him. Each wore a thick veil of river bed dust obviously churned up by the exploding grenades. They looked like the sorriest lot of soldiers he'd ever seen.

"Hey, man, don't shoot," the one with the flag called out. Rosen would've sworn this surrendering Italian had spoken with a New York accent.

"You speak English?"

"Sure, man. We're Americans just like you. I'm from Brooklyn."

"Yeah," another soldier said, "most of us come from Brooklyn or somewhere in New York."

"So what the fuck? Why are you wearing Italian uniforms?"

"Just 'cause we're from New York don't mean we forget that we're Italian. All of us guys still got family in Italy."

"Yeah, we signed on to help. My mom's got three sisters and two brothers over there."

The group casually surrounded Rosen as if they were all old buddies. Most of them looked relieved that they'd stumbled into a safe exit from Mussolini's clutches, perhaps regretting that they'd signed on with his forces in the first place.

"You got any food on you, Pal?"

Rosen leveled his rifle at the one who'd spoken. "No, not enough for half the Italian army. Walk ahead of me. That way." He gestured the direction with his rifle.

The Italian soldiers from Brooklyn gave Rosen no argument. They walked orderly but very slowly back up to the top of the ravine. Rosen led them to the dirt road where his unit had been assembling while waiting to move out.

A guy wearing the helmet of the military police and an armband printed with the letters MP stood at the crossroad directing tank traffic. Rosen and his captured prisoners approached him.

"I got some Italian prisoners of war, here," Rosen said. "Maybe you'd know what to do with them?"

The MP looked confused. "Private, who's your commanding officer? Who are you with?"

"I guess I'm alone, but I need to turn over these guys to you so I can get back to my unit."

The MP drew his handgun. "Jesus Christ, Private, where'd you find them?"

"Down in the *wadi*," Rosen called out as he turned to leave. "They're Americans, fighting on the Italian side. They're nice guys. They won't fire on you."

Rosen left the company of Italian stragglers in the hands of the MP and headed back to his unit. When he reached the area where he'd last seen them, he discovered that the Ninth Division trucks had already pulled out. His entire unit was gone.

He hadn't been down in the *wadi* that long, had he? Maybe in all the confusion of their departure, no one had missed him. After all, he was only one soldier out of a whole unit. But burning in the back of his brain was the fear that if word had gotten to the captain that Rosen was missing, he would be in exceptionally deep shit.

"So where'd the Ninth go?" he asked every soldier he could find.

"They left; all their trucks headed out."

"Yeah, but where?"

"North, I think."

"But where?"

Someone finally said, "Sbeitla."

Rosen grabbed the guy's sleeve, trying to stop him from walking away. "Where the hell's that? I never heard of it."

"Shit, man, I ain't never heard of any of these fucking places they got here in Africa. Just go that way." The soldier pointed toward the road.

Rosen ran at first then slowed to a walk. He walked and walked. He noticed an occasional road sign, but he sure couldn't tell if any of them pointed the way to Sbeitla. The signs were all printed in Arabic.

Finally up ahead he spotted a town, actually more like a gleaming small city with brilliant white buildings. It had to be Sbeitla. He picked up his pace, but then he noted something odd; the entire town seemed to be floating in the air just above the sand next to the road. He hurried to the spot and realized that he'd just witnessed a mirage. He'd read about this unusual phenomenon that sometimes occurred in the heat of a desert, but he hadn't understood how surprisingly real a mirage could appear.

He continued walking until an American infantry truck finally came along and he was able to hitch a ride. The infantrymen told Rosen that he'd already walked 15 miles with about the same distance yet to go.

Once he'd traveled the 30 miles to Sbeitla, he located the spot where his division had set up camp at the top of a small incline. It didn't take long for Rosen to discover that he'd been missed.

"Where the fuck were you?" his buddy Carlyle hollered at him.

"Jesus," Johnson chimed in, "are you nuts? Why'd you desert?"

"I didn't desert," Rosen said. "I swear. I just got left behind."

"And how, exactly, did that happen, Private?" Sergeant Miller had come up from behind. He didn't sound happy.

Dozens of guys now surrounded Rosen and the sarge.

"Hey, look," Dago yelled. "Rosen's back."

"This better be good," Sergeant Miller said. "Your story better be a fucking masterpiece."

Kaminski and Marcus from the floor scrubbing incident with the general quickly elbowed their way next to the sergeant. They looked thrilled that Rosen had screwed up once again.

Kaminski said, "Ain't desertion a federal offense? Now he'll be sent before a firing squad for sure, won't he?"

Sergeant Miller didn't bother to answer Kaminski's question or the flood of other comments bantering from every direction.

"Shut up," Miller yelled. "The lot of you shut the hell up." He turned to face Rosen. "Okay, Rosen, where the fuck were you?"

As carefully as he could, Rosen told his story. By the time he finished, Kaminski and some of the other guys were holding their sides to keep from laughing out loud.

"He's like the greatest fuck-up the army has ever known," one guy called out.

"You can ask the MP," Rosen said. "He'll tell you I captured those guys."

"You captured a bunch of Italians from Brooklyn." Sergeant Miller said it more like a statement than a question. He squinted at Rosen and scratched at the shadow of his beard along his chin.

"Yeah," Rosen pleaded. "They surrendered to me just like I told you."

A muscle in the sarge's jaw rippled as if he were clenching his teeth, disturbing the cigarette that dangled precariously from the corner of his mouth.

"Report to the captain's tent at the top of the hill in exactly one hour." The sergeant then turned back to the men. "You jerkwads act like you ain't got nothing better to do. Move your asses right now, or I'll find plenty to keep you busy."

The hour's wait was pure agony. Rosen trudged up the hill and found Captain Blimp, Sergeant Miller, and First Lieutenant William Rybka, the captain's executive officer, waiting for him just outside the captain's tent. A clerk was standing next to the officers writing on a note pad. Rosen approached, saluted, and waited at attention. Color rose in the captain's face; he looked like he could stare down a German tank.

The clerk came forward and joined the group of officers. He spoke first. "Captain, Sir, this is Private Morris Rosen. He deserted at El Guettar. An infantry truck brought him back."

"No, no, I came back on my own," Rosen tried to explain.

The clerk was immediately in his face, so close his nose almost touched Rosen's. The clerk roared, "You stand at attention, Private. The captain will tell you when you may speak."

No question the captain's edginess had spilled over onto his clerk and Sergeant Miller. They both were standing a lot straighter than usual.

Captain Blimp's chin rose. He glared at Rosen with savage concentration. There was no question that he'd recognized Rosen as the soldier who'd found him quivering in his own boots in the ravine at Thala.

Rosen had every intention of keeping the captain's secret close to his chest, but the captain had no way of knowing that. Even if he told the captain in confidence that his secret was safe, the captain would never believe him. Rosen held the power to expose the chink in the captain's armor, to make him the laughing stock of the whole division. Rosen had a sinking feeling that the captain wasn't going to go easy on him no matter what the offense from this time forward.

The captain's anger had curled his lips back into a snarl. "Private Rosen, I don't know if you're familiar with military law," he began, "but under the Articles of War, desertion is a military offense punishable by death." The captain looked as if he would be delighted to personally carry out Rosen's punishment right then and there.

Sergeant Miller and Rip stepped toward the captain and conferred with him privately, but Rosen could hear enough to understand the gist of what they were saying. Apparently word had gotten to Sbeitla from more than one source that Rosen's outlandish story about the Italian grenades and the surrendering soldiers was actually the truth. They reported that the Italians from Brooklyn had indeed been rounded up by the MPs. The prisoners then sat patiently in a field, waiting until trucks arrived to pick them up. They'd offered no resistance and had been formally treated as prisoners of war.

An even deeper, ill-tempered flush rose in the captain's face. His nostrils flared. Looking into his eyes was like staring directly into a roaring fire. It brought to mind the intense inferno of Latham's machine shop forge. Rosen waited while the captain composed himself. He had no idea what he could say to improve his situation, so he kept his mouth shut.

"Private, this army doesn't have room for a goof-off like you. Desertion is a serious offense no matter what commendable endeavors you were supposedly trying to carry out. But I've decided that instead of standing you in front of a firing squad, I am placing you on a summary court marshal for the duration of our stay at Sbeitla. Sergeant Miller, I'm putting you in charge. I expect you to take care of his punishment detail."

It turned out that General Patton had just ordered a rest period for Rosen's artillery unit. After this brief respite, his unit would go right back into battle on the front lines. Patton intended to keep up the pressure on the retreating Germans and Italians, so Rosen hoped his punishment detail wouldn't last too long. He'd no idea what a court marshal was all about, but it had to be better than facing a firing squad.

He soon learned that the army could invent all sorts of resourceful methods of punishment even in the middle of a desert. While the other men spent the rest period cleaning up, shaving, sleeping, or just sitting around playing cards and dice, Rosen was assigned to KP. He scrubbed every pot the kitchen staff owned, and when the pots were all clean, he dug holes. He never understood what the army—or anyone else—intended to do with all the holes he'd dug, but he knew enough not to ask.

Rosen was the brunt of every joke in the unit for a few days, but that he could take. He'd feared that the captain was searching for any excuse he could find to do away with Rosen—permanently. Rosen kept the secret of the captain's gutless conduct in the midst of battle to himself and did everything he could to maintain a substantial distance between himself and his unwanted nemesis.

Chapter 20

Minor battles lashed across North Africa. Rosen's division fought mainly in Tunisia, but the Italian forces and the remaining Germans put up a meager defense. In a few confrontations they surrendered without firing a shot just as the Italians from Brooklyn had gratefully surrendered to Rosen in the *wadi* at El Guettar.

By now the Allied forces in North Africa had finally gained air support, and the Axis armies realized that they'd been defeated on this front. The Germans escaped North Africa from the Cape Bon Peninsula and regrouped on the island of Sicily. The Allied armies could thank Rosen's divisional artillery and its incredible victory at Thala for their subsequent takeover of North Africa. But at this point in the war, it was doubtful that Thala would ever be rightfully recognized as the turning point for victory in the African campaign.

The Ninth Division was loaded onto Landing Craft Infantry (LCI) transport ships with all their gear. With approximately 200 men squeezed into each flat-bottomed LCI, this enormous fleet departed at once for Sicily.

The weather was clear and balmy, so unlike the extremes of hot and cold they had experienced in the deserts and mountains of Algeria and Tunisia. Shreds of high clouds drifting in the distance couldn't begin to blot out the sunshine. Rosen was pleased that the Mediterranean Sea sparkled as brilliantly blue as it had been described in his story and geography books from school, but the men saw mostly the great runnels of boiling white froth churned up in the wakes of so many swiftly moving ships.

"This ain't too bad," Dago said. "I ain't even sea sick."

"I'm just happy no one's shooting at us," Carlyle said.

Johnson was trying to write a letter against his knee as the ship bounced from wave to wave. After his pencil punched a hole in the paper, he folded the letter and stuck it into his shirt pocket. He noticed Rosen was watching him. "Hey, Rosen," he said, "how come I never see you writing a letter?"

"He ain't got a wife or a girl back home," Dago quipped. "You write to your wife 50 fucking times a day."

"I know. She made me promise to write every chance I got."

Rosen said, "I don't have a girl, but I wrote to my sister Molly when we were in Casablanca. I'm going to write to her again after we land in Sicily."

His one letter to Molly paled next to the handful of letters he'd finally received from her just before they'd departed for Sicily. The news from home wasn't much, except that his older brother Hy, short for Hyman, had been drafted into the marines. Rosen had thought that by now Hy would've enlisted just to get away from their father's tyranny, but Hy was clearly conscientious about working at odd jobs to help their mother. He'd done more than his share ever since Rosen had been hauled off to reform school.

In one of her letters, Rosen had read that Molly was terribly frightened because poor Hy had been sent to ferret out the Japs who'd taken over so many of the Pacific Islands. She didn't know which was worse: a Jap or a Nazi. Rosen didn't know either. Too bad he and his brother hadn't linked up here in the European Theater.

"What about your mama?" Dago asked. "Don't you write to your mama?"

Rosen snapped out of his reverie from home. "My mother can't read, but my sister reads my letters out loud to the whole family."

"Oh."

Carlyle smiled. "Is she pretty, your sister?"

"Sure. She's a real cute kid."

"I'll bet your sister is smarter than you are."

"Hell," Dago said, "everybody's fuckin' smarter than Rosen."

"Well, I captured a whole bunch of your relatives hiding out in a ravine at El Guettar. They weren't too bright."

The laughter swelled between the guys who'd overheard that crack.

Carlyle said, "Have you heard, when we land, we'll be issued brand new rifles? It's about time they retire these ancient Springfield babies."

Rosen said, "Yeah, 'bout time. Our old Springfields go back to World War I. The sarge said we'll be getting new carbines with clips that hold ten shots."

"I'd like to get me a fuckin' machine gun, rat-a-tat-tat." Dago pretended he was shooting up into the air.

Rosen remembered the hideous thunder of the machine gun that had hammered into Creasy back at Thala. That Stuka gunner had probably been just as happy to blow away Creasy and other Americans as Dago would be to take out a few dozen Germans.

All boys played soldier at one time or another, but they were no longer acting out pretend battles in the dusty vacant lots of their childhoods. The war was changing all of them. Dim-witted farm boys like Friar Tuck and street-wise punks such as Dago and himself were going through a slow transition. Previously harmless American kids were evolving into highly-skilled killers.

Rosen shut out the conversations going on all around him. Maybe it was better not to build too many friendships, to form bonds with the other guys. If he kept to himself, he wouldn't feel the bitter stab of pain that came along with seeing a friend die in battle.

    Most of the men didn't know much about Sicily except that it was the largest island in the Mediterranean Sea and it belonged to Italy. The Ninth was ordered to keep up the pressure on the retreating Germans. They started from the southern shore where they'd landed at Licata, marching north through the center of the island and passing by Mount Etna, the island's active volcano. The Eighth Army traveled on their right along the Adriatic; the Third Division covered the Mediterranean coast on their left. British troops blended in with the Americans. The patrols thinned out into smaller parties so their widespread sweep would be as thorough as possible.

    They walked and they walked, rousting all the Italian and German forces they encountered along the way. During the second week, they came to Troina, a small town on the top of a hill, where they stumbled into an unexpected German stronghold. The Germans had taken the town and were in a good position to fire directly down the hill at the Americans.

    Rosen was quickly dispatched to observe the Germans from a position on a plateau atop another hill almost a mile away. When he reached the top, a lone general was already posted on this plateau, gazing through his binoculars. While Rosen set up his radio contact to the commanders below, he admitted to himself that Generals always seemed to gravitate toward his observation posts. He hoped this guy wouldn't give away his position as General Patton had done at El Guettar. Remembering Patton reminded him to make a quick check to see whether his chin strap was fastened. It was.

The general wasn't looking so Rosen popped a mulberry into his mouth. Fresh fruit was usually unavailable to the troops, certainly not something offered in their little ration tins. He savored every bite of the plump, sweet berries he'd picked earlier that morning. He'd already devoured several handfuls, and the rest he'd stashed in his jacket pocket so he could carry fresh berries along on his mission.

The general strolled over to Rosen and his field radio. "I'm General Roosevelt. Is this the best observation point around here?"

"Yes, Sir. It seems to be."

"Where are you from?"

"Pittsburgh, Sir." At least this general was a friendly sort, not grouchy and abrupt like Patton.

The general asked him a few more questions. Rosen answered directly, but he didn't pose any questions of his own. He'd learned not to speak out of turn. He was actually growing a lot smarter about respecting rank the way the army demanded.

General Roosevelt watched with interest as Rosen tossed another mulberry into his mouth. "Private, what have you got there?"

"Mulberries, Sir." He held out a handful. "Help yourself."

"Why thank you. How did you come across mulberries way out here in the field?"

"One of the men, an Italian fellow, pointed out a tree to me. Said his family raised silkworms. The worms eat the mulberry leaves, not the berries."

"Interesting. Very sweet berry. Tastes like the blackberries back home."

"Yes, Sir. Have another."

"Thank you, Son." General Roosevelt picked a few more out of Rosen's hand and walked back down the hill munching on mulberries.

Rosen didn't make an immediate connection with General Roosevelt's name as he should have. Later that day he learned that he'd shared his hand-picked mulberries with Brigadier General Theodore Roosevelt, Jr., eldest son of President Teddy Roosevelt. He should have mentioned that he'd seen President Franklin Roosevelt in Casablanca riding in a jeep with Churchill. He was certain that somehow the two presidents were related.

After about three weeks of raking through the Sicilian countryside, Rosen and four other soldiers approached a small farmhouse. About thirty miles to the east, Mount Etna sat like a squatting sentinel, belching out a thin but constant stream of smoke. The farmhouse looked deserted, but they could never be certain. The Germans managed to hole up in totally unsuspecting places.

"C'mon," Rosen said to the infantryman walking closest to him. "Cover me while I go in."

Rosen held his rifle in firing position and booted the door open with his foot. It swung inward with a hollow creaking sound. A dew of sweat covered his brow. His pulse throbbed in his ears. No matter how many times he'd investigated what looked like an abandoned building, he always felt his heart speed up when he took that first step inside.

He entered cautiously. The place smelled of garlic and vinegar, but it looked clean enough. Rosen checked all possible hiding places. There weren't many. The humble furnishings were sparse, very old. Much of it had probably been hewn by a local carpenter's hand, perhaps by the man who had lived here.

He always wondered about the displaced families that had scattered when the gunfire approached. What were their secrets? Where had they gone? He would never know. It was like reading an adventure story without a plausible ending. Rosen hoped the uprooted families would return someday and find a way to reclaim the lifestyle they'd enjoyed before the rude invasion of their simple existence. It seemed outrageous that armies could disrupt the lives of so many so completely.

Rosen walked toward a small table that sat below a window. It held a neatly-arranged display of old post cards. He picked up one and turned it over. The message had been scrawled in Italian, but he was certain the gist of it was a variation of: "Wish you were here."

He wondered whether his sister had a collection of something as simple as post cards or stamps. He remembered from reform school that the teenage girls were always a twitter about things that made no sense to him. Maybe Stella—the only girl whose name he remembered—had a post card collection. No, he smiled to himself. She probably collected Nancy Drew mysteries.

Rosen went outside and saw four guys from his party emerging from one of the doors in the lower half of a rickety, weather-beaten barn.

"All's clear," the one they called Red signaled to him. "No Krauts, no cows or nuthin'. Just a lot of garbanzo beans."

"What's that?"

"Man, you don't know what a garbanzo bean is?"

Rosen ignored the jab and went inside. Sure enough a pile of hard, round beans (instead of the bean shape that he remembered from his mother's cooking) lay heaped on the floor. They were too dry to be of much use. They sure didn't have time to soak beans for cooking the way his mother used to do. Besides, since he'd never seen beans like this before, he figured it was probably something they ground up to make feed for the livestock.

Red called in through the barn door. "Find anything in the house?"

"No."

"Might as well bed down in there for the night. It's as good a place as any."

"Yeah. At least it'll be dry if it rains."

They entered the house and dropped their packs. Red settled on the floor next to Rosen. "So," Red said, "what are you going to do after the war?"

"I don't know, probably move away from Pittsburgh, far away."

"You ought to go to Kansas. That's where I'm from."

"What's so great about Kansas?" another guy chimed in. "New York's where it's happening. Kansas is nothing but miles and miles of fucking corn fields."

"How do you know?" the guy from Kansas shot back.

"Some guy in boot camp told me."

Rosen stretched out on the floor and closed his eyes. He'd heard stories about places all over the U.S. It seemed that every guy he'd met loved his home town. Rosen wanted no part of Pittsburgh or his father or his Uncle Jack. If he lived through the war, he'd move somewhere new, somewhere that held no sad memories.

They took turns keeping watch outside and sleeping inside. One of the guys commandeered one of three beds in the house, but Rosen and the others slept on the floor. Using someone's bed seemed far too invasive.

The next morning, they headed out once again. A few hundred yards up the road, they found an abandoned German 88-mm gun minus the prime mover, a device on wheels that they used to tow the weapon behind a truck.

"Looks like someone left here in a hurry," Red said. "The gun's still in good condition."

"Mover's gone. That thing's too big to carry," one of the other men said. As he spoke, he headed toward the long-barreled gun favored by the Germans for anti-tank and anti-aircraft warfare.

"Wait," Rosen said, remembering something one of the sergeants had explained about explosives. "Don't go near it. It's probably booby-trapped."

Just as he'd thought, Rosen spotted a string attached to the trigger mechanism. As they'd retreated, the Germans left behind mines and booby traps wherever they could, anything to slow down the Allied troops. Rosen's party gave the gun a wide berth and continued up the road.

They'd walked less than a mile when a sudden burst of enemy fire rang out through the countryside. They dived for cover but not quite fast enough. Rosen felt a horrendous wallop crash into his helmet. The impact left him dazed for a moment; his ears rang with the hollow echo of gunfire.

Rosen's party returned fire and the German stragglers who'd fired at them quickly sneaked back to wherever they'd been hiding. The artillery barrage had been brief, but Rosen had been hit nonetheless. He felt blood running down his neck, but he couldn't pull off his helmet. It was stuck to his head.

Rosen started running and decided he wasn't going to stop until he located a medic. He didn't want to bleed to death lying in an abandoned field. He was lucky enough to find an infantry medic about a mile up the road, but the medic couldn't get Rosen's helmet loose either.

"Soldier, a piece of shrapnel went right through your helmet. It's stuck into your skull like a rivet. I can't get it loose. I'd need a tool, something like a pair of pliers to get a grip on it."

Rosen reached into his pack and produced the pliers he used to strip wire when he set up telephone lines in the field. "How's this?"

The medic grinned and went to work pulling out the shrapnel imbedded in Rosen's skull. He packed the wound with sulfa powder and wrapped a bandage around Rosen's head. In seconds the bandage was a bloody mess.

"What's your name, Private?"

"Private Morris Rosen."

"Serial number?"

"13086326."

The medic scribbled the information on a pad of paper he'd pulled from his shirt pocket.

"Why do you need my name?"

"Well, Soldier, you just got yourself a Purple Heart."

"Oh."

"If you ain't feeling too much pain, you can go on and get back to your party." With that, the medic sent him on his way.

Rosen examined the hole that went clear through his helmet before he carefully placed it back on his head. He would write and tell his sister Molly that his battered helmet had saved his life.

His head hurt a little, and it was still bleeding, but Rosen hurried to catch up with a group from his division that had just passed by.

Chapter 21

It took General Patton's and British General Montgomery's combined forces only 38 days to capture Sicily, the area Winston Churchill had aptly named the "soft underbelly of the Axis powers." In spite of their success, the Americans counted 25,000 dead and wounded, but Germany and Italy had suffered 167,000 casualties. With this victory sewn up, the Ninth Division went west to Cefalu on the Mediterranean coast for a brief rest while waiting for orders to ship out.

Rumors passed from man to man. Everyone thought Italy was about to surrender. The war would soon be over; they would all be going home.

A colorful tri-motor plane skimmed over Cefalu, possibly heading for Palermo, and the men cheered wildly. They were all laying odds, betting that the plane carried Italian General Bagdolio who would personally surrender the Italian army to the Allied forces.

The guys in the division had no trouble locating enough Sicilian wine to propel them all into a drunken state of euphoria. Except for that first time he'd gotten drunk with Carlyle in Casablanca and a few beers at Tebessa, Rosen hadn't consumed any alcohol. Some of the guys had scrounged wine from the houses they'd searched, but Rosen hadn't been in on any of that. But he now had to admit that the Sicilian stuff they'd pulled out of countless hiding places tasted pretty good. He drank with Carlyle and Johnson while Friar Tuck tried to serenade them with his harmonica. Friar Tuck was too drunk to remember the tune, but no one seemed to care.

Dago, Stringer, and four other guys caught fish in the blue Mediterranean and set up campfires for enormous fish-fries on the beach. Rosen drank wine and ate fish. He unwound the bloody bandage from his head and threw it away. Rosen celebrated with the other guys; he was one of the first to pass out that evening.

The next morning Rosen awoke to the sound of Carlyle and Friar Tuck snoring like two chain saws tearing through wood. He had a headache that pounded against his forehead like a fist. He moved away from the snoring, but he didn't get far. Rip had been looking for him.

"Captain's orders," Rip said. "I'm supposed to send you for demolition training."

"You mean explosives?"

"Sure."

"But isn't the war over?"

"Not yet, Pal."

"Where do I go?"

Rip pointed. "Just outside of Cefalu. You'll see a campsite set up. There's a big sign warning about danger, live explosives."

"I'm supposed to go right now?" Rosen asked.

"Right now. It'll take them two or three days to train you."

Word spread that the Ninth Division was preparing to pull out. Evidently the war wasn't over after all, and no one was going home. While Rosen was off learning how to set and place explosives, his division would be heading to England to train for the invasion of France. All this looked mighty suspicious to Rosen. Captain Blimp had hit upon an easy out, a way to remove him from the division altogether.

Rosen went, expecting to meet up with dozens of other guys, but he was the only one who'd been pulled out of his unit for this impromptu session in demolition training. A group of combat engineers greeted him and put him to work learning how to blow up bridges and set booby traps. About 15 soldiers from other units gradually showed up, but no one else from the Ninth Division artillery.

The engineers emphasized the dangers in any kind of demolition work. This was not a job for the typical army goof-up like Rosen, and he was certain he understood why he'd been singled out for something so hazardous. Captain Blimp hadn't forgotten that Rosen had witnessed his moment of cowardice. He was probably hoping that Rosen would manage to blow off his own head. Or maybe the captain thought that Rosen would screw up so badly, the engineers would have good reason to bounce him right out of the army. Score one for the captain. Leaving Rosen behind for demolition training was not accidental.

But Rosen didn't screw up. He became rather good at handling explosives if he did say so himself. Three days later he returned to the base camp fully versed on TNT. In fact he'd become so interested in explosives that he'd helped himself to a box of fuses and bricks of TNT and carried all of it back to camp. He'd enjoyed learning something new, and he was anxious to apply this specialized knowledge to a job. Of course, no such job had been assigned to him as yet.

He'd no sooner arrived back at the rest camp, when the mess sergeant spotted him. "Hey, Private, I need a man for a work detail."

Rosen looked over his shoulder, hoping a few other privates were hanging around, waiting to get pulled into some crummy kitchen clean-up job, but as luck would have it, he was the only private in sight.

"Yes, Sir," Rosen answered while his joy over learning all about explosives suddenly faded.

"I need a place to bury all the garbage. We can't just leave a mountain of rotting food behind us when we're ordered out."

"No, Sir. I guess we can't."

"Over there, next to the pile of garbage, dig a hole eight by eight by eight. There's a pick and a shovel in the supply tent."

Rosen found the tools and started digging. The ground had been baked hard by the sun. One inch deep he hit rock. The shovel barely dented the surface. The other guys were off getting laid or getting drunk while he was left to carve a trash dump out of solid rock.

It was impossible. He tossed the shovel aside and went for his stash of explosives. Demolition training had taught him that there were easier ways to gouge a hole into rock-hard earth. He had it all figured out. He'd set a charge of TNT just big enough to loosen the dirt.

He knew he needed to place the explosives into a hole, so he used the pick to chip away at the rock. He worked in the hot sun for over an hour until he'd finally chopped an opening deep enough to hold the charge. He was sweating like an old mule by the time he was ready to light the fuse and run out of the way.

The boom was extraordinary. An enormous geyser of earth and rock blasted 100 feet into the air, followed by a thundering rain of teeming dirt. He guessed he'd used just a bit too much TNT, but at least now the earth and rock had been loosened up, so he could easily make a hole to the exact specifications for the cook's garbage.

"What the hell are you doing, Rosen?" Sergeant Miller was standing in front of him before the dust had time to settle.

The sarge was so completely covered with flakes of debris that even his eyebrows had turned white. Rosen knew he was once again in deep trouble. The dust couldn't hide the rage bristling dark in the sarge's eyes or the bulging veins throbbing all over his face.

"Just breaking up the dirt, Sir. I'm making a place for the mess sergeant to bury his garbage."

Miller stood there balling his hands into tight fists. His eyes seemed to burrow two holes straight into Rosen's brain. "Did you notice what's going on over there? Did you even see the officer's tent? Did you bother to notice that the officers were having a nice quiet lunch before you fucking blasted the shit out of the place?"

Rosen stood up straighter and permitted his eyes to drift over the yawning crater he'd just created toward the officer's mess tent. He held his breath while he took a better look. The officers—including Captain Blimp and a full colonel—and all their food had been layered with dirt. The stunned officers simply sat there, glaring at him in blank-faced astonishment.

He definitely would have to pay more attention to the quantity of TNT needed for a charge. Sure, he'd over-estimated the amount of TNT a little, but now digging an eight by eight by eight hole for the dump would be a piece of cake.

Sergeant Miller had moved closer to Rosen. They were now eyeball to eyeball, and Rosen caught a sprinkle of the sarge's spit as he spoke.

"When you're finished with the garbage detail, clean up the officer's tent."

"Yes, Sir."

"Then pack your gear. You're being reassigned as of o-five-hundred tomorrow morning."

Chapter 22

The next morning Rosen found a driver sitting in a jeep ready to transfer him to Palermo. The driver knew nothing about Rosen's orders except that he was supposed to deliver him no later than o-nine hundred that day. He kept his eyes straight ahead as he drove. Rosen crunched down low in his seat next to his pack.

The rumors had turned out to be accurate. The Ninth Division was already on its way to Britain where they would begin an intense period of training and preparation for the invasion of France. Captain Blimp was nowhere to be seen. Rosen didn't know what to think about any of this. The army took care of its own, he guessed. Well, at least, the army took care of its officers. As for Rosen, he'd been left behind. Captain Blimp had stumbled upon a clever way to get rid of Rosen without making a big fuss, and he'd jumped at the opportunity.

Rosen had tried not to get too close to the other guys in his outfit, especially after Creasy had been killed, but the truth was that he felt disappointed about being singled out. The other guys, his friends during the past months, were gone. What if he never saw Carlyle, Stringer, Johnson, or Friar Tuck again? He'd even gotten used to Dago's craziness and Kaminski's constant ribbing. He decided that as long as he remained in the army, he would no longer encourage new friendships. It would be easier if he served his time without attachments.

The jeep dropped him off at the dock in Palermo. A lieutenant approached him. He unfolded a piece of paper and read it before he spoke.

"Are you Private Morris Rosen?"

"Yes, Sir."

"You're a radio operator?"

"Yes, Sir."

"Any good with Morse Code?"

"Yes, Sir. The officers who trained me in radio school said I was very good."

The lieutenant looked at the paper again. "Okay, Rosen. You've been re-assigned to me." He pointed. "Get into that landing craft over there. We're heading out to Salerno."

Palermo, Salerno. These Italian names all sounded alike, but he knew he'd be leaving the island of Sicily now. Salerno was a city in Italy.

Two other guys from different outfits showed up and joined Rosen and the lieutenant in the landing craft. One was a private, the other a sergeant. Rosen wondered if these guys had likewise managed to pull off some serious screw-ups in their own companies. The private maybe, but the sergeant had probably been ordered to go along on this mission to supervise Rosen and keep him in line.

The slow passage to Italy took most of the day. The landing craft transferred them to a naval transport ship that had been anchored well off shore. The transporter then delivered them to a destroyer positioned in the bay near Salerno. A naval lieutenant met them after they climbed up a long, shaky ladder attached to the side of ship. Rosen didn't look down.

As soon as they were safely on board, the two lieutenants fired off questions. They wanted to know just about everything relating to Rosen's skills and past experience in communications. Apparently, like Rosen coming off the widespread campaign throughout Sicily, the other two also had plenty of experience under fire. The sergeant and the private seemed capable, but Rosen was the radio operator, and they needed a good radioman.

The naval lieutenant out-ranked the army lieutenant, so he conducted most of the questioning. The lieutenant apparently already knew plenty about Rosen's checkered past, but he seemed willing to ignore the problems, even the details regarding his court marshal in Africa. The lieutenant was more interested in learning about Rosen's knowledge of shore to ship fire control.

"Your record shows you trained to direct naval gunfire back in North Africa?"

"Yes, Sir." Rosen had no idea why the lieutenant would want a problem soldier like him involved with ship to shore fire control. Captain Blimp had wanted Rosen shot at sunrise.

"You know your way around a Morse key?"

"Yes, Sir."

"Okay, Private, here's the story. The 36th Division is in trouble. The Germans are firing down on them from a stronghold on top of a hill outside of Salerno. Got those poor bastards from the 36th trapped in a corner and they're taking an awful beating. The navy can't get the big ships in close enough to help, so we need a qualified radioman on the shore, right in the thick of things with the infantry, to give us co-ordinates to direct the naval gunfire."

"Yes, Sir."

"This is going to be a rescue mission." He paused. "Rescue missions are always dangerous."

"Yes, Sir."

"We'll be going forward, to link up with the infantry. We'll have to hunker down in the middle of the action, and we'll have plenty of flak coming at us. The lieutenant and I will tell you what information to send back to the ships. You'll be directing naval gunfire from the shore via Morse code. You think you can handle it?"

Rosen felt those familiar little beads of sweat forming on his upper lip. "Yes, Sir," he said, but all the while he was wondering if this was another suicide mission. But they wouldn't send two lieutenants along on a job that was impossible, would they?

Rosen wasn't given an opportunity to ask questions. The five of them slipped ashore in a small Higgins landing craft and immediately found themselves in the heart of a colossal fire fight. Shells rained down from the Germans holding the top of the hill at a deafening pace. From their advantageous position, the Germans were lording it over the trapped Americans and doing some pretty serious damage to the men below. The infantrymen of the 36th didn't have artillery that could fire all the way to the top of the hill to reach the Germans, so they took shelter as best they could. The Krauts were blasting them from one end of the alcove where they'd landed to the other. The 36th didn't stand a chance. Rosen wondered whether any of them stood a chance.

For two long days Rosen and his party crouched behind a wrecked landing craft and other damaged equipment while Rosen tapped out co-ordinates for the navy's attack using Morse code. The other private on the mission carried Rosen's equipment. The sergeant stood guard, covering their backs with his rifle.

The five of them stayed close together. Once the navy got those big 12-inch guns on their cruisers positioned just right, the German onslaught was stopped short. The navy fired away, destroying the German stronghold and giving the men in the 36th an opportunity to advance to the top of the hill. The big naval guns and the 36th kept up their assault until the Germans were forced to pull back.

As soon as the 36th Division had broken out of their predicament and the German infantry and artillery had retreated, the U.S. Navy withdrew from the bay at Salerno and the ships got ready to steam north toward Naples. But before the naval lieutenant returned to his ship, he approached Rosen.

The lieutenant said, "Good work, Son. You did a fine job." He even shook Rosen's hand.

"Thank you, Sir."

Rosen watched the lieutenant walk away. He'd simply called him "Sir" during the entire mission because he hadn't learned the naval lieutenant's name. He hadn't even learned the names of the others. Well, they probably wouldn't remember his name either.

But maybe this marked a change in his luck. He'd done a first-rate job, and he hadn't screwed up any part of it. An officer had shaken his hand rather than dressing him down. A tremendous sensation of pride welled up in his chest, and a surge of boundless energy ran through him. He became aware that a kink of a smile had found its way into the corner of his mouth. He had begun to see the army as a job, a job that he could do honestly and up to the army's standards. For once, he was pleased with himself.

With Salerno secured, word passed from man to man that all available soldiers would be moving north toward Naples. As the navy sailed north, it continued firing at the retreating Germans. But the

German army had received replacements, and they were not to be taken easily even though they were on the run. They fired relentlessly, deploying heavy artillery to sink any vessel that might be useful to the opposition. The harbor at Naples had become a floating junkyard.

    Army transportation rounded up any remaining personnel at Salerno, and Rosen found himself on his way to Naples. The artillery of the Third Division was assembling at a place called the King's Hunting Grounds in the hills east of Naples. They'd set up headquarters inside an enormous crater formed by an extinct volcano. The plan was for the Third Division to push north, toward a little village called Cassino, into the mountains, and eventually all the way to Rome.

    Rosen had received no formal transfer. No papers were signed and passed between officers. In the midst of battle, men and equipment shifted to places where soldiers and their weapons were most needed. The conditions no longer resembled the regimen and discipline of the army bases and schools he'd been assigned to during his basic training. Rosen found himself abruptly displaced from the Ninth Division and delivered into the Third Division, 39th Field Artillery.

Chapter 23

Rosen and the other newcomers to the Third Division quickly fell into line with the old guard. The Third was all business; Rosen hadn't noticed nearly as many West Point graduates in the Ninth Division as he now saw in the Third. First and second lieutenants were everywhere—undoubtedly the generals of the future—coming up the ranks under the steady command of General Lucian K. Truscott, Jr.

Rosen sat with a group of guys awaiting orders. They talked, wondering how soon their outfit would move out. Sometimes the waiting was almost worse than the battles. A few of the men joked and fooled around, but most of the guys had found that they no longer had the energy to engage in useless horseplay. Life had become more difficult. They'd hardened; they'd grown weary of pointless one-liners.

Some of the guys sat on their packs, but Rosen balanced himself on top of his helmet, using it like a tiny camp chair. Jules Posner, nicknamed "Julie" stood nearby. He was a big guy who looked like the kind of bruiser you wouldn't want to provoke. Julie shagged over to the group, and without saying a word, casually kicked Rosen's helmet out from under him.

Rosen landed on his rear end with a thud. "Hey, you stupid son of a bitch," Rosen shouted. "What do you think you're doing?"

The big guy laughed and the others joined in. Big joke. This they thought was funny. Rosen had a mind to punch him square in the jaw just to see how much he'd laugh then, but what the hell. Punching out this big galoot wasn't worth getting busted again.

"You're Rosen?" Julie asked.

Rosen picked himself up and walked away. "Yeah, what of it?" he mumbled over his shoulder.

Julie trailed after him. "You a radio operator?"

"Yeah."

"Sergeant said I'm supposed to pick a team. We'll be working the radios together. You and me and a couple of the other guys."

Rosen grunted. That figured. He always ended up working with guys who were a pain in the neck.

Posner's face lit up when he smiled at Rosen. Up close he didn't seem tough at all. He was a good-looking guy with thick, sandy hair and broad shoulders, the kind of guy the girls went nuts over. Rosen continued to walk away, but Julie caught up with him.

"So where are you from?"

"Pittsburgh."

"Yeah? I'm from Brooklyn."

"I've met lots of guys from Brooklyn," Rosen said.

"You're new to the Third?"

"Yeah, came from the Ninth."

Julie went on and on with the questions. Just what he needed, Rosen thought. A guy who never stops talking.

The Third Division ventured north into the Apennine Mountains. Julie hadn't been assigned to work with him just yet, so Rosen guessed he was off doing his job somewhere else. He wouldn't lose any sleep over Julie's assignment. Rosen was happy to be working alone.

Germans lay in wait at every turn. They hid in bunkers, farmhouses, churches, or any place they could find a hole in the ground. As his outfit inched along, Rosen was sent forward with the infantry to lay telephone wire. Spotty, unpredictable radio reception had become a big problem in this mountainous terrain, so the telephone had become their only way to keep lines of communication open. Rosen dispatched positions, directions, co-ordinates, all kinds of information to the officers who were in charge of artillery. Artillery, the big guns, came from behind and supported the infantrymen.

Rosen had lost track of time. It was either September or October of 1943. It really didn't matter much which month it was; the days somehow all blurred together. He wondered whether today was his birthday. He'd turn 19 on the sixth of October, still very much one of the youngest guys in his unit. It seemed as if he'd joined the army 100 years ago.

They were approaching the little town of Avelino. Avelino was deserted, the town and its people long ago blown to bits by German artillery. Some of the lucky ones had escaped to God only knew where. Once the Third Division had moved in, Rosen saw that the scattering of houses that were still standing looked to be on the verge of collapse. Even the trees had been blasted into topless trunks by artillery fire.

Rosen had grown tired of repairing telephone wire that had been ground to shreds after a tank had rolled through, so he now tried to survey the scene first and then tried to improvise ways to elevate the wire off the ground.

At Avelino, Rosen strung his wire over fences, out-buildings, and as high as the second floor between houses and barns. Tanks couldn't come anywhere near the wire because of the way he'd engineered his set-up. He was kind of proud of himself. His ingenuity would save him a lot of extra work. He'd worked all day, knowing the infantry would be ready to advance come daylight. Word was out that the Germans were just over the next hill; the Third Division was ready to kick some more German ass.

By night fall, Rosen had finally finished stretching the wire from headquarters all the way to his current forward position. He was so exhausted he couldn't possibly walk all the way back to camp where the infantrymen were bedded down for the night. He simply dropped to the ground and stretched out on the cobblestones along the side of the road. His stint in the army had taught him to grab the opportunity to catch some sleep wherever he could no matter how impossible the conditions. So in spite of the hard cobblestones that served as his bed, in a matter of minutes he'd drifted off into a sound sleep.

He was rudely awakened by a kick in his side. Rosen grabbed his rifle and pointed it at the outline of the man who stood hovering over him.

"Who the fuck you kicking, asshole?" Rosen yelled.

"You, Private. Wake up. On your feet."

"What the fuck you doing?"

Rosen squinted, trying to get a better look at this guy. A fragment of moonlight barely filtered through a growing layer of clouds, casting shadows in places that were already dark.

As his eyes adjusted, Rosen noticed other shadowy figures milling about off in the distance, far from discernable in the frail moonlight. He hoped they were only Americans on guard duty.

"Watch your mouth, Private. I need a driver. Now. On your feet."

Rosen had fully awakened and finally realized that only an officer would speak to him like this.

"I want to return to headquarters. The jeep is over there."

"You want to go to headquarters?"

The clouds unraveled just enough for the moonlight to give Rosen a better look at the bar on the guy's shoulder. Holy shit, he'd just cussed out a lieutenant. Now he recognized him. Lieutenant White.

"That's what I said," White growled.

"Sir, I don't know the way." He'd finally figured out that addressing him as "Sir" might not be a bad idea.

"You follow the road. How difficult can that be?"

"I came overland. I didn't follow the road. I was laying wire, Sir."

"Christ on a mountain, Private. Stop your complaining and get in the jeep."

Rosen followed him.

Lieutenant White said, "You have your rifle, Private?"

"Yes, Sir, right here."

"Okay. I'll drive. You be on sharp alert for any snipers."

"Yes, Sir."

Lieutenant White started the jeep. He didn't flick on the headlights. "Always best to drive without lights."

"Yes, Sir." Everyone knew not to use lights at the front. Even the windshield of the jeep had been folded forward onto the hood so it couldn't reflect moonlight. A German sniper would target a light or a reflection in a heartbeat.

The lieutenant followed the road; Rosen rode shotgun. The lieutenant drove carefully at first then picked up speed. Rosen knew Lieutenant White was driving much too fast considering he had no headlights, but Rosen wasn't about to say anything. White was sure to make a big deal about Rosen's outburst of foul language to an officer when they reached headquarters. He didn't need more trouble than he already had. Trouble seemed to follow him wherever he went.

The countryside was probably crawling with Germans, but Rosen couldn't see any actual signs of them. No movement on either side of the road. Moonlight leaked through the trees, but it was still much too dark to identify more than indistinct shapes. He watched the long, black shadows of tall poplar trees forming an almost ladder-like design on the road ahead of them.

Then Rosen spotted machine gun tracer fire off in the distance. They'd left the American infantry behind, so this had to mean they were approaching gunfire from the German front. Holy shit. How was he going to convince Lieutenant White that the jeep was heading in the wrong direction?

"Sir, are we going the right way?" Rosen asked, trying to make it sound like an offhand question.

"I know the way." The lieutenant snapped. He gripped the steering wheel forcefully. Rosen said nothing more.

Rosen watched the road, but kept an eye on that machine gunfire ahead. He looked off into the forest on both sides, then back again to the ladder-like pattern of shadows on the road ahead. Suddenly the shadows cast by the trees disappeared. It took a moment for this to register.

The road was gone.

Rosen yelled, "Stop!"

But it was too late. The jeep was air-born, flying across a deep canyon where a bridge had been blown out. The jeep sailed the full width of the ravine before it plunged down, down, hitting full force into a stone abutment on the other side. The stone abutment was solid and obviously had once supported that side of the missing bridge.

Rosen was knocked senseless for a moment. Loose equipment and a load of tire chains in the back of the jeep had been tossed forward, on top of them, knocking Rosen half-way out of the open side of the jeep. He tasted blood in his mouth. He felt a sharp bolt of pain seizing his back and legs.

"Holy shit," Rosen cried. He turned to the lieutenant. "You all right?"

He didn't answer. Rosen pulled himself back into the jeep and grabbed the lieutenant's shoulder. He shook him slightly.

"Sir, Lieutenant White, you all right?" he repeated.

The clouds parted just enough for Rosen to get a clear view of the lieutenant. He'd been thrown forward, his head crushed against the stone wall. The lieutenant's entire face had been shattered. Blood streamed over his uniform, over the steering wheel, everywhere. Rosen had seen plenty of mangled soldiers during the past year. There was no question.

Lieutenant White was dead.

Chapter 24

Rosen grabbed his rifle and crawled out from under the tangle of heavy chains that had landed on top of him. He tried to pull himself to his feet, but no matter how hard he struggled, he couldn't overcome the pain. He couldn't stand up; he couldn't walk away from the wreck. The forward thrust of the chains and other supplies had shoved him sideways out of the jeep, saving his head from exploding like a pumpkin against the culvert's massive stone wall. He could have been killed the same way the poor lieutenant had been killed. God. He couldn't believe it. Once again, his life had been spared, this time by a bunch of rusty old tire chains.

Pain flashed the length of his body, but he knew he had to get away from the jeep. If a German scout had heard the crash, he'd come to investigate. Rosen checked to make certain the hand grenade he always kept carefully attached to his belt was still there. Radio operators usually didn't carry grenades everywhere they went, but Rosen had decided months ago that he would never allow himself to be taken prisoner. The army had decreed that it was essential to imprint each soldier's religion on his dog tag. Rosen's tag flaunted a bold "H" for Hebrew. He had no doubt that the Krauts would find endless joy torturing a Jewish prisoner of war. He'd steer clear of capture by the Germans his own way.

Rosen winced at the pain that gripped his spine. He took a deep breath and waited a minute. He felt sweat running into his eyes. He wiped it away with the back of his hand and tried again. If he couldn't walk back to camp, he'd crawl.

Finally he somehow managed to drag his body up from the depths of the canyon, reaching the road several yards above. He'd pulled himself into a shallow ditch—most likely intended for drainage—that ran parallel to the road. Following the ditch seemed a safer bet than exposing himself fully.

He spotted another scattering of machine gun tracer fire above the trees. He headed the opposite direction. So for the next two or three hours, he crept along on his stomach, straining himself forward through the mud and underbrush with his elbows.

His shoulders tightened and the pain was agony. His entire body burned with fatigue, but he had to keep moving. The frontal bones of his forehead seemed to be splitting, but he ignored the pain. He continued his slow journey back toward his unit.

It seemed as if weeks had passed before the first whisper of daylight flickered on the horizon directly in front of him. He blinked through his sweat at the glow of the approaching sunlight. Good. Unlike Lieutenant White, he was heading the right way, east, toward his unit's encampment. His ravaged body trembled with exhaustion. He'd left the dead lieutenant and the jeep way behind, but now his progress per hour could be measured only in inches. The sun crept higher in the sky and a gorgeous sunrise bequeathed layered shades of pinks and gold between the treetops.

But suddenly he heard footsteps.

"Jeez," he whispered out loud.

He didn't have time or the strength to crawl away from the footsteps, so he fumbled for his grenade. Then he saw three figures, men, walking toward him on the road. They didn't look like soldiers. Instead of helmets, they wore hats with wide, floppy brims. Rosen let his forehead sink down against his out-stretched arm in relief. They were simply farmers, three Italian farmers who had probably defied their wives and all logic to stay behind to tend their fields.

"Look," one of the men called out in Italian, "it's a soldier, American soldier."

"He's alive," said another.

Rosen released his grip on the grenade. The farmers knelt next to him.

"Are you shot?"

"No, I'm hurt," Rosen answered in his clipped Italian. "Jeep accident. I was trying to crawl back to my unit, to the first aid station, but I'm worn out. Do you have a car or a wagon?"

"No, nothing like that," one of them said. "The German soldiers, they take everything."

The men showed no surprise that Rosen was able to communicate with them in Italian. They conferred and somehow agreed as to which one of them would carry Rosen to the American camp. The two other men lifted Rosen onto the back of the third.

The man shifted Rosen's weight until he was comfortable and then set out at a steady pace, carrying Rosen piggy-back. Rosen dropped his head gratefully against the farmer's broad shoulder.

After twenty minutes, the farmer stopped to rest. Rosen offered him a cigarette and took one himself before giving the man the remainder of the pack. They smoked together like old friends. The farmer showed him a tattered sepia-toned photo of his wife and two sons, and Rosen wished he had a photo of his own to brag about. Maybe someday.

The farmer again hoisted Rosen into piggyback position but with a bit more difficulty this time. In another twenty minutes or so, with the farmer jogging at a steady trot, they reached the Third Division First Aid Station. The farmer smiled, happy because one of the medics had given him a full package of Lucky Strikes and a tin of coffee. He waved and called goodbye to Rosen before he returned to his fields.

The medics examined Rosen, checking for broken bones without the benefit of an x-ray machine.

"You got some nasty bruises, but you'll be all right," a medic said. "We've got to write a report on this, so just tell us everything you remember."

Rosen told his story while one of the medics took notes. The medics exchanged guarded glances. One of them said there was no question; Rosen's unit had to be notified.

Staff Sergeant William Kunz, head of Rosen's radio section, was ordered to investigate the scene of the accident and to report his findings directly to Captain Coates. They kept Rosen in the first aid station while all this was going on.

Sergeant Bill Kunz reported back what he'd observed at the scene of the accident. He said he'd found the body of the lieutenant pinned against the wall, still slumped over in the driver's seat. Kunz had made arrangements to have the lieutenant's body removed from the wreckage. The jeep would stay where it was.

"So, Sergeant, you believe that Lieutenant White was killed in the crash?" The captain said it like he wasn't fully convinced.

"Yes, Sir."

"The lieutenant was driving the jeep like Private Rosen claims?"

"Yes, Sir."

"The bridge was blown out?"

"Yes, Sir. Completely gone."

"So you'd say this was an accident?"

"Yes, Sir," Kunz said. "It's a miracle Rosen wasn't killed, too."

By now everyone knew that Rosen had cussed out the lieutenant prior to the accident. The gossip spread, altering and exaggerating Rosen's comments to outright threats. More than one guy believed that Rosen had killed the lieutenant because he'd awakened Rosen so abruptly. The rumor-mill worked overtime.

Rosen had bruises and pulled muscles but no broken bones. He felt sore all over, but one of the medics firmly suspected he was faking his injuries. Rosen stopped trying to explain. All the army had to offer him was a few days bed rest. His "rest," which consisted of a four-day stay in the first aid shelter, seemed strangely similar to imprisonment while the investigation into the accident continued.

But in spite of all the talk about Rosen openly swearing at Lieutenant White, the accident report clearly stated that the lieutenant had been sitting in the driver's seat when he'd been killed. Clearly, Rosen was not responsible for the lieutenant's death.

Rosen was driven back to his outfit and dropped off without further discussion. New orders from Captain Coates came down, stating that the entire unit would move out in a few days.

Julie Posner had returned to the outfit and for the time being was assigned to work with Rosen. The two of them would work together as a team. In spite of the accident and the lieutenant's death, Rosen was expected to carry on as radio operator and forward observer.

The rumors about the death of Lieutenant White gradually were replaced by more gripes about the state of affairs of the army in general or just plain cussing out the lousy Germans, wherever they were.

Life in the Third Division went on.

Chapter 25

Rosen and Julie were the only two Jews in their outfit. Although they certainly had no way to observe the established Jewish traditions they'd known back home, for Rosen it was a comfort of sorts knowing that he was no longer the only "Jew Boy." Now that they'd traveled side by side and endured battle after battle for so many months, the guys had let up on Rosen about his heritage. Perhaps they'd eased off in part because there were now two Jews to deal with.

Rosen hadn't exactly been looking for Julie's or anyone else's friendship. From the time that Creasy had been killed, Rosen had believed that going through the war without close ties would make more sense. He could fend for himself. But once the unit was on the move again, he and Julie grew to depend on each other in and out of battle. When they worked as a team, they somehow knew how and when to cover each other. They looked out for each other. Without making any formal declarations, Rosen and Julie Posner had formed an honest and enduring friendship.

Together, Rosen and Julie tramped north through Italy. The once beautiful and peaceful Italian countryside was now a shambles. Tiny farmhouses standing near tumbledown barns stood vacant, just as they had in Sicily. Vineyards and surrounding fields had been plowed into dismal ruts by artillery shells rather than tractors. Most of the farmers had fled, their fields left untended. The unknown fate of the displaced inhabitants still bothered Rosen. They'd lost everything because of the war, and in his mind, their stories should not go unfinished. Their lives as well as their crops had gone to seed.

At one farm, Rosen spotted a skinny, abandoned dog trembling in the doorway of a blown-up house. He wondered whether the dog would die. Probably. There was little left for a domestic animal to eat. Many days there was little for the troops to eat as well.

Rosen saw the lonely, abandoned farms as an opportunity to gather fresh food. He didn't mind the C ration tins the army provided for them, but he knew that eating canned, fatty meat month after month was probably not the best diet. From the time he'd gathered the mulberries in Sicily that he'd shared with General Roosevelt, he'd kept his eyes open for growing fruit and vegetables wherever they went.

Rosen figured that any vegetables left behind in the fields were his to harvest. He reasoned that otherwise the food would rot on the ground and go to waste. He shared the produce he reaped with Julie, everything from potatoes to dandelion.

"Hey, Morris, are you sure these are okay to eat? This stuff looks like weeds."

"Greens are good for us."

"Even weeds? It looks like weeds."

"You're from Brooklyn. You wouldn't recognize anything to eat except a blintz."

"A blintz ain't a weed."

Julie always managed the last word. He never shut up, but Julie's constant banter kept Rosen's mind off the brutality of combat that had become the nerve-wracking core of their daily existence. While Julie was talking, Rosen sometimes let his mind wander, sometimes recalling his favorite Altsheller stories about survival in the wilderness. He'd loved those tales about the two boys trapping animals and building fires with little more than their own cunning. Like the boys in the story, Rosen built fires with only two or three tiny twigs. He kindled just enough flame to warm their ration tins. The lowest possible bit of warmth made the food almost agreeable.

Fresh meat was unheard of for most of the American troops fighting in Italy, but thanks to Rosen's ingenuity, he managed to snare rabbits and shoot chickens that he cooked and shared with Julie.

The days in the Italian countryside had bled into weeks while the Third made almost no progress against the many almost impenetrable lines of defense that had been set up by the Germans. Italy would not fall into Allied control as easily as Sicily.

Progress was slow. Major battles in the countryside had dwindled. One day while they were mostly just sitting around, waiting for orders to move out, Rosen was approached by Lieutenant Bailey.

The lieutenant said, "Rosen, I've selected three guys to go into the Apennines to learn mountain climbing. You're one of them."

"Me? You selected me?" He remembered to add, "Sir."

"That's right. Get your gear; I've got a truck waiting for you about a half-mile to the rear. Get moving; you're going now."

Rosen thought this was a heck of a time to go mountain climbing, but he said nothing. He instinctively knew that the brass had something up their sleeves. They might be planning to eventually send him into some steep mountainous spot with his radio equipment to direct artillery fire, but Julie, his partner, was not going with him for this training. Rosen knew it wouldn't do any good to question orders, so he headed for the truck. At least he'd be doing something besides sitting.

Once the truck had delivered the men high up into the mountains, they were greeted by an Italian Captain named Christian. Captain Christian and his Italian Alpini forces knew everything there was to know about scaling a sheer overhang of bare rock or a treacherous mountainside. Christian and his men were small in stature but as muscular as gymnasts. Their arms rippled with thick cords of disciplined muscle. The mountain climbers worked together almost like a troop of commandos.

Captain Christian told them a story about his Alpini soldiers clambering up a vertical cliff on the Italian side of Mt. Blanc without the use of any specialized climbing equipment. Like spiders, they had crept up the rock face all the way to the top. Christian wanted the Americans to understand that just about anything could be done if you knew how.

Rosen and the other two men spent the next four days learning how to use nylon ropes, pitons, and snap links for safety. Rosen was taught how to make a rope trolley that would help him haul his equipment as he ascended into a dangerous position if it ever came to that. They worked hard, practicing on the mountain slopes from dawn until sunset each day.

The Italian troops congratulated the American men on how well they'd learned the art of climbing safely and efficiently. They were sent back to their unit to get ready to break through the German line at Mignano. Once they'd taken Mignano, they'd be able to advance north to the next German stronghold at Cassino.

When they returned to camp, the two men with Rosen both sported a four-day growth of beard. Rosen had a dirty face.

Chapter 26

The winter of 1943 fell like a sledge hammer. A bitter cold seized Italy as gusts of wind rocked the tall pines in the mountains. And then it started to rain. And rain. The clouds that had been glooming overhead opened up and turned the hillsides into rivulets of mud. Everything was layered with mud including the men.

Rosen felt mud oozing between his toes even while he was wearing his boots. He had no idea when he'd last changed his clothes. He hadn't showered in months. He carried his only extra pair of socks under his shirt, pressed against his chest. It took days, but his body heat would eventually dry the socks which remained just as filthy and muddy as before. When he changed into the dry pair of socks, the cold, wet ones took a turn inside his shirt.

Trucks and the heavy artillery could barely navigate the steep mountainous roads in Italy on a good day, but now the roads had become torrential cascades of mud. Tanks and jeeps slid on the muddy roads, skidding into ditches with no hope of retrieval. At times the runoff from the rain formed strong currents that thundered like furious rivers adjacent to the paths they followed. Along the way the rushing channels of muddy water dislodged rocks and uprooted small trees and brush. The mountainside was shifting, but the army forged ahead.

Finally, all trucks and jeeps had to detour, so Rosen and Julie (weighed down with their packs, rifles, and radio equipment) could no longer hitch a ride on a truck as usual. They struggled up the mountainside with the infantry, their feet clumsy and heavy from the thick accumulation of mud sucking at their boots. They headed through the teeming rain toward Mignano, stopping only to return fire when they were overcome by German snipers.

Huge tractors called prime movers had been borrowed from an anti-aircraft unit to haul the 105-mm cannons up the mountainside. The artillery division needed the cannons in place to be able to support the Third Division infantry. Rosen, with Julie's help, went forward and laid telephone wire over the deep trenches of mud churned up by the massive treads of the prime movers.

The rain seemed endless. Rosen took off his glasses and protected them inside his jacket pocket. Seeing the distant mountainside as a blur was better than wiping the rain from his lenses all the time. He'd discovered early on that rain was a problem when it came to wearing glasses, but he could slip them on in a moment if he heard gunfire. Without his glasses, he couldn't hit a target, so he wouldn't be much use to the army. But he wasn't concerned about the army's reputation. For the most part, he wanted to fire his rifle accurately only when it was necessary to save his own neck.

During the uphill movement, the men were too winded to talk and even Julie had let up on his relentless stream of dialogue. Rosen listened for sounds of enemy gunfire, but he heard only the howling wind, the endless drip of rain against his helmet, and the tedious mincing of boots pulling free from the mud. They were all drenched. And so very cold. The cold penetrated all the way through to his bones.

Slope-shouldered, they gradually plodded up mountainous trails through knee-deep mud, leaning forward from the weight of their packs and radios. If nothing happened to upset the momentum of their uphill march, they advanced in spite of the driving rain and mud. Rosen saw how Julie sometimes clenched his teeth as they forged upward. Julie never once complained, but Rosen understood how tired he must be. The men had all gone beyond exhaustion. They tramped mindlessly, like robots with great, clomping feet.

The fast, steady rain bled right through their uniforms. The troops had no way to stay dry or to keep warm. Half-frozen rain slapped all around them. The ground had become so saturated that streams had formed in odd places. They'd never seen so much water and such a relentless surge of mud. The days and nights rolled over each other as the men now struggled through angled sheets of freezing rain. They knew it wouldn't be much longer until this downpour turned to snow.

Deserted farm houses sometimes seemed as if they might be warm refuges, but once they'd entered one of these humble and incredibly tragic structures, they often discovered that the roof or even several walls were missing, completely blown away. Even inside, the men saw their breaths puffing white as they spoke. Some were lucky enough to find old blankets lying amidst the rubble, and they wore these welcome finds like capes over their shoulders. Of course, the rain soaked through the blankets as well. Rosen cut up an old woolen blanket he'd found and wore it under his jacket like a vest.

All traces of color had disappeared from the Italian landscape. Everything that wasn't covered with mud was a bleak gray. The lovely vineyards and olive trees had been left behind in the lower valleys. While they slogged through water and mud well above their ankles, Rosen had visions of the dark winter months stretching before him like a direct view into hell.

"This fucking country is one big mud hole," one guy complained.

"No, shit," said another. "Get used to it."

The men slept in foxholes for protection only to find the holes had filled up to their waists with rainwater by morning. They didn't dare lie down. They slept sitting upright in holes and trenches or next to the shelter of a boulder or bridge. Men grew ill and sometimes vomited in their own foxholes. The stench was disgusting, but there was nothing anyone could do about their painfully sordid conditions. Coughs hacked through the night. The overall gloom among the men worsened as it began to rain once again.

Some of the men complained about painful sores that had developed on their feet after wearing the same wet socks and boots for days on end. Sergeant Armstrong said the condition was called trench foot and warned the guys to report cases of serious infection.

The men carried no antiseptics in their packs, but Rosen remembered reading the word on his army-issue tube of shaving cream. Since he rarely shaved, he always had plenty of left-over shaving cream. He massaged his feet with it when he changed to the dry socks that he kept stashed under his shirt. The shaving cream generated a tingling sensation and warmed his feet—if only temporarily. He was certain he owed his thanks to the shaving cream because he ended up being one of the few lucky ones. He never developed trench foot.

The Allied Forces had battered their way through the German defenses at Mignano by November of 1943. During this push north from Naples, the American forces had counted 3,265 dead, plus additional thousands for Britain and the combined Allied forces. But for all those lost lives, they'd advanced less than 50 miles.

For Rosen and many of the others, the war had become a crash course in disconnecting themselves from life as they'd all known it back home. At night when they bedded down against their cold, sodden packs, they'd dream of home. But home was now a faraway place, no longer firmly vivid in their memories. Most of the men were too cold and miserable to even voice their complaints. It had become their reality. The American soldiers had no choice but to accept the unspeakable kind of existence they were forced to endure while engaged in military combat.

They were exposed to horrendous conditions, and as a result, they'd grown markedly different from the civilians they used to be. Gradually the men had changed. They'd all changed. Rosen understood this and knew it to be true, but he wasn't certain he'd ever be able to explain this difference in his thinking to anyone else. Each man had become an island, fending for himself; it was a constant struggle to just barely survive.

Following the long attack on Mignano, Rosen's outfit was ordered back to Naples to regroup. By now the company desperately needed replacements, and the sick and wounded required more medical care than the medics in the field could provide. Some of the men could barely walk into the temporary headquarters established in the rolling fields beyond the outlying areas east of the city.

Infection from trench foot and even frost bite had taken a greater toll than anyone had expected. The Americans had set up their supply depot and even an airfield adjacent to the tent city that housed army headquarters.

The enlisted men camped in the fields and meadows flanking their headquarters. Naples was almost warm compared to the temperatures at the higher altitudes in the mountains, and best of all, it wasn't raining.

Word spread that the men needed to line up for tetanus booster shots promptly at 13:00. Julie looked at his watch. "That's in fifteen minutes. I can't do it."

"Why not?" Rosen asked.

"I get light-headed from shots. I must be allergic."

Rosen grinned and burst into laughter. "Yeah, right. You're allergic."

"No, I'm serious. The shots they gave us back at boot camp made me light-headed."

"Okay. Does that mean you passed out?"

Color rose in Julie's face. "Yeah."

The guys were already milling around a tent that housed the medical staff and supplies. Rosen went to the front of the line, got his shot, and walked back to Julie.

"It was nothing. A stick in the arm and a medic crosses off your name."

"They got our names written on a list then?"

"Sure."

"Well go through the line again and say you're me."

"What, are you nuts?"

"Go ahead. I don't want to pass out in front of the whole outfit. Please."

Rosen was laughing, but he went back into line and waited. The process went quickly and the medic didn't even look up when Rosen stated that he was Jules Posner. Rosen received two shots and Julie had none. In thinking about the way they put their lives on the line each and every day, it didn't seem like a big deal.

Following his second tetanus shot that was meant for Julie, Rosen scrounged a bar of soap and washed both pairs of his filthy socks in his helmet. After his socks had dried, Rosen began to massage his feet with his shaving cream.

"What the fuck are you doing?" an infantryman named Stretch asked. Stretch was a tough-looking guy, over six-feet of muscle.

"Rubbing this stuff on my feet."

"What the hell for?"

"Maybe he's gonna shave between his toes?" a guy named Kenny joined in. "He ain't got a hair on his chinny, chin, chin. Maybe he got whiskers between his toes?"

They laughed and quickly pulled in a few other guys to watch.

Rosen replied, "I don't know what's in the shaving cream, but I didn't get trench foot like all the rest of you."

Kenny frowned, knitting his eyebrows closer together. "I got a couple of sore spots. The doc said it wasn't too bad, no infection yet, but I guess it can't hurt to use the shaving cream."

"Nope, can't hurt." Rosen pulled on his clean socks. The extra pair went under his shirt.

Some of the other guys continued to poke fun at him, but Rosen noticed that Stretch and Kenny and a few others carefully swabbed their own feet with Barbasol shaving cream.

Later that afternoon a two and a half-ton army truck pulled up and parked near where the Third division had camped. It seemed odd that nothing was loaded on the back of the truck except an old upright piano. Like wildfire the word soon spread. Al Jolson had just arrived in Naples, and he was getting ready to entertain the troops in a matter of minutes.

The enlisted men fell into place, sitting behind the truck on the ground or balanced on their helmets. Rosen and Julie Posner found great spots close to the front. The excitement mounted, but a few groans rang out as orderlies began setting up folding chairs directly in front of the soldiers already seated on the ground. The chairs had been lined up for the officers. When the officers filed in, their eyes glided over the enlisted men as if they weren't really invading their territory, as if they had some God-given right to sit wherever they wanted even if that meant blocking the view for the others.

Al Jolson climbed onto the back of the truck along with his piano accompanist, but he didn't look happy. He began waving his arms while conferring with his piano player. The buzzing conversations among the men calmed as they strained to hear what Al Jolson was saying. Finally Mr. Jolson walked to the very edge of the truck bed which served as his stage. He indicated the officers, pointing with his index finger and called out to them.

"No, no, no," Jolson said. "No chairs. You must sit on the ground like everyone else."

The stunned officers looked to each other for a ruling in this most delicate situation, but Jolson stood his ground. He said he had no intention of performing until the officers agreed to his demand.

The chairs were quietly folded and removed from the field. The officers sat on the ground, risking a little dust on the seats of their pants and a momentary slump in their customary dignity. The troops went wild, cheering Al Jolson's decision to level the playing field if only for an hour.

Without the benefit of a microphone, Mr. Jolson sang his heart out while the piano music echoed throughout the hills. The men were thrilled with every song, applauding and whistling at full volume. But at the very end of his performance when Jolson sank to one knee and belted out the song, "Mammy," the crowd went silent, listening to every word with spellbound attention.

Rosen wasn't the only one who wiped a tear from his eye.

Chapter 27

After the division had re-grouped at Naples, they continued their push to the north. Their next objective was to capture the town of Cassino. Towering over the town was the mountain peak known as Monte Cassino, famous because it was crowned with a magnificent Benedictine abbey founded in 530 AD by Saint Benedict. This highly-esteemed religious shrine had been home to the monks of the Benedictine Order for many centuries.

Cassino was situated on the formidable German Gustav Line that, according to Hitler, had been fortified to render it completely impassable. Stretching across the narrowest part of the "boot" of Italy, the Gustav Line had been designed to cut off the advances of the Allies once and for all.

The Germans had crammed fifty miles of heavy artillery into place along the Gustav Line to hold back the Allies, but they hadn't depended on artillery alone. They'd also cut down thousands of trees to build physical barriers complete with carefully-placed booby traps. Hundreds of houses had been blown up to give the German gunners a clear, unobstructed view of the countryside.

Cassino was a major strong point in the blockade intended to prevent access to Rome, and the Allied commanders were determined to break through. They believed the Germans had taken over the abbey itself because a constant stream of artillery fire rained down from the mountaintop. The Germans held the high ground, and they took advantage of their enviable position to slaughter Allied troops.

The Allies went all out, sending in additional units from Poland, France, India, New Zealand, Canada, and North Africa, as well as the units from Britain and the United States. A sweeping offensive seemed the only way to take out the German gun emplacements on Monte Cassino.

It was Christmas 1943. Supplies were running low. Rosen's division needed C rations and ammo. Somehow the American Red Cross had gotten through from the rear and delivered crates of donuts and huge aluminum containers of coffee to Rosen's outfit. The donuts had been on the road for some time, and then more rain moved in, making the donut delivery a soggy disaster. So much for a gesture of glad tidings and good will at Christmastime. The men complained bitterly.

The guy they called Stretch took a bite out of a waterlogged donut and promptly spit it on the ground. "What the hell? We need real food. How about a turkey dinner, not this shit."

Rosen didn't even bother with the donuts. "At least the coffee is hot," he said.

Julie said, "Yeah, it's better than drinking muddy water from our canteens."

"No shit," Stretch shot back, "but the coffee reminds me how goddamn cold I am inside."

They gave up on the donuts and any more thoughts of Christmas and went back to fighting in the line. The Allied troops were trying to ascend a very narrow, treacherous dirt road that switched back and forth up the side of Monte Cassino toward the abbey. They slowly stalked their way up the muddy trail. Steady German gunfire hammering down from the top of the mountain peppered the hillside, landing in explosive bursts all around them. Every so often a soldier would slip and fall face down on the slippery, half-frozen mud. If he picked himself up and started cussing about the mud and the goddamn war, they would all feel relieved. The ones that fell and never stood up again were the ones they didn't want to talk about.

God, it was cold. A heavy ground mist rose up all around them. The lifeless landscape of nearly frozen mud provided little cover for Rosen and Julie. The land had been stripped bare except for an occasional skeleton of a splintered tree, with naked branches dangling much like the shattered limbs of some of the men. The houses and barns that might have offered protection for the soldiers had been bombed into fragmented junk. A little church had been blasted to pieces. All that remained was half of the fallen steeple, its iron bell listing crookedly over the mud. Rosen and Julie faced outrageous circumstances, but like everyone else, they did their jobs.

The infantry of the Third Division had been sent back to Naples to prepare for the next move on the generals' chess board. The men had no idea what that move would be, but the war they were trying to wage at Cassino sure wasn't working. Rosen and Julie had been left behind with the 39th Field Artillery to do whatever they could to help the combined Allied infantry divisions mount their attack on Cassino.

Rosen and Julie had moved in close to the infantry, Rosen calling in directions for artillery fire on the radio. A shell exploded close to them, and they both hit the mud, dropping for cover.

"You okay, Buddy?" Julie asked.

"Yeah," Rosen answered, "but my eye." He reached for his glasses.

"You get glass in your eye?"

"Shit." Rosen held up his glasses to show Julie that one lens had cracked into a pattern that resembled a spider web, but fortunately the glass hadn't cut his eye.

Rosen and his shattered glasses were sent back to headquarters at Naples via a supply truck. He walked across the spot where Al Jolson had recently performed for the troops, remembering that Jolson hadn't played favorites with the brass. The entertainer had won the hearts of all the enlisted men that day.

While Rosen waited around for his lens to be replaced, he noticed that everyone in the rear echelon wore shoe packs, thick rubber boots with warm felt linings. These boots were intended for the men who had to spend weeks on end walking and even sleeping in the rain and mud. He'd noticed that the supply truck driver had worn the same fancy footwear, but at least the driver drove back and forth to the front.

Damn, Rosen thought, the shoe packs had been confiscated by officers who spent most of their time inside tents. Rosen had never seen a single infantryman or artilleryman on the front wearing these protective, warm boots, but he sure had heard about numerous cases of frost bite. Guys on the front were losing toes to the cold, but back in headquarters at the rear, everyone from the cooks on up to the generals in command had warm feet.

Rosen had gotten a day off from combat to have his glasses repaired, but he returned to Cassino feeling let down. The army permitted the rear echelon personnel to have it pretty easy while the guys who were in the line of fire suffered. He just couldn't shake it out of his head. He could still envision officers walking around wearing the warm shoepacks intended for the enlisted men in the front lines. Didn't anyone care? He couldn't understand how the brass could so coldheartedly disregard the needs of the American soldiers.

By the time Rosen returned to the front line, the sky had darkened and it had begun to snow. He found Julie and the rest of the men shrunken down against the cold. The landscape seemed dissolved behind the swirling snow. Rosen could barely catch his breath. Each word they spoke wheezed into a steamy cloud of vapor quickly swallowed up by the icy air around them. The gunfire from above had tapered off, but that meant a huge barrage would soon follow. During these chilling periods of quiet there was no sound except for their heavy, labored breathing and their cold, crunchy steps against the snow. The siege continued like this for days; men were sent in to replace those who'd been killed or wounded, but it seemed hopeless. It didn't take a general to tell them that they'd reached a stalemate at Cassino.

British Prime Minister Winston Churchill finally outlined an ambitious plan for the Allies to break the stalemate. He proposed a surprise amphibious landing intended to circumvent the Gustav Line by sea and to land at a beachhead about 30 miles south of Rome. The Third Division had been ordered to depart from Naples and re-enter Italy by landing craft, well behind the fortified German lines.

Sergeant Armstrong began passing the word that orders had come down for many of the men in the 39th Field Artillery to withdraw from Cassino and return to Naples with the rest of the Third Division. Once Armstrong located Rosen and Julie, he told them to head back to Naples to re-group.

Rosen and Julie had been selected to link up with thousands of other soldiers who were on their way to mount the surprise landing at Anzio.

Naples, Italy
Left: Morris Rosen. Right: Julie Posner

Chapter 28

Prime Minister Winston Churchill had convinced the British Chiefs of Staff that a different approach had to be initiated at once. In Churchill's opinion, the stalemate at Cassino and along the Gustav Line was nothing short of scandalous. He designed and proposed a strategic battle plan that came to be called Operation Shingle.

Operation Shingle established a plan to withdraw battle-tested British and American troops from the ranks. Their combined forces would then invade Italy under the overall command of Major General John B. Lucas. Rosen's outfit, the Third Division, would depart Naples and make a surprise landing at the beachhead of Anzio. At the same time, the British First Division would land at a nearby seaside resort called Nettuno. Arriving at these two beachheads by sea would place the Allies well behind the German line and only 30 miles south of Rome.

The plan sounded simple. Once the beachheads were established, infantry and artillery would spread out and advance inland. By then it was assumed that the American Fifth Army would have finally overtaken the Germans still holed up at Cassino. The Fifth Army would then be able to circle around heading west and connect with the Third Division. This tactic would cut off any possibility of escape for the Germans. The enemy, according to Churchill, would be completely surrounded and thus easily crushed. Rome would be secured by the Allies in a matter of days. As the men readied for departure from Naples, they were not all as confident as Mr. Churchill.

The dockside at Naples was a beehive teeming with activity. Thousands of men were preparing to depart. Like Rosen and Julie, many of them had just marched in from Cassino, and they were so exhausted that the captain ordered a few days rest time. As wasted as they were, anticipating the landing was not conducive to taking it easy. Rosen spent most of his down time checking out his radio and telephone equipment. There was always something that needed repairs, and intuitively Rosen had somehow figured out how to overhaul almost any radio part that had broken down.

Sergeant Armstrong barked out orders, but he wasn't a gruff old bulldog like Sergeant Miller from the Ninth. His parents had left Scotland and arrived in New York just in time for him to be born in the U.S. The guys teased him about being a tightwad

Scot, but he took it all in good spirits. He was actually the first officer that Rosen felt he could call a friend.

"So," Rosen asked the sarge, "why the big rush to get us loaded?"

Sergeant Armstrong took his time filling his favorite pipe with tobacco. That pipe was always in his mouth, but he managed to talk around it. Rosen still hadn't tried pipe smoking, but thanks to all the free cigarettes the American tobacco companies supplied to the troops, Rosen, like so many others, had gotten hooked on the nicotine in cigarettes. Smoking seemed to fill the time; it was something to do when a guy was tired or nervous or scared. That covered most of them most of the time.

Sergeant Armstrong finally said, "All this is what the army calls logistics. We've been ordered to make our landing by January 22 or it's no go."

"Why's that?"

He shrugged. "Just following orders. The landing crafts will drop us off on the coast of Italy and then they'll sail on to their next mission."

"Where's that?"

"I don't know, but my best guess is Britain. They'll probably need every LSI we've got to move our troops across the channel for the invasion of France."

Rosen said, "The guys from my old division, the Ninth, went to Britain to train for the big invasion."

"So I heard."

"When will it be? Soon?"

"I don't know exactly when they'll invade France, but I do know we'll be going in first."

"Why's that?"

"They need more time to regroup and prepare for that invasion. They're probably also waiting for some decent weather."

Rosen remembered his geography. "Yeah, it's pretty cold up there this time of year."

Sergeant Armstrong nodded. "I heard that Eisenhower's on his way to fine-tune their training. Meanwhile, like it or not, we're going in."

"Figures." The army had sent him directly into hell many times. Nothing surprised him anymore.

"If it'll make you feel any better, it came straight from the top that we were supposed to select only our best men for this landing."

"Well, at least I've graduated from being a chronic screw-up to one of the best," Rosen said with a smile, but nevertheless he felt a rampant queasiness uncoil in his gut.

He'd been culled out of the Ninth Division because Captain Blimp had stockpiled plenty of reasons why he wanted to get rid of him. It had never occurred to him that he'd ever reach the point of being considered one of the best.

Sergeant Armstrong smiled back at him. "The guys at the top also figure that since we'll be keeping a couple of German divisions busy at Anzio, the Krauts will have fewer men available to send to France."

Kenny and Stretch worked next to Rosen and Julie at the dock, checking radio equipment and weapons and loading their packs with ammo. Rosen was off to one side, trying to stretch a condom over a pistol when Kenny spotted him.

"What the hell are you doing, Rosen?"

"Got this pistol I wanna keep dry."

Kenny took a closer look. "That's an old .32, isn't it?"

"Yeah, army issue."

"Where'd you get it?"

"That new lieutenant gave it to me. He was issued a brand new .45 caliber, and he didn't want to carry around two pistols."

"So ramming it into a fucking condom is your way of carrying a weapon?"

"Should keep it dry during the landing. If I can get the whole thing in here, I'll tie a knot on the end."

Kenny shook his head. "Looks to me like you're trying to stuff 200 pounds of shit into a 50 pound bag."

Rosen chuckled. "There. I did it." The condom was stretched to the max, but it hadn't torn.

Kenny said, "Remind me someday to tell you what you're really supposed to do with a rubber."

While the men packed their supplies, the army brought in a couple of those weird-looking vehicles everybody called ducks. A duck sailed like a boat, but when it reached shore, it could drive right up onto the land like a truck. The brass had ordered the men to load all the 105-mm howitzers onto the ducks. Normally they used LCTs (Landing Craft Tanks) to transport tanks and large equipment, but someone at the top apparently wanted to experiment. Maybe a couple of generals had gotten together and brainstormed this idea, finally coming to the conclusion that using the ducks would be an improvement over the old tried and true method. The men never learned who actually came up with all these bright ideas. They just followed orders.

The first duck headed away from the beach at Naples riding very low. The howitzer was much too heavy for it, and the duck promptly tipped over and sank. After a lot of hollering back and forth, the second howitzer was loaded onto the second duck a bit differently. The duck sailed away somewhat steadier than the first, but it, too, was swamped by a wave and found its way to the bottom of the Bay of Naples. Rosen didn't know much about things like the laws of gravity, but he figured he knew more than the guys in charge of the lost howitzers. Two big guns and two amphibious ducks had been sacrificed. The whole thing seemed like a very expensive bright idea.

January 22, 1944, the men frantically completed last minute preparations before boarding the landing crafts. They put on their life vests and settled into the LCIs. Rosen tucked the .32 caliber pistol he'd cosseted inside the condom into his belt. He wanted to take it home as a souvenir for his younger brother Sidney. The kid would love it.

Anzio was only about 50 miles north of Naples, but the landing crafts moved slowly and deliberately distant from the coast to avoid detection. They planned to quietly travel under the cover of night. The sea was choppy, the waves cresting into stiff white peaks. Some of the men started vomiting before they'd sailed even a thousand yards, but something like seasickness never deterred the army. Men hung over the sides of the crafts and heaved until their guts ached. Sea water sprayed over all of them as the LCIs bounced head on against the waves.

Julie said, "Well, this is it, Morris. We're on our way."

Right, he thought, on our way to what? Walking into the face of danger time and again had involved far too many close calls for Rosen, yet he'd somehow managed to avoid getting killed. Maybe luck was still with him.

"Yeah." Rosen finally answered. He now had his eye on the guy next to them. He looked like he was ready to puke.

Julie didn't seem to notice the sick guy. He shouted over the roar of the engines. "Hey, Buddy, you ever think of getting married?"

"Me?"

"Yeah, sure."

"I don't even have a girl back home."

"I was seeing two girls for a while, but I want to propose to Leatrice. She's really something."

"So who's the other girl?"

"Thelma."

"What's wrong with her?"

Julie thought a moment. A spray of water smacked him right in the face. "Nothing. Except she talks too much. You know what I mean?"

"Shit, man, you never stop talking yourself." Rosen said.

"Not like Thelma."

Rosen said, "Which one is pretty?"

"They're both beautiful. Both gorgeous."

"Oh."

"Another thing, Thelma doesn't like my parents very much."

"She wouldn't be marrying your parents."

"I know that. But Leatrice likes my folks; she's real sweet and easy going."

"So get with it. I'm hearing that you're in love with Leatrice." With that the craft bounced against another big wave and they were both drenched. Rosen took off his glasses and swabbed the lenses against his sleeve.

Julie wiped his eyes. "Yeah. I guess I really am in love with Leatrice. And she's smart. Leatrice is smart. You'd like her."

"So if Leatrice is smart and beautiful, what are you waiting for? Ask her to marry you."

"What if she turns me down?"

"Why would she turn you down?"

"I don't know."

"Then you can always ask Thelma."

"No, really. That would be awful if Leatrice turned me down."

"Shit, I'd turn you down because you talk too damn much."

Julie punched him in the arm. Rosen just laughed. He knew all too well that Julie wouldn't shut up until they landed. He couldn't help it. Julie always talked a blue streak when he was nervous.

Chapter 29

Hundreds of Landing Craft Infantry transport ships had ferried the men away from Naples in a wide arc. The LCIs had been escorted by a flotilla of U.S. Naval ships. Their departure went smoothly; no one interfered.

Julie continued to ramble on and on about his plan to propose to Leatrice. The noise of the ship more often than not drowned out his voice, but he continued talking anyway. Rosen gave up trying to work in a word edgewise. He figured Julie was just thinking out loud, bouncing his ideas off Rosen. Once Julie had finally made up his mind to write his letter of proposal to Leatrice, he started to expound at great length about his ambition to become a hot-shot salesman.

Julie said. "I tell you, I'm good at sales. I know I could make a decent living as a salesman."

"If a salesman has to be full of shit, then you'll be fantastic," Rosen said flatly.

Julie laughed and nudged him with his elbow. "Hey, I think the boat has slowed down."

"Relax will ya'. Sarge says we're not going to land until closer to daybreak."

Eventually the sound of heavy artillery fire and the flare of rockets off in the distance managed to quiet the men, even Julie. Their naval escort was off shore at Anzio, firing at the beach.

"Sarge," someone asked, "how many Krauts do you think are waiting for us?"

Sergeant Armstrong said, "We don't know. The navy is trying to knock off anybody on the beach before we even get there."

Rosen heard a lot of quiet mumbling all around him. A lot of the guys were saying whatever they said when they fingered their rosary beads. He wondered how many fisherman and farmers would be killed in the crossfire. If this landing was a surprise, no one would have warned the locals. Then again, maybe the whole damned country had been evacuated by now.

Sergeant Armstrong spoke up. "We'll be going in soon. Try to keep the sand out of your rifles. You see any Germans, shoot them, but keep moving. We'll go forward and form a perimeter. We should be able to secure this whole area in a day or two."

Rosen removed his pack and hitched the straps over just one shoulder because the pack could pull him under if the currents were strong enough. He'd decided to just let the pack sink if he had to, but he would hold on tight to his rifle and his telephone and radio. The men were all loaded to the hilt with equipment. At the last minute, they inflated their life vests with compressed air capsules. The landing craft moved in as close to the shore as possible, but Rosen and Julie still landed in chest-deep water when they jumped off the LCI.

The men scuttled across the sand by the hundreds. It seemed as if they'd pulled off a complete surprise. Even though no one was shooting at them, they crouched low, obscured by darkness. The moon wasn't full and a bit of cloud cover further dimmed the pre-dawn sky. At first they were basically running blind, running inland away from the beach.

Soldiers stumbled and even ran into each other, but they forged ahead. So far there had been no opposition to their landing. The only sounds were made by the men themselves.

"Move it."

"Keep moving."

"Let's go. Get your ass over that fence."

"Move faster, goddammit. Get out of my way."

Then Rosen heard someone say in a much quieter tone, "Hail Mary, full of grace."

The darkness of night had finally drained away. Rosen had expected dawn to be a blazing hell of gun fire, but that wasn't the case at all. There were no fire fights; the Germans were nowhere in sight.

The sky to the east grew rosy with brilliant pink ribbons radiantly highlighted against shredded layers of clouds. As the day brightened, they were able to travel faster, steadier. They moved constantly, keeping up a fairly brisk pace for hours. The Third Division connected with the British, and they now trudged along together. They paused only for food and to relieve themselves. Altogether 36,000 men marched inland, covering the land like a swarm of locusts.

They came upon farmers walking to their fields. Some were already at work, bending over a hoe, or walking along side a disinterested horse. The farmers waved and called hello. The troops waved back. The Italians—or at least the Italian farmers—seemed genuinely happy that their quiet countryside was being trampled by a horde of invading soldiers.

Rosen had pretty much lost track of time. By the second day they were approaching the foothills. The landing had been a complete success, and he was glad he'd taken part in such a triumphant mission. His only crisis had been the discovery that he'd somehow lost the pistol he'd shoved into the condom for safekeeping. He figured it must have fallen out of his belt when they'd jumped into the chest-deep sea water upon landing.

The march inland continued for another full day before word came from the rear that all troop movement should stop. They'd advanced 20 miles across the valleys and into the foothills. Then the orders were further defined to force the men to pull back.

"What's going on?" Julie asked.

Stretch put down his pack. "Shit if I know. It doesn't make sense. We've marched halfway across Italy, and now they're telling us to go back."

A guy named Cunningham came rushing up to Rosen and Julie. "Captain says stay put. General Lucas wants us to wait, pull back to that valley we just passed through." He pointed.

"It doesn't make sense," Rosen said. "I can't believe he'd want us to go back the way we just came. We should be blowing bridges and setting out mines." General Lucas was obviously being cautious, but this was nuts. Didn't the general realize he was being far too cautious?

Cunningham reminded Rosen of a choir boy, with his fair skin and rosy cheeks. Rosen knew all too well the endless jabs a baby-faced guy had to endure, and he felt sorry for the poor kid. It was hard enough for the 18 and 19 year-old guys to come across like men in this war without looking like little kids half their age. So many boys were scattered among the fighting men. At least Rosen wasn't the only one.

Today Cunningham was madder than a hornet. "The generals don't know shit. We have to follow their fucking orders, but I tell you they don't know shit. Lucas wants us to circle the wagons. It's crazy. I tell you he don't know shit." Cunningham had briefly summed up how most of the guys felt.

So they withdrew from the high ground they'd already taken and pulled back to a low-lying valley that had once been rich, fertile farmland before the war had torn the country to bits. They stayed rooted in this position for nine days just waiting for the next set of orders.

Julie wrote out his words of proposal to Leatrice. "Hey, Morris, tell me if this sounds all right?" He read the letter out loud.

"Yeah, it's good."

"No, really, tell me what's wrong with it."

"Nothing. It's good."

"But this has to be perfect, you know what I mean?"

Rosen clutched his chest. "I'm swooning. It's the most beautiful letter ever written in a wheat field somewhere in the middle of fucking Italy."

"You think she'll say yes?"

"Of course she'll say yes."

A mail courier arrived that same evening and Julie relinquished his heartfelt letter. A bag of mail had also arrived for the troops. Rosen got two letters from his sister Molly and Julie received three from Leatrice. Yeah, there was no question in Rosen's mind. She was probably anxiously awaiting Julie's proposal. But their high spirits were overshadowed by a Dear John letter that Sergeant Armstrong had received from his girlfriend.

The Dear Johns were the worst. A letter like this slammed a damper on the recipient's buddies as well. Poor guy had a war going on all around him while his girl had hooked up with some 4-F bastard back in the states. Rosen was glad he didn't have a girl back home. Sergeant Armstrong hadn't been the first to get the boot while he was helpless to do anything about his girlfriend's lack of patience.

Maybe he shouldn't blame the sergeant's girl. Maybe it was simply too hard to wait.

Then all hell broke loose. While the 36,000 Allies sat riveted in place in the valley, the Germans had brought in eight divisions, 100,000 troops, from the Balkans. They quickly spread out and took positions in the very hills the Allies had just relinquished.

The Germans controlled all roads plus the railroads coming from the north. They brought in heavy artillery and rockets, surrounding the Allies while they were lined up like sitting pigeons in the valley. When the Germans began firing, the pounding was non-stop. The Allied soldiers ducked for cover but there were very few places to hide. The Germans were in the hills, shooting down at them, blasting away as if every Kraut had six guns.

"Holy Christ," Stretch yelled as he hit the dirt. "It's like they're shooting fish in a barrel."

"What are we supposed to do?" Kenny shouted.

"Try not to get shot," Rosen called back.

"The Krauts got us pinned. The lousy sons of bitches are everywhere."

Rosen and Julie jumped into an irrigation ditch for cover. At least it offered some protection. Kenny and Stretch followed. They fired back at the Germans, but their fire didn't seem to matter much. The Germans had the protection of the hills.

"Get down," Rosen cried. He tried to get through on the radio, but all he heard was static.

The earth seemed to be exploding in all directions. Shells hit close. Too close.

"Are we going to fucking die like this?" Cunningham cried.

Rosen pulled him down into the ditch next to where he and Julie had dug in. "Use your rifle instead of your mouth."

"They're beating the hell out of us."

"Yeah, I know. Just shut up and fight back."

Chapter 30

It went on like this. They took cover wherever they could by day and slept in holes at night. Rifle and machine gun fire pounded in their direction but at the moment it was coming from a fairly comfortable distance. Rosen heard every round. His hearing remained acute in spite of the incessant gunfire; he was always watchful.

Julie had taken a hit with a spray of shrapnel and he was off somewhere being treated. Rosen was grateful Julie was alive and would soon recover. He thought back to his personal vow to steer clear of taking on Julie or anyone else as a friend. But in spite of his vow, in the madness of war, bonds developed whether a guy sought them out or not. Rosen didn't know how it had happened, but Julie was now his closest buddy.

Rosen's outfit ran toward another deserted farm and took refuge behind the dilapidated house, its walls already riddled with a barrage of bullet holes. The Germans were out there somewhere skulking about the countryside, but most of the men had chosen to wait this one out, thinking the Germans would eventually grow tired and crawl back into their bunkers for the night.

"Wait here," Rosen whispered to Stretch.

"Where are you going? Stay down."

Rosen ignored him and slipped to the corner of the farm house. He shouldered his rifle and pulled off a single shot into a nearby clump of fruit trees. A high-pitched inhuman wail followed by a heavy thump against the ground brought Stretch rushing to his side.

"You nail a Nazi sniper?"

"No."

"Then what the hell are you shooting at?"

"I shot a cow."

"You what? Are you nuts? Why the fuck would you shoot a cow?"

"Meat. We'll have steak tonight."

"You shot a fucking cow? I don't believe it. How are you going to cook a whole fucking cow?"

"We'll build a fire, but we're gonna have to wait until dark to butcher it."

"Butcher it? With what?"

"I'll borrow a bayonet. You can help."

"Help you butcher a cow? Won't there be fucking blood and guts when you cut it up?"

"Sure."

Stretch gave an involuntary shudder. "Count me out. I don't want some poor cow's blood on my hands."

Rosen laughed. So much for Stretch the tough guy. Stretch was a lot like Julie when you got right down to it. They both tended to get a little squeamish at times. He smiled to himself, remembering how he'd taken the tetanus shot for Julie. Maybe that was just the way it was with these big bruisers. They talked big, but they were soft on the inside.

Rosen said, "As soon as it's dark, you can gather some dry sticks so we can build a little fire, unless gathering wood is too upsetting for you."

"Fuck off." Stretch muttered, but then added, "I'll get your goddamn wood."

A fog-like veil closed in on them while they waited for nightfall. Gradually, the crack of retorts from gunfire on both sides slowed as it usually did after dark. Finally, the shooting ceased altogether. No sense wasting ammo when they couldn't see each other. And men had to sleep even though they were in the middle of a war, even the seemingly tireless Germans.

Rosen was carrying one of the new carbines that didn't use a bayonet, so he borrowed one from an infantryman. He looked out, checking for traces of gunfire before he left the protection afforded by the house. Carefully, he approached the dead cow.

Rosen got a firm grip on the bayonet and tried to penetrate the thick cowhide. The bayonet wasn't sharp enough. He prodded and jabbed at the cow, but the bayonet was useless. He gave the bayonet back to the soldier and searched through his pack for his pocketknife. He couldn't locate the knife, but since he seldom shaved, he did have plenty of brand new razor blades. He retrieved his shaving supplies from his pack and set to work, tediously skinning and butchering the cow with nothing more than a single-edged razor blade. His hands were slathered with blood up to his wrists.

Rosen cut uneven slabs of meat from the cow's side while Stretch started a small fire behind the house. They skewered the meat on sturdy pieces of baling wire they'd found on the ground. They moved in close to the fire and held the steaks over the flame. Bits of fat dripped from the meat, sizzling and sputtering and sending up wisps of wonderfully aromatic smoke. Gradually the implausible aroma of roasting beef attracted other guys from the unit and Rosen and Stretch were soon surrounded.

"Hey, what the fuck?" one guy moved closer. "What're you cooking? Where the hell did you get meat?"

"Rosen's always cooking something for himself," said another.

Rosen picked up on the insinuation. "There's plenty of meat. A whole cow. Help yourselves. Cook all you want, just keep your fires small and hidden well behind the building. We don't want to invite the Krauts over for supper."

While Rosen and Stretch savored their meal, the others kept coming. They used their own knives or Rosen's razor blades to sever generous slices of raw beef from the carcass. Several fires were started behind the old farm house, and that evening the entire unit dined with more enthusiasm than they had in months.

At the time Rosen had no way of knowing that in all probability he'd shot one of the few remaining domestic animals in the valley. Farm animals that had been left behind had fallen victim to the Nazi shelling just as so many civilians had fallen. When the Americans first landed, the valley had also been a wonderful sanctuary for birds, but they, too, were now gone, silenced by the war. The birds had scattered to the four winds so completely that now not even the trill of a common barn swallow could be heard. Even the steadily plodding, clucking chickens had all vanished.

Sadly, nothing in this entire valley would remain untouched.

Chapter 31

The Nazis were relentless. From their position of strength high in the hills, they shelled the trapped Allies, hammering away, day after day. The unnerving sounds of the war never ceased. Even when the gunfire died down somewhat at night, Rosen couldn't shake the sensation of heavy artillery fire echoing and throbbing inside his head. In his mind he relived the scream of shells streaking through the air and the hideous explosions that followed. When he tried to catch a few minutes sleep, the war ruptured his dreams, sending visions of German tanks dancing against his closed eyelids. He never fell into a deep sleep for more than a few minutes at a time; the slightest noise awakened him.

The shelling went on for days; days turned into weeks. The combat at Anzio had been raging on for a full month. It seemed that cries of "Medic!" were always followed by another volley of artillery fire. The dead and wounded were carried away and replacements continuously streamed in. The Allied forces at Anzio had grown to 100,000 soldiers, but even so, they were still grossly out-numbered by the Germans. The German troops had increased in huge numbers as well.

Rosen came within inches of getting shot dozens of times. The only positive note in this bloodbath had been the Luger he'd taken from the body of a dead German officer. He cleaned the weapon against his pant leg and carried it with him in his pocket or lodged in his belt. He finally had a great souvenir, an impressive German pistol, to take home to Sidney, his younger brother. He hoped he'd live long enough to deliver it in person.

American and British soldiers were being killed at an alarming rate, and still the battering continued. The Germans had the Allies surrounded; Rosen never felt safe. None of them did. The Allies had dug into the fields as best they could, but it was almost impossible to stay out of harm's way.

In a few spots they'd discovered wine cellars or barns that had been built into a hillside that could be used to store supplies or house the officers' command posts. Most of the farmhouses they'd attempted to use for shelter in the beginning had been blasted into splinters long ago. American bulldozers, brought in from the center of operations set up at the beach, pushed tons of earth into great knolls that the troops now used for protection. They were actually building their own encampment.

The men carved out and shored up crude caves directly into the mounds of dirt, but many were hit and killed in the very same trenches and holes they'd hollowed out for cover. Each cavern shielded as many soldiers as they could possibly cram inside. Some even tried to make light of the situation by referring to their hand-made caves as "home." They spent their nights crowded together, enduring much like prisoners of war but in their own camp. The men of the Third division existed but just barely.

Rosen continued to direct gunfire, crawling from trench to trench laying wire as the shelling unleashed its terror all around him. The Allied soldiers were exposed to enemy fire all day, every day. The persistent barrage not only killed troops outright, but the deluge rattled every membrane of their hearts and souls. Operation Shingle had been a complete disaster. Instead of providing an answer to the stalemate at Cassino, the troops who'd landed so audaciously behind enemy lines at Anzio now needed rescue themselves.

Then the Germans rolled out the most terrifying weapon as yet seen during the war. The Germans had mounted a pair of 280-mm guns on two flatbed railroad cars. Each gun weighed 94 tons with a barrel over 70 feet long that could easily lay waste a target over 30 miles away. The Germans silently slid the guns toward the Allies by rail, fired, and then withdrew the guns into railroad tunnels. With the big guns so quickly shifted out of sight, the Allies had no way to retaliate even after they'd finally gained air support. The Allied bombers simply couldn't spot the tunnels where the Germans hid their enormous guns.

The Americans named this devious weapon Anzio Annie. They couldn't tell whether the Germans were using one big gun or many. But one thing was certain: the American Sherman tanks were no match for Anzio Annie. The Germans even fired shells from Anzio Annie at the naval ships anchored off the coast west of the beachhead. Quite a few reached the targeted ship. The men came to instantly recognize the distinctive squeal of the long drawn out delivery of one of her shells.

"Incoming!" someone would yell.

They'd all duck for cover.

"Sounds like fucking thunder."

Rosen, Stretch, and Cunningham huddled together. Dirt spewed all over them. The non-stop pounding sucked their moral fiber right out of them.

"They're beating the hell out of us," Cunningham hollered.

"Just keep your head down."

The slaughter was horrible. The medics worked tirelessly; litter bearers hauled the wounded to field hospital tents set up in the rear closer to the beach. The quartermasters buried the dead quickly and without ceremony, but all the men carried the incredibly heavy weight of so many deaths along with them. Rosen cringed every time he saw a man so badly shattered there was barely enough left to bury. He'd seen so many demoralizing sights that he wished he could erase forever from his mind. He tried to forget, but he couldn't. No one could. The gruesome sight of the hundreds of soldiers who'd been blown to bits since this battle had begun haunted every one of them.

Rosen wondered how many had died unloved, how many would be quickly forgotten? His poor mother would be terribly saddened if he were killed. And who knew how his brother was faring in the Pacific campaign? He prayed for at least one of his mother's sons to return to her, alive and well.

Many of the weapons carried by the American infantry seemed like pea shooters compared to the horrifying might of Anzio Annie. Thousands of replacements and tons of equipment had been brought in by sea, but the Allied troops were still getting soundly beaten. The beachhead where they'd originally landed had turned into a busy center of operations, larger by far than most of the nearby Italian villages.

Assignments were chaotic, shouted out to the men over the roar of the big guns. Orders changed at the whim of a sergeant or the demand of a captain. At times they had only seconds to comply with the most recent command. They all did the best they could.

Since they'd met up with the likes of Anzio Annie, all artillery fire was now being launched from the biggest guns the naval ships had to offer, making Rosen's skill in directing ship to shore gunfire especially valuable. Rosen and Sergeant

Armstrong had been assigned to team up, and they now worked together directing naval gunfire against any enemy post they spotted up in the hills. Sergeant Armstrong gauged decisions for the navy's shelling, but more and more he was now asking Rosen's advice to double-check his call. Rosen had become proficient at calculating the co-ordinates which he then radioed to the ships off shore using Morse code. Unfortunately, they would knock out a German nest only to see two more spring up to take its place.

Julie had been cleared to return to combat since his wounds hadn't been life-threatening, but Rosen had no idea where Julie was dug in at the moment. Most likely he'd been assigned to another radio team, and he could be anywhere on the crowded Anzio plains. The guys tended to stay close, working in tight little clusters. Rosen couldn't identify guys no more than fifty feet away.

Stretch was now carrying Rosen's equipment for him and they worked well together, but Stretch wasn't Julie. Rosen never would've guessed that he'd actually miss Julie's non-stop banter and his steady stream of questions.

Chapter 32

The morning of February 24, 1944, dawned cold and foggy. It had been raining on and off for several days. Rosen was still working with Sergeant Armstrong and Stretch still carried his radio equipment. Rosen and the sergeant were directing fire from a squadron of destroyers and the big cruiser, "Philadelphia."

Stretch helped Rosen lay telephone wire over muddy fields that had been scored into gaping trenches by artillery shells as well as the even deeper trenches dug in by his outfit. They worked on their hands and knees in the mud, trying to keep their heads down. Their telephone line extended across the battlefield from a naval officer's post to their own forward position. Rosen's job was critical and exceptionally nerve-wracking in light of the fact that the intense bombardment by the Germans never stopped.

That day Rosen planned to set up his observation post on a higher berm to provide better reception for ship to shore signals. Some of these high spots occurred naturally in the terrain, others had been rammed into place by the bulldozers. The elevation would also give him a better view of the action.

The fog had made it increasingly difficult to direct naval gunfire accurately, and to make matters worse, an American team of Special Services commandos known as Darby's Rangers were covertly proceeding into the area, hoping to make a surprise frontal assault against the German infantry. The Rangers had crept up from the rear, quietly advancing toward the line during the night. Rosen and Sergeant Armstrong had received word that the Rangers were ensconced in a ravine that must have been a dry river bed. At first they'd moved in almost close enough to actually provide some desperately-needed help, but now the Germans had the Rangers surrounded. Their position didn't look good.

The Germans were especially aggressive on this particular morning. German infantrymen boldly marched along next to their tanks, shooting at anything that moved. The enemy attack escalated by the quarter-hour. Rosen and the sergeant were frantically trying to divert the naval gunfire away from the ravine that shielded the Rangers and toward the Germans that surrounded them. It was an insanely tight situation.

The white fog was gradually lifting from the ditches, rising over the scattered high points. Rosen reached the top of the berm where he had a better view of the German tank assault directed at the squad of Darby's Rangers. But suddenly a German tank materialized through the remaining fog seemingly out of nowhere. It reared up the side of the berm and opened fire. Infantry bullets as well as machine gunfire from the tank sprayed Rosen and his party.

A sharp pain tore savagely into Rosen's left knee. As he slid down the side of the berm, he saw Stretch and Sergeant Armstrong collapse into a trench at the bottom. They'd all been hit. The tank rolled away and the German soldiers moved on, apparently satisfied that all three of them had been killed.

Rosen clutched at his knee and then looked to the others. Sergeant Armstrong and Stretch were lying flat in the mud. Rosen dragged himself down into the trench, closer to Stretch.

"Holy shit," Rosen muttered to himself. Stretch had been killed instantly when he'd caught machine gun scatter in the stomach and chest. When a guy is blown apart like that it doesn't do any good to try to help him. Rosen had no idea what anyone could do with the devastating mess that had once been Stretch.

Rosen took Stretch's grenade from his belt and crawled toward the sergeant.

"I'm hit," Sergeant Armstrong said when he saw Rosen approaching him.

"Yeah, me, too. I got it in the knee."

"My arm." The sergeant lifted his arm slightly. His hand was trembling. No, actually his whole body was trembling. "Call a medic. We need a medic."

Rosen looked around. Bullets were flying hot and heavy. "Yeah, but I don't want to call out just yet. The area is still lousy with the goddamn Krauts. You just hang in there a little while."

Rosen put pressure on Sergeant Armstrong's bloody arm and bandaged it as tightly as he could with the sergeant's handkerchief. He lifted the sergeant's head slightly and supported him against his shoulder. He cradled the sarge and offered him water from his canteen.

"No water. How's Stretch? He was hit, too. Where's Stretch? Go see if Stretch is all right."

"He's fine," Rosen lied. "Nothing could take down that big brute."

Sergeant Armstrong slowly moved his good arm and dragged his hand over his heart. It was then that Rosen noticed a growing red stain spreading across the front of the sarge's jacket. God, he hadn't spotted that wound at first. The sarge had taken more than one bullet, maybe one in the back. Rosen raised his head to yell for a medic, but just then another German tank rolled by. Machine guns paid out a volley of shells directly over their heads; the ground shook from the rumble of the massive tank treads. Rosen ducked down, shielding Armstrong, and lay perfectly still.

"Rosen, stay here with me until the medic comes."

"Sure, I'm right here."

"Thanks."

"It's okay. I'm right here. We'll be able to flag down a medic soon."

"Do something for me, Rosen." Now the sergeant's lungs bubbled when he spoke, the familiar sound of a severe chest wound.

"Sure, Sarge. Anything."

"Tell my father I died like a soldier."

"Shut up, you're not dying." God, Rosen wished he had an ampule of morphine. He'd jab it into the sarge himself. He looked around again for a medic, but he didn't dare raise his head too high. Gunfire was thundering overhead in every direction.

"Tell him I was brave to the end. You have to tell my father."

"Hell, we're gonna walk out of here. We just have to hold on a little while longer until I spot a medic." An explosion rocked both of them; that one was close, too close.

"Tell my father."

"Hey, just hang on. It's only a flesh wound; you'll be around to tell him yourself."

"Tell my father."

"Sure, stop worrying I'll tell him." Rosen blinked back his tears. None of this talk would matter much when it was all over, but he wanted the sarge to hold on a bit longer. Maybe the doctors could save Armstrong. Rosen couldn't just let him drift away.

"I wanted to write to my girl one last time before she gets married."

"Just hold on. You're gonna be fine. You can write to her."

Sergeant Armstrong stopped talking, but he continued trembling. He looked over Rosen's shoulder to the east, toward the sound of the latest machine gun volley. His eyes stared vacantly. Rosen held him close, like a baby, until the trembling stopped.

"Sarge? Sarge? Can you hear me?"

He didn't respond.

Sergeant Armstrong was gone; he'd died in Rosen's arms.

Chapter 33

Rosen sat there stunned. Damn this war to hell. Why Sergeant Armstrong? He'd been a good man. One of the best, and now the poor guy would go home in a bag, or he'd be buried at fucking Anzio. No American should be buried at this bullet-riddled hell hole. It just wasn't right. He'd seen hundreds of guys get hit, but the loss of Sergeant Armstrong had a bitter impact he hadn't expected.

Rosen was breathing rapid, shallow breaths; his throat had tightened. The searing pain in his leg no longer mattered. He was even forgetting to duck when the shells came whistling over his head. Was there any sense to what the Allied troops were doing here at Anzio? He couldn't think of a single good reason for all the lives that had been lost. Sergeant Armstrong and Stretch were dead, but the battle went on, still bellowing with non-stop thunderous shelling.

He thought for a moment about taking the sergeant's pipe from his pocket, just a little something as a remembrance. But he decided the pipe should stay right where it was. He would never forget how the sarge puffed away on that thing, sometimes even when the fire had gone out long before. Besides the pipe would only serve as a grim reminder of Sergeant Armstrong's pointless death at the hands of the goddamn Nazis. Rosen didn't need to be reminded that he'd lost another friend. He gently laid the sarge flat on the ground.

Another round of machine gun shells cracked into a Sherman tank to his left. A hideous boom followed. That was another one that came much too close. God help him, would he be next?

He remembered telling Julie that he'd wanted to live through this fucking war so he could one day vote for president of the United States. Some of the older men, like Julie, had cast absentee ballots in the last election. Rosen was 19. The way the bullets were flying overhead, he was afraid he would never see 21.

He'd almost forgotten about the constant throbbing in his knee. He wriggled his pack off his back and searched for his pocket knife. He slit open his bloody pant leg and stared at the wound. Holy shit. He'd taken a machine gun bullet deep into the flesh above his kneecap. It wasn't bleeding profusely, but it looked god-awful. He yanked his first-aid kit from his pack and took out an envelope of sulfa. He squeezed a generous swath of the yellow powder over the wound and then wrapped several lengths of gauze around his knee, tying the gauzy ends in a knot. He had no tape.

The knee wasn't a mortal wound, and he was pretty sure he could endure the pain. As far as he could tell lying there in the mud, the medics were not yet out searching for casualties. They were smart to lay low because today's horrific fire fight blazed on indiscriminately. Rosen knew he had to remain alert and wait until nightfall when the litter-bearers combed the fields for the wounded.

He just wanted to make certain he would not be taken alive. He'd taken Stretch's grenade, so now he had two. He wanted three. Two he'd throw at any approaching Germans; the last one he'd save to blast himself to kingdom come.

Rosen spotted a soldier on the ground about 20 feet ahead. He lay deathly still. Rosen dragged himself to where the soldier had fallen and checked him for signs of life. Goddamn. The poor guy had lost most of his face and his brain had been laid bare. His nucleus, his essence had spilled out onto the mud. Rosen took the dead soldier's grenade and pulled himself further along, to a spot next to a blown-up tank. The remains of the tank would offer some protection, and it wasn't too far from a path the litter-bearers might travel come nightfall.

Now he had three grenades, and he settled down to wait. Shells shrieked overhead all day long. Dozens of dead infantrymen lay ahead; plenty more had fallen behind. Rosen believed that today's casualties numbered in the hundreds, way more than usual. The heavy, sweaty odor of fear that usually surrounded the troops had been replaced by the smell of blood, the smell of death.

Rosen kept still. The sounds of battle were especially unnerving now that he was stuck out in the open and unable to run for cover. Just let those lousy Kraut bastards come back to see if he were actually dead. He'd be waiting. He'd toss one grenade into the German search party for Stretch. The second one would be for Sergeant Armstrong. The third would be his way out of Anzio, out of the war, out of everything.

He leaned against the tank and waited. The pitiful cries of the men who'd been wounded filled his head, their agony resounded everywhere. He tracked the movement of the sun across the sky. Hours had gone by, but he'd have to remain calm until dark. He didn't dare call out until darkness fell. He'd lain in the field all day long and was anxious for nightfall. It would grow colder after sunset, but Rosen didn't care. The cooler air would clear his head and keep him alert.

At last the sun sank to the west and gradually kindled the sky with fiery color. The sunset brought with it a slowing of the monotonous chittering of gunfire. Finally the countryside grew mysteriously quiet. His surroundings seemed cold and still for a short time until Rosen finally heard footsteps. The litter-bearers would be looking for the wounded, but the Germans would also send out parties to finish off the wounded men who hadn't died. He clutched the three grenades and waited.

It was a gloomy, moonless night, so Rosen could barely see his own hand in front of his face. He repressed a shudder. Then he heard something coming from the German side, a noise. It sounded like leather creaking, maybe boots. The Germans wore impressive leather boots of a much better quality than those worn by the Americans. He pulled the pin from the first grenade. The sound drew closer, but Rosen was ready.

"Halt," Rosen yelled. "Who goes there?" He waited a beat and then called out the current password: "Bitter." He waited to hear someone call the counter-sign, the word: "Sweet."

No response.

Rosen's back stiffened. He got ready to throw the live grenade. Again he called, "Bitter."

He heard a man's voice say, "Jesus Christ, anybody know what's the fucking password?" The voice had a decidedly Brooklyn accent, just like the band of Italians he'd captured in Tunisia.

Only an American would come up with: "What's the fucking password?" instead of the correct counter-sign, the word, "Sweet."

Thank God, the men who were approaching were Americans. Rosen began to tremble. His hand shook so uncontrollably he almost dropped the grenade.

"Come quick," Rosen called. "I've got a live grenade in my hand!"

"Jesus, Buddy, why'd you pull the pin?" One of the litter bearers quickly slipped the pin back into place and grabbed it from Rosen. He then let out the deep breath he'd obviously been holding.

"The sound of your footsteps seemed to come from the German side."

"Yeah, I guess we missed you the first time we passed through here. We just came back to give one last look around. There's so many poor dead bastards piled up, you wouldn't believe it. The fuckin' Krauts were mighty busy today."

The litter bearers carried Rosen on a stretcher until they reached an aid station where several jeeps awaited the wounded. They had nothing like an ambulance, so they simply placed his stretcher right on top of the hood of a jeep. One guy steadied the stretcher from the passenger's seat while the driver proceeded down a rutted road to the field hospital. The field hospital was within walking distance of the same beach where they'd landed a month earlier.

Rosen's stretcher was pulled from the jeep and lined up on the ground next to dozens of other stretchers. The jeep hurried back to collect another casualty. The medics had so many wounded in the line-up that they assessed those who needed immediate care and those who could wait. Rosen's bullet wound was deep, but since he'd administered his own first aid, he would have to wait for medical attention. It had begun to rain again, yet another drizzling, bone-chilling rain. Lying out in the open, the wounded soldiers simply got soaked as the stretchers stacked up.

When his turn finally came, Rosen was carried inside a dimly-lit tent that had been dug into the sandy soil about two feet deep. By digging in, the tent now had a lower profile which meant a reduced area for the Germans to target. Problem was, even with the tent protected somewhat, gunfire still rained down on the medical personnel. The sign of a bright red cross displayed on a hospital tent supposedly marked it as neutral territory, but the Germans could always claim that a hit to a field hospital was purely "accidental."

Rosen had heard about the nurses and physicians who'd been killed in the line of duty even as they attempted to operate on the wounded. Casualties who'd been brought in for treatment were further wounded or killed as they lay on hospital gurneys. He saw the holes left by hundreds of shells that had penetrated the canvas tent.

Being so close to the sea, they'd also dug down too close to the high water table. The medical teams in the field hospital had to stand in two inches of mud and water while they desperately tried to save the lives of their patients.

Doctors, nurses, aides, and litter bearers rushed back and forth inside the crowded tent. The doctor who approached Rosen was covered in blood. He was a big man with dark eyes. He looked as if he hadn't slept for a week.

"I'm Dr. Schneiderman."

Someone had given Rosen a shot of something for his pain, and he was beginning to float on a thin, drug-induced haze. He remembered that in Yiddish and German the word schneider meant to cut. He almost laughed out loud. How very appropriate. The surgeon's name identified him as a man who cuts.

Dr. Schneiderman stood by while a member of his staff cut away Rosen's pants leg. As they lifted him from the litter to an operating table, the surgeon noticed the butt of Rosen's souvenir Luger poking out from his belt.

"What do you have there?" Schneiderman asked.

"A German pistol."

"Is it a Luger?"

"Yes."

"May I see it?"

Rosen rolled to his side, nearly losing his balance on the narrow table as he slowly retrieved the Luger. He slapped it into the doctor's hand.

"Here."

The doctor smiled as he admired the sleek lines of the pistol. "May I have it?"

You son of a bitch, Rosen thought. As he saw it, he had no choice. He figured it was either give the surgeon the Luger or wake up without his leg.

"Sure." Rosen said. This time he laughed out loud in spite of the pain.

"Okay," Schneiderman said, "give this soldier another shot for the pain."

He vaguely felt the pressure of the injection then all went black.

Chapter 34

Rosen awoke to the roll and pitch of the sea. He heard the moans and cries of the wounded all around him. Some screamed the same horrible screams he'd heard on the battlefield. But this place was different. He wasn't lying deep in mud out in an open field. It was enclosed, airless, dark. He found it hard to breathe. The stink of sweat and smoke from cigarettes almost choked him.

Perhaps he was having a bad dream or he'd gone out of his head with hallucinations. Then he remembered being picked up by the litter bearers and the doctor in the field hospital who'd taken his Luger. That bastard. It wasn't a dream. He was on a lower deck in a ship, and he had a plaster cast on his left leg from his hip to his ankle. A shiver ran through him even as he felt his own sweat soak his arm pits.

Rosen questioned anyone who walked by, and in bits and pieces he learned he was on an LST

(Landing Ship Tanks) headed for Naples. The LST had just delivered tanks and supplies to the Americans stranded at Anzio, and its return cargo consisted of the dead and wounded from the battlefield.

When the ship docked at Naples, those with the more serious wounds were rushed ashore first. The lower decks were slowly emptied and two men carried Rosen's stretcher topside. The sun and a fresh sea breeze felt good against his face after lingering so many hours in the awful stench of the ship.

A long line of drab military ambulances waited at the dock, and one by one the stretchers were carried to emergency vehicles and shoved inside. Each ambulance carried as many men as it could hold; three other wounded soldiers had been squeezed in with Rosen. The high-pitched wail of the sirens spiraled away, taking flight into the morning air.

The majority of the wounded from this shipload had already been delivered to a well-established hospital in Naples, and it had been quickly filled beyond its usual capacity. Rosen's ambulance was diverted to a brand new hospital facility that had been constructed during Mussolini's regime.

The hospital was so new it almost sparkled. A complete team of American physicians and nurses decked out in clean, crisp uniforms had just arrived from the United States. Boxes filled with medical supplies stood stacked in the corridors waiting to be unpacked. With the arrival of Rosen's ambulance, the hospital swung into its first full day of actual operation.

Rosen and the three other soldiers who'd arrived in the same ambulance were taken into a bright, sunlit ward and placed on the incredibly white sheets of four brand new hospital beds. It had been a long time since Rosen had even seen clean bed sheets. The whiteness hurt his eyes. In fact he'd never been anywhere so impossibly clean, white, and quiet.

Three female nurses smiled and greeted him warmly. Their white nurses' shoes squeaked against the shiny new floor. The nurses circled his bed and scrubbed away the months of grime that had crusted over his entire body. They soaked his hands one at a time in a small basin to remove the accumulated filth and blood. He wondered if the blood caked under his fingernails was his own or Sergeant Armstrong's. Rosen enjoyed this first-class fussing and scrubbing as the nurses groomed him for surgery.

Then a full colonel in a freshly-starched uniform entered the ward, and the nurses scurried away from Rosen's bedside. They stood at attention directly behind the colonel. Rosen never did catch the colonel's name, but he listened attentively as the colonel went into a thunderous speech about the real heroes of this war. It took Rosen a minute or two to realize that the colonel was referring to guys like him, the unsung heroes of battle. It was astounding. Four battle-weary guys who'd been shot at Anzio had caused a full colonel to swell with pride and respect for the soldiers of the American army.

The colonel presented Rosen and the three other men with Purple Heart Medals beautifully displayed in velvet-lined cases. He removed Rosen's medal from the case and pinned it on his hospital gown while the entire nursing staff watched in rapt admiration. He followed the same ritual for the other men. When the colonel had finished, he clicked his heels and briskly saluted the men with the kind of decorum that only a dedicated officer could muster. They quickly returned the honor.

While Rosen was being prepped for surgery, a wave of new casualties flowed into the hospital. Rosen saw the last of having several nurses attend to him at once. He was pretty sure the colonel's individual Purple Heart ceremonies would have to be forsaken as well. Purple Heart Medals would probably now be shuffled out to the wounded like cards.

Rosen's cast was removed, and he was wheeled into surgery. At the field hospital Dr. Schneiderman had packed the wound with Vaseline gauze, so now the gauze had to be extracted before the wound could be cleansed and stitched. Rosen was back in his hospital bed with the cool white sheets when he awoke. He was under mild sedation for the next few days and he drifted in and out of sleep, not even waking long enough to eat. But then, he wasn't hungry. Whenever he came out of his distant haze, he felt his knee throbbing like a bad toothache. It was better to close his eyes and let sleep take over.

On the fourth day a surgeon came to look at Rosen's wound. A furrow of concentration creased his forehead for a moment then he actually screwed up his face as if he had something really awful to announce.

"Private, I guess you've noticed the dreadful odor emanating from your knee."

"Yes, sir," Rosen said. He knew the doctor was not just passing the time of day. "Then it's not just the medication I'm smelling?"

"No, it's not medication. I'm afraid gas gangrene has settled into your knee and it's out of control."

Rosen wasn't absolutely certain what gas gangrene was, but he was well aware of the distinctly foul odor seeping from his knee.

The surgeon said, "This wound should show signs of healing by now, but that hasn't happened. We're going to take you back into surgery."

Rosen was once again wheeled into the operating room, but his wound was not even stitched this time. When Rosen awakened, the surgeon returned to his bedside.

"Soldier, I'm afraid we're going to have to amputate your leg."

"Amputate?"

"Yes. I'm sorry, but the gangrene will spread throughout your body and kill you if we don't take off that leg." He paused. "It's the leg or your life."

Chapter 35

Rosen's mind floated somewhere above his frozen senses. A foggy place inside his throat uttered just one word: "No."

He wasn't certain whether he'd said the word out loud. He said nothing more. He tried to ignore the beginning of a headache; his mind was reeling.

Back home in Pittsburgh, he'd seen many men who'd lost a leg during World War I. These poor souls competed with the kids for the privilege of selling newspapers on street corners. Rosen always let them have their corners while he ran inside shops and public buildings where the one-legged men couldn't manage. Rosen had always done a good job of selling his entire daily allotment of newspapers, and he was always willing to share his regular customers with the crippled newspaper men.

Now he'd be one of them, a cripple, hobbling around for the rest of his life on crutches, with one trouser leg folded up and fastened in place with over-sized safety pins. He couldn't find words; he felt deflated.

One of the Red Cross volunteers who'd followed the surgeon to Rosen's bedside spoke up. "Excuse me, doctor, could I have a word?"

The doctor turned suddenly, as if he'd forgotten she was standing at his elbow. She was a stunning woman, with enormous eyes and sensuous lips. The doctor studied her for a moment before he nodded. Perhaps it was the first time he'd noticed her good looks. He smiled and followed her to the corridor.

Rosen couldn't hear what the woman was saying, but he saw her pointing toward something off in the distance. He figured it had nothing to do with him. What could a good-looking dame like that have to say about a poor slob who was about to lose his leg?

The doctor returned. "I've agreed to hold off on your surgery for one day."

"Why?"

"That Red Cross worker, Madeleine Carroll, wants me to try a new drug they've just started using at the British Hospital in the next building, right across the driveway. Seems she volunteers over there as well. In fact, she's running over to the British Hospital right now to pick up a vial of the drug for you."

Rosen managed to maneuver himself up on one elbow. "You mean this drug will cure the gas gangrene?"

"She says it can save your leg. We'll see."

"Madeleine Carroll you said?"

"Yes, she's rather famous in Britain; she's a movie star, an actress. She starred in a splendid film called The 39 Steps. Alfred Hitchcock directed it. Took the wife to see it. My wife loves movies that have a bit of mystery and suspense."

Rosen hadn't seen that movie or any others for that matter. He'd never had extra money to spend on movies, but he was impressed that a famous lady from the movies was volunteering as a nurse's aide in not one but two hospitals. Rosen was doubly impressed that she had enough compassion to try to save his leg.

Madeleine Carroll returned from the British Hospital and entered Rosen's ward in less than twenty minutes. She smiled at Rosen as she handed a large glass vial of a milky-white fluid to the surgeon. Miss Carroll hurried off to help elsewhere, and the doctor used the largest hypodermic needle Rosen had even seen to inject the fluid into his rear-end.

The dying flesh festering in Rosen's knee showed noticeable improvement the very next day. Two days later the surgeon stitched the wound and set it in a cast. The news was great. The gorgeous actress had brought him the best gift imaginable. The gangrene had miraculously disappeared. He wouldn't lose his leg after all.

"What was that stuff the doc gave me?" Rosen asked an orderly who worked in the ward.

"Doc said it's something brand new, a kind of wonder drug."

"What's it called?"

"Doc says they call it penicillin."

After a few days, Rosen was able to pull himself up onto crutches. He teetered out of the ward, shaky on the crutches, and tried to locate this angel named Madeleine Carroll. She'd saved his leg with the British penicillin, but she'd never returned to his ward. He wanted to thank her for her gift, for his leg, but he never spotted her again. The orderly who seemed to know everything about everyone told Rosen that Madeleine Carroll now limited her volunteer work to soldiers in the British Hospital.

While Rosen recovered in the hospital, he heard the latest news regarding the progress of the troops still out on the line. Everyone was eager to share whatever information they had.

The Germans had captured the entire Darby's Rangers unit that had tried to infiltrate the Allies' position on that fateful day when Rosen had been shot. The Nazis rounded up all one-thousand of the Rangers and blatantly carted them into the center of Rome. They paraded the prisoners through the main streets of the city like cattle, anything to further disgrace the Americans.

German airplanes had also dropped thousands of propaganda leaflets over the beachhead and battlefields at Anzio. Printed in English, the pamphlets publicized the humiliation suffered by the Darby's Rangers and advised the Allies to give up. Unconditional surrender would be their only way out. The Americans and British dug in a little deeper.

Rosen also learned what was happening regarding the stalemate at Cassino. Churchill and the American Chiefs of Staff hadn't considered that the 5th Army wouldn't be able to break out of that bind as scheduled. Rosen's Third Division had not been able to take Cassino. A regiment of Gurkhas from India who were a specialized unit in the British army and a division from Poland had also failed. The American press had dubbed the area "Purple Heart Valley." Many of the Allied commanders now firmly believed that the abbey afforded the Germans a position that no one could overcome by land.

Allied leaders conducted intense debates over the need to bomb the Germans out of the abbey at the top of Monte Cassino. The destruction of an ancient religious shrine seemed abhorrent but nonetheless necessary for an allied victory.

On February 15, 1944, a wave of Allied Flying Fortresses began the assault on the beautiful Benedictine holy place. The abbey and the village below were reduced to rubble as tons of bombs carpeted the countryside and the mountain. Dozens of civilians who had taken refuge in the abbey were killed.

Sadly, the Allies learned that the Germans had never actually occupied the abbey. Their gun emplacements were all over the mountainside just below the abbey walls, but none had been situated inside the abbey itself. The Allied commanders had taken a tremendous gamble and lost. The Allied bombs naturally blasted away massive amounts of stone which landed in heaps next to the fractured craters. By re-arranging the building blocks of the ancient abbey, the bombers had inadvertently provided the enemy with additional and far better places to hide.

The Germans then spread a world-wide propaganda attack denouncing the Allies for destroying the sacred monastery that the Germans claimed they had intentionally avoided. Even as the German troops moved into the abbey's rubble to dig in additional strongholds, German officials under Hitler condemned the American bombings as an unspeakable crime.

When Rosen was finally released from the hospital in Naples, Cassino was still in German hands and the battle at Anzio persisted. Since their initial landing, 20,000 Allies had died at Anzio.

The Germans were now launching unmanned glider bombs into the offshore naval warships. The U.S. Army quickly deployed more naval warships to the site as replacements. The additional warships shelled the Germans but Anzio Annie was still on hand to shoot back. The constant thunder of the big guns continued to shake and unravel the once-peaceful valleys that surrounded Anzio.

General Lucas was replaced by General Lucian K. Truscott, the former commander of Rosen's Third Division. The men welcomed Truscott's command, but, for the soldiers dug in at Anzio for so many grueling weeks, there seemed to be no end in sight.

Chapter 36

Rosen remained in the hospital at Naples for six weeks. By that time the new hospital overflowed with hundreds of additional casualties that had been brought in by the shipload every few days from Anzio. Rosen spent his time exercising his leg and thudding up and down the halls on his crutches. His knee had been so badly damaged that he could no longer straighten it completely. He was determined to exercise and strengthen his muscles until he could regain full use of his leg. By his sixth week he'd graduated from struggling with the crutches to walking with a cane.

He was taken from the hospital to a Replacement Depot in Naples. It was actually another army tent city the soldiers had nicknamed "Reppel Deppel." There he was issued a uniform and told to wait for his orders. The first thing he did was cut off all the tags from his new clothing. At least he'd learned a few things since he'd enlisted. In a matter of days back on the front, however, his spotless new uniform would be crusted over with mud like everyone else's.

Reppel Deppel served as a point where the wounded could rest until they were re-deployed. The soldiers who'd lost a limb or their eyesight were sent home, but the army desperately needed men, and most of the wounded were experienced soldiers. They joked among themselves that they were well-seasoned soldiers who hadn't learned when to duck.

Rosen watched as many of the now-recovered casualties were sent off to Britain for the D-Day invasion of France. The build-up of troops in Britain was already extensive, but the commanding officers continued to add to their numbers. The problem was that the impasse at Anzio was also still in full force, and men were desperately needed there as well. After reviewing his records, there was no question. Rosen's ability to precisely direct naval gunfire and his skill with Morse code meant the army needed him back at the front at Anzio.

In May, 1944, he was still walking with a cane when he boarded a supply ship for his transfer. During his absence, thousands of additional troops had arrived at Anzio to build up the reserves of the Third Division. The beachhead looked like a small city. They'd set up portable shower facilities that actually were equipped with soap and hot water. They could now rotate the troops to the rear for showers and clean uniforms, and each man was given two brand new pairs of socks. Civilized treatment like this reminded Rosen of the steak dinners the Ninth Division troops had been served before they'd headed out toward the horrendous battle at Thala.

Hundreds of tanks had also been delivered to Anzio and these sat in orderly rows along the beach. The build-up had been gradual, but there was no question the Third Division was gaining ground. Plans to launch a major attack and finally break through the German lines were in the works. At the moment Rosen's outfit had been pulled back to the rear for rest, another sign that the break-out was drawing closer.

When they weren't resting, the men prepared and trained. They refined their skills at hand-to-hand combat and charging with a bayonet. They were given specific instructions about moving through mine fields and blowing up enemy tanks. In addition to endless practice and drills, they heard lectures about the tactics planned for the break-out. Some days it felt as if school were in session.

For a change there had been no leaks from the command posts, so the men had no idea when they would be ordered to march into the hills and advance into the German strongholds. Every man in the division was itching to give the Krauts a little payback for all those months of relentless bombardment. Even though no date had been issued, the men could feel the static in the air. A successful break-out and an end to the nightmare of Anzio would bolster the entire war effort in Europe, especially giving confidence and lending support to the upcoming invasion of France.

Rosen was issued a rifle and told where to report for duty. He couldn't figure out how to shoot his rifle with a cane dangling over his arm, so he threw the cane into a ditch. He limped slightly, but he figured a limp wouldn't slow him down too much.

The morale of the troops seemed much improved. Rosen heard guys singing the Third Division theme song and whooping it up like a bunch of kids. They'd all learned the words though no one could remember who'd actually made up the song:

> *I'm just a dog-faced soldier*
> *with a rifle on my shoulder,*
> *and I eat a Kraut for breakfast every day.*
> *So feed me ammunition,*
> *keep me in the Third Division,*
> *your dog-faced soldier-boy's okay!*

He hummed along with the many repetitions of the theme song that he heard from groups gathered for training or a cigarette after chow. Rosen searched through the scores of Third Division men waiting in reserve until he finally connected with Julie, Kenny, and the choirboy, Cunningham. Julie's jaw tightened and his eyes flickered when he spotted Rosen. Julie jumped to his feet and immediately began smiling and slapping Rosen on the back. Julie looked bedraggled, but then they all did.

"You look like you've been run over a few times," Rosen said.

"At least once a day," Julie answered. "I'm afraid Leatrice won't even recognize me."

"Ah, she'll know it's you the minute you start in talking."

They hugged and laughed, thrilled that they'd reconnected. Rosen was glad his buddies were still alive, especially Julie. Kenny slapped Rosen on the back just as a fresh rain of artillery fire scudded overhead. They all ducked for cover.

Rosen still worked the radio by day, but Julie had been assigned to a night detail. Every evening several men were sent out by jeep to prepare forward positions for the upcoming break-out. Julie was ordered to dig in gun emplacements for the big artillery guns, a job especially designed for a guy Julie's size. Rosen hadn't pulled this detail, but he went along most nights just to keep Julie company. As long as he was there, Rosen picked up an extra shovel and helped Julie dig.

The Germans were pulling back. Their numbers were dwindling and rumor was that they were low on ammunition. They would level a tremendous bombardment one day but wouldn't fire a single round the next. The time for the break-out was approaching. They'd trained; they were ready to bust out of hell. It couldn't come soon enough; some of them had been trapped in the trenches at Anzio for almost five miserable months.

While they slowly pushed forward, replacements kept pouring into Rosen's outfit. Many were fresh off the boat, brand new recruits from home. A big, beefy Native American guy from one of the reservations out West was told to check in with Rosen when he returned from working the night detail with Julie. He'd been ordered to carry Rosen's radio.

The guy couldn't have been more than 19, but he was at least six-three, and he looked like he could tear apart a Sherman tank with his bare hands. He approached the men and just stood there, glaring at Rosen, Julie, Cunningham, and Kenny. The big Indian held his arms away from his body, slightly flexed like a weight-lifter getting ready to heft an enormous barbell.

Kenny looked up at the gigantic guy for a moment then said, "How!"

The man didn't respond.

"Well, if you don't know how, I ain't gonna tell you." Kenny laughed at his own joke like it was the funniest thing he'd ever heard.

Julie said, "What's your name?"

The big guy seemed to growl when he spoke. It was hard to understand him, but he mumbled that everyone called him Black Foot.

"I'm Julie. You'll be working with Rosen and me. We'll show you what to do."

"Sure, I guess you Jew Boys know all about everything, don't you?"

Rosen and Julie simultaneously clenched their fists. They'd been through the worst of this war ten times over, and everyone in their unit knew it. It had been a long time since anyone had come off sounding like a Jew-hater, at least openly and in front of them. This big dumb Indian had no idea who he was messing with.

Cunningham started to laugh. "You got a lot to learn, Cochise, and you'd better learn it fast."

"Don't call me Cochise."

"Hey, Cochise, you got a bad attitude or something?"

"I said don't call me that."

"Aw, gee, I forgot."

"Fuck off."

"You're supposed to go on a detail with Rosen, ain't you?"

"So what?"

Cunningham slapped his knee and started to laugh. "You're new here. You ain't never heard that the guys who work close to Rosen have real bad luck, have you?"

"What's that supposed to mean?"

"Like he's a fucking jinx. Guys who go off with Rosen usually come back in a fucking bag."

Black Foot's face grew red; veins bulged in his thick-set neck, but he remained silent.

"Rosen even polished off a lieutenant. Damn near got himself shot at sunrise for that one."

They all laughed, even Rosen, though he didn't find Lieutenant White's jeep accident at all funny. It was one of those things he didn't want to think about. Besides the jeep accident, he'd experienced many other close calls, too many occasions when he'd been within inches of catching a fatal bullet. Sergeant Armstrong and Stretch were dead, but he'd lived to return to Anzio. He still felt spooked about poor Creasy catching a whole string of machine gun bullets no more than twelve inches from him. And there had been others. Maybe Cunningham was right about him being a jinx.

Black Foot scowled, but he went face-to-face with Cunningham. "You think I can't hold my own against a light-weight Jew Boy?"

"You big dumb son-of-a-bitch. Don't you know that every time you call one of them a Jew Boy, you're hammering another fucking nail into your own coffin? Those two guys look out for each other. Watch your back when you're out with Rosen."

"What do you mean?"

"Ain't you been paying attention? I just told you that if you go out with Rosen, you might not come back, if you get my drift."

Rosen didn't agree with or dispute Cunningham's threat. He stared at Black Foot until the big guy began to squirm.

Black Foot stormed over to the sergeant. Rosen couldn't hear every word of their conversation, but he knew Black Foot was asking questions about his upcoming assignment with Rosen.

The next morning a replacement for Black Foot reported to Rosen. He stated that Black Foot wouldn't be able to carry Rosen's equipment that day because somehow he'd accidentally shot himself in the foot.

Chapter 37

The Third Division had been ordered to spearhead the break-out from Anzio. Additional reinforcements continued to arrive, building the level of Allied troops to almost 300,000. They would finally leave the beachhead and the plains of Anzio behind after so many months of bloodshed and devastation. Once again they would fight their way inland, capturing the very same hills they'd taken when they'd first landed. General Lucas, who'd been widely criticized for pulling back the troops after a completely unopposed landing, had been replaced by Major General Lucian K. Truscott, Jr. Under new leadership, a well-coordinated attack was ready to move forward.

The troops were issued canisters containing smoke bombs intended to create markers to identify their lines, but some of the men were not told how and when to use the bombs. They threw away the canisters as they marched—one less thing to carry—

but Rosen attached his smoke bomb to his belt. He'd always liked gadgets, just as he'd been fascinated with the electric toaster he'd "lifted" from the store window when he was a kid.

It still hurt to remember how his father had turned him in to the police knowing well in advance that his son would be sent to reform school, but somehow his hatred for his father had mellowed. His father had been a tyrant, but after several years of separation from him, Rosen now saw the old man in a different light. He guessed, if anything, he pitied his father. Rather than assuming the role of a loving husband and father, he'd chosen to be a stern dictator. But now that he'd thought about it, Rosen was glad he'd let go of some of that old hatred. Living in trenches with live ammo flying overhead forces a guy to think differently about what's really important in this world.

Just as the Ninth Division had done at Thala, preparations for the breakout were made in absolute darkness. The Americans cut through the German barbed wire as all personnel were rounded up and sent into the line as added support for the infantry. The cooks and their kitchen helpers, mechanics, truck drivers, and even the quartermasters were called into service. Rosen had never before seen all personnel sent forward like this, and for the most part they looked like the most mismatched bunch of soldiers ever pulled together. Up to now these guys had performed what everyone else called "cushy" jobs in the rear, fairly well-protected from the worst of it. They didn't look at all confident when Truscott ordered them to carry .50 caliber machine guns right along with the regular infantry.

Hundreds of tanks went first, creaking into the night and dragging behind sled-like contraptions filled with infantrymen. The sleds shielded the men from land-mines and also created a safe path for the men following on foot in straight lines directly behind the tanks. Rosen traveled by jeep to the rear of the infantry so he could direct artillery fire, aiming high over the heads of the marching infantry and landing well into the German positions. The big guns of the field artillery brought up the rear, some two miles behind the infantry.

Abandoned wheat fields had grown to shoulder height, and the Allied troops circumnavigated the fields when they could to safeguard the crops. The country had already been tragically ravished, so this made little sense, but preserving some poor farmer's crop seemed the least they could do. By the thousands, they moved inland, slowly at first, heading boldly toward the enemy encampments. Then the artillery barrage began, and the Americans finally broke through the German lines.

At daybreak the following morning, they were able to view the damage their artillery fire had done. Hundreds of German troops had been cut down; the rest had actually begun to retreat to the north. The machine gunfire leveled off by the cooks and the mechanics had done some good. The additional fire power had made a difference.

Rosen and the others advancing along with him had reached a high point in the foothills as the morning sun climbed in the eastern sky.

"Hey," Cunningham said. "Look behind you. You can see all the way to the beach."

Rosen turned and got a good look at the lay of the land in the valley below. The area stretched for miles. Maybe it was just his imagination, but it looked as if the ground on which they'd fought had taken on a reddish hue, the color of dried blood. He suddenly flashed on that foggy morning when Sergeant Armstrong had died in his arms. There was no question that the fields of Anzio were now rich with American blood.

Rosen instantly appreciated what a tremendous advantage the Germans had held over them for so many months while they'd occupied the high ground and constantly shelled the Allied troops below. The lousy Kraut gunners had enjoyed a panoramic view of everything the Third Division was doing from their perfectly-elevated look-out posts. He wondered whether the Krauts had a good laugh over the way they'd forced the pathetic Americans to grovel in the mud.

The infantry had marched beyond artillery support, so the artillery leap-frogged forward, reaching the summit of the first hill by late afternoon. They came upon a road that skirted along the ridgeline near the town of Cori. By the time they'd reached the road, they were moving at a steady pace, advancing north in rapid pursuit of the retreating Germans. The sound of air support approaching from the south cheered them on. But then to everyone's surprise, the American P-51s circled around and began to bomb their fellow American soldiers.

"Holy Christ," someone yelled.

"They must think we're Krauts," yelled another.

Rosen and a band of infantrymen took cover behind a big pile of gravel. The American bombs kept falling. Horror-struck soldiers were killed as they cried out to the pilots who, of course, couldn't hear them. The pilots had mistaken them for the retreating Germans probably because they'd advanced up to the top of the hill much more rapidly than anticipated.

"We gotta let them know we're fucking Americans. They're gonna kill all of us."

Most of the infantry men had tossed away their smoke bombs to lighten their loads. They had so much to carry as it was, so it seemed logical to exchange the weight of a smoke bomb for more ammo on their belts. Rosen, however, still had his clipped right there where he could see it. He set off the cylindrical device and tossed it out over the pile of gravel onto the road. It clanked up and down like a Mexican jumping bean while it generated a huge plume of bright yellow smoke. As the yellow smoke rose, the P-51s banked and turned away from their location. Immediately, the planes were gone and the bombing stopped.

"They saw your smoke!" one of the infantrymen cried.

"How did you think of that?"

"Well," Rosen said, "that's what the smoke bombs were for, weren't they?"

They waited on the road until someone yelled out, telling them to turn left. They were on the road that led directly to Rome.

It took the men in Rosen's party two days to reach Rome because they encountered fire fights all along the way. Plenty of German stragglers had remained loyal at their posts, trying to take out as many of the advancing troops as they could. The Allied soldiers had fanned out in all directions, covering the land as far as the eye could see. United and exhilarated, they continued to proceed forward through the beautiful Italian countryside south of Rome.

Rosen was overjoyed that he was finally out of that mess at Anzio. He moved to a forward position and reported back to the artillery, but they'd reached a point where there wasn't a whole lot to report. It was a wonderful spring day and the Germans were high-tailing it out of their way. They didn't have to fire the big guns. What more could they ask for?

Then Rosen spotted a cherry tree fully laden with cherries just waiting to be picked. He climbed into the tree and began to feast upon one luscious cherry after another. Delicious. He hadn't quite reached his fill when a sniper's bullet whizzed right by his head. He managed to nose-dive out of that tree in record time. One of the nearby infantrymen nailed the sniper.

Rosen turned his attention back to scanning the landscape for the enemy. Oh, well, maybe he'd find fresh fruit in Rome.

Chapter 38

On June 4, 1944, the liberation of Rome turned into a loud, exuberant parade as thousands of American troops, tanks, jeeps, and trucks crowded into the city. Of course, the Germans had already fled, but the Italian people couldn't resist the opportunity to show their genuine appreciation to the soldiers who had forced the Germans out of their capital. They'd lived in terror of Nazi cruelty long enough. The Germans had raped their women and murdered innocent children. The Third Division had finally brought them hope. The war had destroyed everything except their spirit.

Rosen rode through the center of Rome in a jeep. He waved to the thousands of citizens who'd jammed the streets, hoping to get a closer look at their American knights in shining armor. He felt just as important as the officers who smiled and nodded beneficently at the wildly-energized throngs of people. Maybe the officers—or more precisely the generals—actually believed that they'd performed this miracle all by themselves.

Italians waved American flags or white handkerchiefs; some of the men stood at attention and saluted the troops as tears rolled down their cheeks. The crowd pulsed close to the parading troops, tossing fresh flowers onto the jeeps, tanks, and trucks. The people were drunk with happiness and very drunk with Italian wine. Wine bottles passed from citizens to the soldiers; older women cried and blessed themselves; younger women kissed the American men over and over. Many young women were boosted up into the already-crowded jeeps, and they rode along with their liberating heroes as part of the parade.

The men pressed slim Italian cigars into the hands of the soldiers. Rosen got his cigar lit easily enough, but once he drew the pungent smoke from the dark tobacco into his lungs, he went into a coughing fit. Thankfully the other guys were too busy with wine and women to worry about Rosen. His coughing went unnoticed instead of turning into a big joke—on him.

Once the Romans drifted back to their homes and the celebration ended, the Third Division was pulled out of line. The division was scheduled to move to southern France, but first the men were sent to bivouac in the outskirts of Rome for a brief rest period. The men clustered into tents, but the officers commandeered several once-grand and beautifully-appointed villas in the hills overlooking Rome as their temporary headquarters—the spoils of war.

Anything they did was okay as long as it elevated the comfort of the officers. Rosen wondered how the officers would respond if the owners returned and objected to this flagrant occupation of their homes.

News spread throughout the camp about other battles and victories in this god-awful war. The good news seemed diluted now that the war had already gone on far longer than any of the brass had ever anticipated, but everyone wanted to hear, to know how the other American troops were faring.

When the Allied troops had finally broken out of the standoff at Anzio, one Third Division regiment came across a German stronghold at the nearby village of Cisterna. The village itself had been bombed beyond belief, but the Americans took the ruined village away from the Germans who'd remained behind to defend it. This victory came with a huge price tag, however, since 995 members of the division died in the attack. Within a few hours, the offensive at Cisterna had racked up the greatest number of Americans killed in a single day during the war.

Right about the time the Allies had executed the breakout from Anzio, Cassino had finally also been liberated. French troops had helped the American armies to force the dwindling number of Germans down from their lofty placements on the mountain. The Allies stormed Cassino and the German army gave up and pulled back.

It was assumed that those German soldiers who'd lived to retreat from Monte Cassino had already headed toward northern France. Hitler had enough military intelligence to accurately predict that the Allies who were assembling in Britain were gearing up for an invasion of France. Hitler wanted a hard-hitting defense waiting for them in the wings. He intended to bring any plans for an invasion of France to a speedy and demoralizing halt.

With the liberation of Rome bolstering Allied morale, the troops all over Europe kept up the fight. The war raged on, and Rosen heard rumors that the countdown for the invasion of France had begun.

Several days into the rest period, Rosen and his outfit were trucked into Rome to see a special show at the opera house. Irving Berlin, who was a veteran from World War I, had arrived in Rome with a USO company of his own. To celebrate the liberation of Rome, Irving Berlin presented "This Is the Army," a show he had written for the combat troops. The opera house sparkled with lights for the first time in many months, and the ushers were dressed in American colonial costumes, complete with red coats and powdered white wigs.

The troops were orderly enough as they filed into the magnificent old theater, but they soon got into the spirit of celebration and began whooping it up. Some of the guys pulled condoms out of their pockets and blew them up like balloons. They tossed them from the upper balconies and the guys bounced the "balloons" back and forth all over the orchestra section on the main level. Mr. Berlin wore his old WWI uniform that evening, and he took no offense at the raucous behavior of the men. He sang along with the other performers, and, although he was rather short in stature, by the end of the show, the troops thought Irving Berlin was ten feet tall.

Following the show, Rosen went back to their rest camp and heard that Lieutenant Bailey—who had recently been promoted to Captain Bailey—wanted to see him. Rosen had no idea what to expect, but he'd learned to follow orders.

"Private Morris Rosen reporting, Sir."

"At ease, Private," Bailey said. "I've been reviewing your records."

"Yes, Sir."

Rosen felt his ears grow hot. The captain had probably heard that he'd climbed the cherry tree when he should have been on the lookout for enemy activity. He stood very still, waiting for the captain's wrath to come down on him.

"Why the hell are you still a private? You've been in this war almost two years."

"Yes, Sir." He wasn't about to plead his case by volunteering an explanation about Captain Blimp, the court marshal for desertion, the TNT explosion, Lieutenant White's accident, and all the rest of it.

"I heard you threw out a smoke bomb when we were taking friendly fire from the air."

"Yes, Sir."

"Good thinking. Okay, you're now Private First Class and I'm putting you on limited service."

"Sir?"

"The limp, Rosen. You're still limping from that hit you took at Anzio."

"Oh. Yes, Sir."

"You're going back to Naples to catch a British transport ship to France."

"Yes, Sir."

"You'll be assigned to a new outfit. The Third is going on without you."

"Yes, Sir."

Rosen thought for a moment about Julie. He'd be losing another friend, but at least he wasn't losing this one to a German bullet.

"You'll report to 7th Army Headquarters. They need a good forward observer. Report to the master sergeant after you land."

"Yes, Sir."

He'd finally been promoted, and he'd been placed on limited service, whatever that was. For the first time, he thought that perhaps he might actually survive this war and someday return home.

Chapter 39

Rosen sailed to St. Tropez on the French Riviera via a British transport ship. As far as he could tell, he was the only American enlisted man on board. An amphibious landing craft came to the ship and ferried Rosen and a few British soldiers ashore. Thousands of deliriously happy French citizens and soldiers lined the beach and greeted each of the Allies like old friends.

Rosen had been ordered to report to the Signal Section of the 7th Army Headquarters. He soon learned, however, that the upper echelon officers from headquarters would not land until the area had been completely secured. But, except for an occasional sniper's bullet fired by a Frenchman who still sympathized with Hitler, the coast seemed peaceful enough. Most of the Germans had already fled to the north. The master sergeant told Rosen where to bunk until official headquarters were set up.

The French were ecstatic. France—or at least southern France—had been liberated. It didn't take long for the French wine to begin to flow. For the next two days, Rosen became caught up in the spirited celebration. People gathered in the town square where a band—consisting entirely of very old men—played patriotic songs almost non-stop. A woman who was a celebrity with a local opera company sang the "Marseille," the French national anthem. Apparently this was the first public performance of the anthem since the German occupation, and the people wept as they attempted to sing along. No one remembered the words to the second and third stanzas, but the opera singer brilliantly carried all of them right through to the end. It seemed the hearts of these brave people were about to burst with appreciation and joy.

On Rosen's second day at St. Tropez, he and a few members of the Free French Underground, French civilians who'd fought against the Germans, were standing in the square trying to communicate. In spite of their language differences, the French seemed to understand Rosen. Their hands flew with gestures in a straight-forward sign language. Just then a German staff car boldly rumbled into town and stopped right in front of Rosen and the resistance fighters.

A German general in full military dress got out of the car and presented himself, announcing he wanted to surrender to the Americans. The general's hands trembled anxiously, and a film of sweat covered his face. Little beads of perspiration rolled down his temples, eventually soaking into his stiff collar.

Like a circling of sharks keen to attack, the Frenchmen wanted blood. The French were ready to shoot the general on the spot, but Rosen insisted that the surrender of an obviously important officer should be handled properly by the American Army. After all, the intelligence officers might be able to pry some valuable information out of a guy who was running this scared.

Rosen took the general into custody, and quickly frisked him for weapons. He found no weapons but he did take the general's impressive-looking hat away from him. Once the general was in Rosen's hands, the Freedom Fighters swarmed all over the poor, unsuspecting sap who had obediently driven the general into town. They snatched the German driver out of the staff car and began to thrash him with their fists. Rosen decided not to interfere. After all, the French had taken a lot of abuse during the last two years.

Rosen walked the German general to headquarters and turned him over to the military police. With the general secured, Rosen headed for a café. Capturing a prominent general, he reasoned, deserved a drink or two. He'd developed a taste for wine since he'd become a soldier, and there was no sense letting all that free-flowing French wine go to waste. Just showing up wearing his American uniform guaranteed him all the complimentary wine he could possibly drink.

It was broad daylight outside, but one step into the café transferred Rosen to a dark, smoke-filled getaway. The place smelled of musty old wine that had spilled to the roughly-hewn wood floor over the years. Once his eyes had adjusted to the faint light, he found a few Freedom Fighters at the bar and joined them for a toast.

They poured wine for him and pounded him on the back. Glasses were raised for a toast Rosen didn't quite understand, but he went along. He'd swallowed just a few sips of a wonderful red wine when suddenly an explosion rocked the entire café. The windows imploded into the bar area along with hot shrapnel from a bomb that had gone off right outside the building.

People screamed and ducked for cover; the serene little café caved into a pile of shattered glass and debris. The air was almost too thick with dust and smoke to breathe. Many of the civilians were so badly injured that Rosen feared they'd been killed. It took a few minutes for him to realize that a searing fragment of shrapnel had ripped through his pants and was now deeply imbedded in his right thigh. At least it wasn't the left leg that was still weakened from the hit he'd taken at Anzio.

The French went into a routine that sadly they'd performed countless times before. Litter bearers and medical people appeared seemingly out of nowhere. While the French rescue workers aided the injured citizens and Freedom Fighters, an army medic found his way to Rosen who was still sitting, unmoving, at the bar.

"You hit, soldier?" the medic asked over the screaming and crying.

Rosen took a moment to nod then pointed to the blood seeping from his leg. "Here," he said.

"Jesus, just when you think it's over, it ain't over." He cut away a section of Rosen's pant leg and took a closer look. "I need to pull out this hunk of metal with my pliers."

"Okay," Rosen said, still stunned, still absorbing the disastrous commotion reverberating all around him.

Right there on the bar stool, the medic yanked out the shrapnel and stitched up Rosen's wound. No pain medication, not even a bullet to bite.

"In about ten days, you can cut loose these stitches and pull them out yourself," the medic said as if removing sutures were no big deal.

Oddly, Rosen didn't find anything unusual about performing such a procedure. Of course he could remove his own stitches in ten days. Any soldier worth his salt could tear out his own stitches.

"Who set off the bomb?" Rosen asked.

"Probably one of those French bastards, you know the sons-of-bitches that still sympathize with the fucking Nazis. It had to be one of them; most of the Germans are long gone."

"Yeah," Rosen answered. He never did learn the source of the bomb.

When Rosen reported to 7th Army Headquarters the next morning, he enlisted the help of a clerk to mail the general's hat to his sister, Molly. Good, he thought. He had finally latched on to a fairly spectacular souvenir that would find its way safely back home.

Chapter 40

Rosen walked into the temporary 7th Army headquarters to report his latest shrapnel injury. He felt ill at ease at first, but the master sergeant just laughed. He recorded the event but didn't cite the location. The master sergeant diplomatically avoided mentioning that the bombing had taken place just outside a bar and that Rosen had received medical aid while sitting on a bar stool. But then it was common knowledge that all sorts of unusual injuries plagued army personnel.

He looked around headquarters for the other enlisted men, but there were none. General Wooley headed up all operations assisted by two full colonels, ten captains, and the master sergeant. To this impressive group they'd added Private First Class Rosen.

"What do we have here, Rosen?" one of the full colonels said. He'd been reviewing Rosen's orders which also contained a brief summation of his record. "You're a Private First Class?"

"Yes, Sir." Rosen drew himself up to his full height. This was the first time someone had recognized his long-awaited promotion.

"Well, this will never do. We can't have a PFC handling sensitive codes and communications."

"But, Sir, I've worked directing naval gunfire; I know Morse code."

"Sure, it says that right here." He slapped the paperwork with the back of his hand. "And your former captain sent you here because you need to be on limited service."

"Yes, Sir."

"Let me look at this. You were awarded two Purple Hearts while in combat before you suffered a shrapnel injury here in France?"

"Yes, Sir."

Rosen's heart was sinking. He'd obviously landed in the wrong place, and he was certain the colonel planned to bounce him right back into battle. He'd be ordered to rejoin the front line of his old division. The Third was now heading north through France on its way to Germany.

"Well, son, we need your expertise in communications, but we can't have a PFC doing the job."

"Yes, Sir," Rosen barely whispered.

He smiled. "So I have to promote you. You're now a corporal. Congratulations, Corporal Rosen."

Rosen was so rattled he almost forgot to return the colonel's salute.

After they'd exchanged their very serious-looking salutes, the colonel shook Rosen's hand. "Welcome aboard, Corporal."

The 7th Army Headquarters had located its first home in France in a grand old hotel nestled in a stand of towering pine trees. The magnificent stone building, with copious stone chimneys, had been blessed with minimal damage from German bombs. The elegant retreat stood high on a hill overlooking the golden sands of the French Riviera and the blue Mediterranean. In its day it must have been a wonderful vacation resort for the privileged-class with "old" money. Rosen hoped that someday it would be restored to its previous elegance. A rude scattering of army jeeps and battered trucks parked haphazardly on the circular drive in front of the hotel seemed completely out of place.

Rosen's assignment at army headquarters went into full swing. The First Signal Battalion was now attached to headquarters, and thirty people in this section reported directly to the officers in charge. Headquarters was the main center for communications in the area, responsible for deciphering German code, as well as sending out radio signals and supervising telephone lines. Rosen assisted the signal section wherever he could by setting up their communications equipment. Every day, all day, there was always some new job or an urgent errand awaiting Rosen's attention.

When he wasn't out working on downed telephone lines or setting up new ones, Corporal Rosen was put to work as a glorified office boy. He reproduced documents and drawings using a gelatin-filled pad that was capable of holding an image long enough to make as many as fifteen to eighteen copies of the original. The officers barked out orders whenever Rosen entered the room.

"Rosen, I need three copies of this, on the double."

"Yes, Sir."

"Corporal, deliver this to the General. Wait for his response."

"Yes, Sir."

"We got a switchboard down over at the signal section. Do you think you can fix it?"

"Yes, Sir."

The officers sent him on endless errands, but he soon discovered that he actually enjoyed this kind of work. He felt like a free agent because when he had a job to do outside of headquarters, he went alone. He had a jeep he called his own, and no one tagged along issuing orders. He was never accused of goofing-off or taking too long to complete an assignment. He also liked the idea that, for the most part, no one was shooting at him.

Rosen felt as if he were on an extraordinary vacation while headquarters occupied the old hotel, but as the army moved, so did their headquarters. The Third Division moved steadily north, liberating one French village after another as they swamped the retreating Germans. When the infantry and artillery moved out of range of headquarters, Rosen was sent forward to reconnoiter their new post and report back via telephone when the site was secure. Each time a different headquarters was established, Rosen stayed at the new position and waited for the rest of the staff to pack up and join him the following day.

He was now a part of the rear echelon, and it turned out this assignment was by far the best chapter of his army experience. He didn't miss the irony of the fact that he'd always resented the men who'd worked in headquarters while he was in the direct line of fire during all those many months of combat. He'd discovered, however, that the officers in 7th Army Headquarters were different from guys like Captain Blimp who were all pomp and no substance. For the most part, these were men who'd been drafted out of corporations and universities back in the States because the army coveted their unique skills and many years of experience in communications.

The colonel who'd promoted Rosen to corporal had been the former head of AT&T in Philadelphia. Several of the captains at army headquarters had been college professors, mostly mathematicians who'd been pulled into service to help break German codes. Men who could help the war effort in any way possible were snapped up from many different technical fields back home and given instant commissions as officers.

Summer drifted into fall, and on October 6, 1944 Rosen celebrated his 20th birthday. A couple of the guys in the signal corps bought him a few beers, and he received a letter from his sister. That same week he had a chance to drive his jeep to the spot where his old division was camped, but he couldn't locate Julie. Julie was alive, though. One of the guys reported that Julie had been sent out somewhere on an assignment.

Another cruel winter was soon upon them. Rosen and army headquarters had gradually inched north into central France along the Rhone River. They were still south of the area where a horrendous conflict called the Battle of the Bulge was now in progress. That icy battlefield was blanketed in a deep, heavy snow, with howling winds delivering the most penetrating cold imaginable. It was cold enough where Rosen was stationed, but reports trickled in about the hardships the soldiers further north faced while trying to fight in drifts of snow that piled up over five feet high in constantly changing patterns. Many had died of exposure; frostbite was common. He couldn't imagine fighting in weather even more miserable than last winter's cold in Mignano and Cassino.

For the infantry and artillery in Rosen's outfit, the fighting was intense and progress was painfully slow, but in his current assignment at headquarters, well behind the front lines, he was safe. He usually carried a rifle with him, sometimes left behind in his jeep, but he never fired a shot. The extreme pressure of living in a trench, with ammo blasting all around him, still haunted him, but he'd been liberated from those incredibly miserable years. Rosen now understood why the citizens in the Italian and French villages were so grateful when the shelling finally stopped.

Every day Rosen came in close contact with experts in code and communications who worked at headquarters. Many of the Frenchmen who purported to assist and advise the Americans spoke German as well as French, so it was difficult to tell who was a spy and who wasn't. The French who were German sympathizers had a way of screwing up army objectives, so the officers were now in close liaison with French officers. American officers who were fluent in French frequently came in for a briefing or a staff meeting.

While one of these briefings was in progress, Rosen was in an adjacent room jotting down his orders for the day being dictated by one of the colonels. As usual, the colonel had a long list of jobs he wanted Rosen to perform. All of a sudden a deep stentorian voice boomed into the room from the corridor.

"Rosen!" the voice roared.

Before he looked, Rosen had already identified the bellow. No one but Captain Blimp sounded like that. Rosen took a deep breath. He turned around slowly to face him, but before they made eye contact, Rosen noticed the gold oak leaf on the voice's shoulder. Captain Blimp was now Major Blimp, and apparently he'd studied enough French in high school to enable him to get a job as a liaison officer. Of all the rotten luck; his nemesis had caught up with him.

Rosen bit back the word he wanted to shout. Inside his head he was screaming: "Shit" over and over.

"Yes, sir," Rosen finally managed.

The major ignored Rosen and rushed right past him to the colonel's side. "I want you to know that this man was in my command in Africa." He pointed to Rosen.

The colonel didn't mention the flaming red flush that had suddenly consumed the major's face, but he must have guessed that something was up. The colonel thought for a moment, giving Major Blimp a long, hard stare. He finally said, "That's okay. I think he'll get over it."

Major Blimp's red face smoldered to a deep purple. He spun around and left as quickly as he'd arrived. Rosen never saw him again.

Chapter 41

One poor guy had been drafted by mistake in spite of the fact that he'd been granted an official exemption from military service. Raymond W. Deacon was an engineer who designed landing gears for American aircraft carriers and was desperately needed at his job back home. The army explained the confusion simply by calling Mr. Deacon's situation an unfortunate SNAFU. Army talk for: Situation normal. All fucked up.

Deacon was older than most of the men, even some of the officers, and he certainly was not familiar with life under fire. General Wooley insisted that Deacon should remain at headquarters until the army could arrange the paperwork necessary for his discharge and subsequent return to the States. Meanwhile, Rosen was assigned to take care of him and make certain that he was kept safe. The general didn't want the president and the entire U.S. government coming down on him for failing to protect a man who was vital to the defense effort.

Rosen got along well with all the officers at headquarters, and Deacon also took an immediate liking to him. Deacon was impressed by the way Rosen picked his brains about his work as an engineer. In fact, Deacon had duly noted that Rosen was inquisitive about everything. Deacon admired Rosen's curiosity and the two became fast friends.

Once again 7th Army Headquarters had moved north, this time into Alsace-Lorraine. As the army advanced, the Germans were forced to retreat back into their homeland. The Germans had occupied this French province since 1940, and now that Alsace-Lorraine was in the hands of the Americans, France took back possession and control of its former territory.

Deacon was still Rosen's responsibility and, no matter what tasks Rosen had to perform, Deacon usually tagged along. Headquarters had packed up and moved further north, this time to occupy a set of low buildings that had formerly been used by the Germans as army barracks. Rosen guessed that the Germans had fled in a hurry because the place was a mess. A small mountain of junk filled the entire west end of the larger building.

The colonel said, "Rosen, we need to make room for the officers to set up bunks."

"Yes, Sir."

"And find a spot for you and Deacon to bed down."

"Yes, Sir. What do you want me to do with the stuff the Germans left behind?"

"I'm sure the French have already taken anything of value."

"Yes, Sir."

"Just toss the whole lot outside. We probably won't be here very long."

"Yes, Sir."

Deacon and Rosen worked together in the old barracks to scratch out a decent place to bunk. They picked through the heap of rubble, throwing aside old mattresses, bedding, and trash left by the German troops.

"Nothing but a load of junk in here," Rosen said. "Junk the Nazis didn't take with them when they ran for their lives."

Deacon chuckled. "Be glad they ran, or else they'd be breathing down our necks."

"Hey, look at what I found," Rosen said. He held up an old violin and bow he'd pulled out from under a pile of debris.

Deacon took the instrument, handling the dusty old violin very carefully, almost with reverence. "It looks like a good one."

"The strings are all broken."

Deacon nodded. "Yes and two strings are missing altogether."

When Rosen held up the bow, a stringy black spider web dangled from one end. "I'll bet this belongs to the violin."

Deacon smiled as he took it from Rosen. "Right, this is the bow for the violin. The horsehair strings need to be cleaned and tightened."

For the next two days, Deacon worked on the violin. He took some of Rosen's regular field wire and stripped away the outer layer of copper. He took the steel wire from the center core and used it to re-string the violin. Deacon fussed with the wire, tuning and adjusting the instrument until Rosen started to hear sounds that were more than just squeaky noise.

When Deacon propped the violin under his chin and began to play, Rosen couldn't believe his ears. Deacon played a beautiful melody that turned the old German barracks into a symphony hall. Rosen stopped what he was doing and sat down to listen. There was absolutely no question in Rosen's mind: Deacon was a genius.

"How far did you go in school?" Deacon asked him one day.

"I finished the eighth grade."

Deacon frowned. "When this war is over, you should go back to school. Go to college."

"But I didn't even go to high school." Rosen said flatly.

"Doesn't matter. You're smart. You can make up whatever you missed in high school. Son, believe me on this; I know you can do it."

Rosen scratched his head. "Well. . ." He was certain he could finish his high school education one day, but college? How could he ever pull that off?

Deacon continued, "Rosen, you're too smart to throw away your life working at some menial job. You're probably smarter than half of the generals running the show in this war. Go to college."

Raymond Deacon was the first person who'd ever mentioned college to Rosen. He hadn't received any counseling when he'd graduated from the eighth grade because, thanks to his father, he'd gone straight into reform school. And now here was a highly-intelligent man advising him to reach for the stars, telling him he could do it. Mr. Deacon believed Rosen could succeed in college.

Rosen thought about Deacon's advice for days. For the first time, Rosen understood that he did not have to spend the rest of his life laboring as a machinist. He believed Deacon was right. College was the answer. If he lived through this war, he'd figure out some way to resume his education where he'd left off. Deacon's words had not fallen on deaf ears.

Raymond Deacon was finally picked up by the military police and escorted to the closest airfield. Deacon carried with him the old violin that he had brought back to life. He and Rosen shook hands, and Deacon again reminded Rosen of his promise to return to school. Rosen would miss his friend, and at the same time he realized how very much he was indebted to him.

Leatrice and Jules Posner
March 25, 1945

It was now April of 1945, and Rosen had received word that his buddy Julie Posner had returned to the States and married his sweetheart, Leatrice, on March 25, 1945. He wished he could've traveled to New York for the wedding, but headquarters wasn't giving out passes. They were fully involved with the paperwork required for working out schedules to send the men home for discharge. The few men who were issued passes during this time period had friends in high places, and Rosen had no such connections. Rosen was glad that Julie had survived the war and that he'd married his girl. He planned to visit Julie and his new bride in New York as soon as his hitch in the army was over.

Headquarters had followed the troops all the way into Augsburg, Germany. The war was coming to an end in Europe although Germany's actual surrender had yet to take place. Of course, the United States was still at war with the Japanese in the Pacific. Rosen thought about his brother, Hy, fighting that nasty battle, probably enduring more suffering than Rosen even wanted to think about. In his last letter from his sister Molly, he'd learned that Hy's outfit had been sent into Okinawa.

Rosen pulled out a few maps stored at headquarters for those who wanted to follow the war in Japan. Okinawa was nothing more than a slender little island that looked no bigger than Long Island in New York. Okinawa. Even the name sounded strangely foreign, so distant from the life they had both known as boys in Pittsburgh. Word had spread that Okinawa was the last stronghold the Americans had to defeat before the final invasion of Japan. He hoped his brother and the rest of the marines in his outfit would give those Japs plenty of grief.

One of the captains called Rosen into his office. He was smoking a cigar, leaning back in his chair. With the war winding down, the captain, like the rest of the men, looked much more relaxed than usual.

"We have a dignitary from Hollywood coming to visit us."

"Sir?" Rosen had a hunch that this would turn into a baby-sitting assignment for some starlet or the other. He wouldn't complain.

"You ever hear of Cecil B. DeMille?"

"Isn't he a big Hollywood director? A guy who makes movies?"

"That's the one. I believe you know the way from here to Dachau, don't you?"

"Yes, Sir. It isn't far."

"Well, Mr. DeMille wants to film the liberation of a concentration camp. The army will be going into Dachau tomorrow to take care of the prisoners and get them the hell out of there, and DeMille wants to record all this on film."

"Yes, Sir."

"I'm assigning you to his camera crew for as long as they need you."

"Yes, Sir."

"Show them the way to Dachau and then stick around and help out in any way you can."

"Yes, Sir."

The camera crew had its own driver and a truck filled with cameras and other equipment. Rosen sat next to the driver, a guy from California, and gave him directions to Dachau. Film-maker, Cecil B. DeMille, followed in a staff car.

The 20 kilometer drive didn't take very long, but it was time enough for Rosen to reflect on what they might encounter once they'd arrived.

Word had spread that the Nazis had set up death camps all over Eastern Europe. They'd imprisoned Jews, Poles, Gypsies, Slavs and anyone else who'd offended their need for Aryan purity. The first death camp had been unearthed near Lublin, Poland by Soviet troops. As one horror story after another reached the American soldiers, some claimed that not even the Nazi bastards they'd come to despise could be that cruel.

Who could believe the outrageous stories about gas chambers and mass murders? But then the Soviets revealed more ghastly stories about additional death camps that they'd discovered. Even so, many remained unbelieving, but most of the skeptics were not Jews. Somehow, in his heart, Rosen knew the reports were accurate. As a Jew, he'd been assailed by anti-Semitic insults and wisecracks for as long as he could remember.

The more Rosen heard about such atrocities against the Jewish people, the more sickened he'd become. He'd always read that the Germans were peaceful, gentle people. They'd farmed their land, planted vast orchards, raised goats and chickens, and quietly tinkered with the intricacies of cuckoo clocks and music boxes.

But then Hitler came into power. He had transformed a whole nation into fanatic extremists. Hitler and his firmly-indoctrinated followers had taught the German people to believe that, above all, the Jews were responsible for all their problems.

The Jews somehow interfered with Hitler's plan to establish a perfect world. It was rumored that Jewish women and children had also been incarcerated and tortured in concentration camps under the most deplorable conditions that anyone could imagine. Adolph Hitler and his Nazi bullies picked on innocent people who had no way to fight back. The Jews, in fact, had been taught to turn the other cheek, not to fight back. As a whole, they were not violent people. Their ethnic origin seemed to be their only crime.

Rosen assisted the camera crew as best he could, but they were experienced and knew exactly how to set up and get those cameras rolling. Rosen soon learned that he could help best by just staying out of their way.

The German guards had all fled, and American soldiers were waiting in place to usher the prisoners out of Dachau. Medics, trucks, and ambulances stood by. No one knew what to expect.

While he stood around waiting, Rosen noticed the fancy scrolled wrought-iron lettering that had been fastened high above the heavy gate. The ominous-looking black sign loomed over the gate like a bold proclamation. Rosen was able to translate the German into English because he understood Yiddish.

The sign publicly stated their shameless Nazi slogan: "Work Makes You Free."

When the crew had the cameras in place, they signaled Mr. DeMille. They stood near the gate, ready to proceed inside. Cecil B. DeMille slowly studied the scene before him, gathering his thoughts. He seemed to be planning his strategy, deciding on the best possible camera angles. He drew his eyebrows together into a frown and stood that way, perfectly still. Then finally, he pointed to Rosen who was standing nearby with the crew.

"Soldier," he said, "open that gate."

Chapter 42

And so, with the cameras finally rolling, 20 year-old Morris Rosen stepped up to the entrance of the Dachau Concentration Camp. He pulled the heavy gate open slowly; the cameras followed him inside.

The American soldiers stiffened in horror as they unbolted the doors to the barracks. The prisoners did not rush out to freedom as they had expected. Most did not have enough strength to even stand up. So thin they barely looked human, the prisoners lay cramped together on lice-infected wooden pallets that served as beds without even a bit of straw for a mattress. The Nazis probably had enough consideration to give their animals clean straw to lie upon.

The German guards had fled, leaving their prisoners who were mostly Jews to die. No one knew how long it had been since the prisoners had been given any food, and from the looks of them, their rations had been no more than a few scraps a day even when the guards had been in residence.

In spite of the rumors, up until he'd actually walked through that gate, Rosen had no idea how ruthlessly the Nazis had treated the Jews. He couldn't even begin to comprehend how deeply the Jewish prisoners had suffered. No one could. Almost as if in a daze, Rosen wandered away from the camera crew and started to explore this intensely gruesome scene on his own.

He passed huge brick ovens with the doors flung wide open that were still filled with bones and ash. Hollow-eyed human skulls resting upon the powdery ash stared back at him. He shuddered and hurried away from the ovens. He rounded a corner beyond a large brick building and walked into what looked like a railroad yard.

Rosen came upon a train of box cars that apparently had been wheeled into the camp before the Germans had fled. In their haste to escape with their own lives, the German guards had not had time to unload this shipment of at least five car loads of prisoners.

The men and women in this latest shipment were dressed in their tattered civilian clothes, marked with the insidious yellow star that identified them as Jews. Apparently they'd been forced to lie flat on their backs on top of one another, stacked into the cars like so much firewood. A few on the very top of the heap in each car spilled over the edge, legs twitching, arms moving slightly.

God help them, Rosen thought, some of these starving, beaten souls were still alive. The prisoners who were alive had been left to die on top of the already dead. Even those who'd fallen out of the railroad cars and landed on the ground lacked the strength to get up and run. He had to tell someone that he'd found a few who were miraculously moving, breathing.

Rosen hurried past lopsided mountains of bodies that had been dumped from previous railroad shipments. The stench of decaying human flesh was unbearable; he could barely catch his breath. The piles of decomposing bodies stretched forward along the path all the way to the end of the railroad yard.

He bolted away from the horror of it all. Cold chills throbbed through his every nerve. As he rushed toward the rescue officers to report what he'd seen, his chest grew so tight it hurt to breathe.

"Sergeant," he called to the first rescue worker he spotted. "In the railroad yard, over there." He pointed. "Some of the people piled upon the dead are still alive. In the box cars. They're still moving."

"Jesus," the sergeant muttered. "Okay, we'll get them out of there."

Rosen watched as several men from the rescue team headed toward the box cars. An iron fist squeezed his heart until it was barely limping in his chest. He felt the ice in his veins grow colder, yet his skin was damp with a vile, hot sweat.

Little wonder people didn't believe the stories about the concentration camps. Humans simply could not do what the Nazis had done, yet here it was. He had seen the inconceivable end results of Nazi brutality with his own eyes.

He went back to the barracks to escape the mounds of dead bodies and the overwhelming stench of death. He shook his head to dislodge the sights he'd just seen. The images didn't fade, but instead, pierced like an arrow through his brain. He entered a barracks that had just been opened by a rescue team. Trembling visibly, Rosen sat down next to one of the camera men. He sat on his hands to keep them from shaking.

The American soldiers pulled ration tins out of their pockets and tried to feed the starving prisoners. Some did not have enough strength to swallow. Those that could gobble the food forced too much into their shrunken stomachs too quickly. After a few minutes, they vomited, unable to keep the food down. The soldiers were then cautioned by the medical team not to feed them at all. The medics feared that too much food might actually kill the most-severely emaciated. Giant pots of soup were delivered by army trucks to give the prisoners a slower, carefully measured intake of nourishment. Army doctors and nurses frantically tried to assess what needed to be done.

As the shriveled, disoriented men tried to swallow water from American cups, Rosen spoke to those who seemed most alert. He found that it didn't matter whether they were German, Polish, or

Hungarian. Most Jews could converse in Yiddish, their own privileged language. While they sipped water or the warmed soup that had been brought in, Rosen tried to communicate with anyone who was able to speak.

Rosen spoke to them in Yiddish. "Where are you from?" he asked one man.

"Turka, in Poland." His faded voice croaked pathetically.

A shiver raced up Rosen's spine. His father was from Poland. Turka sounded familiar. "Do you have a family?"

"Gone. I had a wife, four sisters, my parents, all gone."

Rosen had to place his ear very close to the prisoner's mouth to pick up the words. Rosen's eyes had grown moist; his skin tingled, pebbly with gooseflesh.

"So what's that you're asking him?" one of the medics said.

"Just asking where he's from. This man's from Poland."

"You speak Polish?"

"No, Yiddish. I'm a Jew."

The medic shook his head. "Damn. This must be awful for you. Goddamn Nazis."

Another medic told Rosen to find out when the men had last eaten.

Rosen spoke to as many Jews as he could. The prisoners said they hadn't been fed for many days; they'd been left to starve to death. Most were naked, but a few wore filthy black and white striped uniforms that hung on their bodies like shredded, limp rags. They looked to Rosen and their rescuers with cautious disbelief. They'd obviously heard so many lies in the past that they trusted no one.

"It's going to be all right now," Rosen said over and over in Yiddish. He came close to tears every time he made that particular promise. "We're American soldiers. You'll be okay as soon as we get you to a hospital."

Some of the men wept. Some squeezed Rosen's hand with a feeble grip.

Rosen's voice cracked but he kept repeating, telling the prisoners that their suffering was over. They would soon be out of this horrible place.

The tales were tragic and all very much the same. Some had no idea what had happened to their families; most believed that all their family members had been killed. In some cases wives and mothers had been murdered right before their eyes. And their children? Well, the children had been taken into forced labor, or they'd been slaughtered on the spot when their crying and whining disturbed the Nazi guards.

Most of these drained and defeated men had a hard time speaking out loud, as if they feared some sudden, absolute form of punishment might be unleashed if the guards overheard them talking. They whispered, telling Rosen about the men and women who'd been abruptly wrenched from their barracks never to be seen again. Tears filled their swollen, diseased eyes. The prisoners wouldn't—no they couldn't believe that the German guards were gone. The concept of liberation had drifted beyond their understanding. They'd been through so much; they couldn't accept as true that their suffering was over.

Rosen asked another man whether he had family.

"Every one sent to the gas chambers, even my little girl, Hadra." The man tried to sit up but lacked the strength.

Rosen's blood ran cold. He put his arm around the man's skeletal shoulders to support him. His bones protruded like sharp edges. Rosen said, "I'm sorry about your family. But you'll be okay now that the rescue team is here. They're going to take you to a hospital."

Tears slipped down the man's cheeks. "They worked my brother until he dropped dead from sheer exhaustion and lack of food. The Nazi guards then tossed his body into a cart like a dead animal and hauled him away to the ovens. They forced us Jews to throw our own people into the ovens." The man began to sob. "They made us do it."

Rosen nodded, trying to show the man he understood, but no one could understand the unbelievable carnage the Nazis had brought about. A Jew was of little use to them; a dead Jew was a nuisance, so much garbage to be disposed of as quickly as possible.

Rosen wandered around, talking to the prisoners who had enough strength to speak. His ability to translate their Yiddish back into English for the medical people was helpful, but Rosen didn't feel his minimal help would make a big difference. He tried his best to offer the men hope, but he feared the worst. These walking skeletons had been so terribly damaged that he knew many would die even as the rescue efforts took place. Rosen felt emotionally bankrupt just by virtue of witnessing the agony that the Germans had inflicted upon the Jews.

The heavy burden in his chest continued to make it difficult for him to breathe. He'd lived through an impossible deluge of bloodshed during the course of the war, but even the cruelty of seeing his buddies die in battle could not compare to the shameful devastation he was witnessing now.

As he moved from one barracks to the next, searching for survivors who could talk to him, he covered his face to ward off the smell of death. Rosen tried to get his mind around what he'd witnessed at Dachau, but the reality of what had happened here was beyond his comprehension, beyond human belief.

He simply couldn't understand why the Nazis had held such utter contempt for not just a few Jews, but all Jews. They'd treated Jewish men, women, and children as if they were a lower life form that did not qualify as a human being. And for so many years the Germans had used deceitful, underhanded means to cover up what was going on in their hideous death camps. To the rest of the world, the death camps had masqueraded as work camps for their prisoners. But now that Germany had been defeated, the Allied troops had finally exposed the Nazi's deepest, most monstrous secrets.

Rosen could take no more. He'd seen too much of the deceit and death that had taken place in Hitler's Germany. He finally walked out through the same gate he'd opened for Cecil B. DeMille's cameras as the infantrymen and the medical staff began the painfully delicate process of transporting the prisoners to hospitals.

At Thala, Salerno, Mignano, Cassino, or even at Anzio, Rosen hadn't fully understood exactly why Hitler had to be defeated. He'd been a boy who'd simply recognized that he was an American soldier doing a job that had to be done. He hadn't been aware of the insanity behind Hitler's thinking. Now for the first time Rosen saw the reason for this war. He understood why Hitler and his army had to be stopped, why all those Allied soldiers had not died in vain. They'd died to stop a mad man.

As Rosen trudged away from Dachau, he'd had no way of knowing that by the time the war in Europe ended, the Americans and the Soviets would uncover more than 100 such death camps. He had yet to learn that of the 9 million Jews alive in Europe in 1933, two-thirds had been killed in death camps. By 1945, Hitler and his regime had murdered six million Jewish men, women, and children.

Chapter 43

On April 12, 1945, American President Franklin Delano Roosevelt died. FDR had served as president for more than 12 years, so most of the younger soldiers like Rosen could not remember a time when he did not preside over the White House. They'd counted on their president's expertise and guidance to pull America through this war.

But then, less than a month later on May 8, 1945, the Germans finally announced their unconditional surrender to the Allied forces. The darkness of war had lifted and people were ready to celebrate. Civilians and soldiers alike went wild. Rosen fired off a flare gun from the front steps of army headquarters at Augsburg, Germany.

Celebrations rang out wherever Americans troops were stationed, but it wasn't the pure jubilation as they'd experienced in Rome. The celebration was inundated by German soldiers coming forward, pleading to surrender into American hands. American personnel had to halt their celebration in order to take the surrendering Germans into custody. It seemed that the Germans had also shown their pension for extreme cruelty in their treatment of the Russians, and the Germans understood that, given the chance, the Russians would gladly shoot every one of them.

The German women threw themselves at the American GIs, but orders had been issued from the generals at the top to prohibit any and all American military personnel from fraternizing with the enemy. Some of the guys got into some real hot and heavy fraternizing just the same.

One of the captains asked Rosen to drive him to Bertchesgarten, Hitler's hideout and vacation headquarters high on the German side of the Bavarian Alps near Augsburg. Bertchesgarten, also known as the Eagle's Nest, had been initially captured by the Third Division, but now it had become a looting and pillaging ground for army personnel from all the divisions stationed in Germany. Soldiers of every rank found their way up the steep mountainside to investigate Hitler's luxurious, secluded hideaway.

Hitler's Eagle's Nest offered an incredible view of the surrounding countryside, but Rosen and the captain hurried inside, wanting to see where the madman Hitler had spent his time, dreaming up his contemptible, insane strategies for ridding the world of those he considered sub-human.

Rosen and the captain joined the others who were picking through Hitler's confidential letters and papers and looting anything of interest or value. Rosen passed over beautiful silver trays, flatware, and goblets, dozens of art treasures, and valuable old books that probably would become priceless as time went on in favor of checking out Hitler's private wine cellar.

Rosen was still too young and naïve to realize the future value of Hitler's belongings. Rosen knew only that the man had been an evil maniac. He wanted nothing to do with Hitler or his treasures. Rosen was thrilled to settle for getting drunk on Hitler's exclusive reserve of French champagne.

The army had established an elaborate point system to help the officers determine the order of discharge for the men. Points were given for time overseas, the number of campaigns fought, battle wounds, and military decorations. When the points were added up, Rosen had the highest score of anyone at army headquarters.

The colonel announced that Rosen was indeed the first eligible for discharge, but he had another plan for Rosen. Instead, he offered him a commission as a second lieutenant if Rosen were willing to stay on with the army and go to the Far East, to the war in the Pacific. Rosen's stomach clenched. Just because the Germans had surrendered didn't mean the Japanese had relaxed their battle tactics in the Pacific. In fact the Japanese had stepped up their efforts to defeat the U.S., and Rosen's brother was still fighting in Okinawa.

But Rosen remembered his many discussions with Raymond Deacon. He had learned enough about himself to understand that he wanted to go to college and learn about all the mysteries of higher education. He wanted to learn and understand philosophy, the sciences, and higher math. He wanted to read books beyond SWISS FAMILY ROBINSON. He recalled a time when Deacon had quoted something from Shakespeare. He'd marveled that someone—even someone like himself who'd completed no more than the eighth grade—might someday be able to attain that same level of sophistication.

Although Rosen was still capable of making stupid decisions, he had definitely grown up. He still looked young and innocent enough, but he'd changed in ways that couldn't be detected just by looking at him.

He'd faced and overcome the challenges of combat, which was bad enough, but he'd also seen things that would pull at his heart and soul for the rest of his life. The horror of what he'd witnessed at Dachau would stay with him forever. No one who experiences what Rosen had experienced remains unchanged.

He'd gone into the war as a 17 year-old kid who wanted nothing more than to become an airplane mechanic. That hadn't worked out, but he'd become a valuable asset to the army without really setting out to do more than fulfill a kid's dream of going off on an exciting action-packed journey. In his imaginative daydreams about the adventure stories he'd loved to read as a boy, he'd always been an inadvertent warrior.

As soldiers, all the men in Rosen's outfit had seen things, done things that their minds couldn't handle. So many had gone over the edge, their hopes destroyed, their dreams twisted into haunting nightmares. Rosen wanted to move on, to leave the horror and devastation of the war behind. He'd done his share and that was all he could do. He turned down the colonel's offer of a commission.

He arrived at an army airfield with 100 or so other soldiers for the flight home. They would travel light, no packs, no rifles, for the first time in years. They were divided up into five bombers nick-named Flying Fortresses, about 20 men per plane. This was Rosen's first air flight, and he secretly hoped he'd have a window seat so he could observe the world below from an incredibly high vantage point. The other men were hastened into the bomber, hoping only to have a reasonably comfortable place to sit; windows were not even an option in a bomber, except for one special seat. The glass-enclosed bombardier's section in the very nose of the plane could hold only one passenger. Rosen was pushed into that coveted special position, landing there again by chance.

Rosen had a bird's eye view of France and Spain before they flew south over the Rock of Gibraltar. His plane stopped at an air base in Africa to refuel before the Flying Fortress soared over the Atlantic Ocean non-stop to Miami, Florida.

During the long flight across the Atlantic, Rosen had plenty of time to think. The war hadn't seemed all that remarkable while he was in it, but now at a safe distance he realized what an incredible feat the Allied soldiers had accomplished. Rosen had managed to walk away from the war in one piece, but so many had died, especially at Anzio. There was no redeeming all those lost lives. The Third Division had suffered more combat deaths during WWII than any other division in the U.S. armed forces. Rosen would feel a sense of pride in the division's determination and bravery for the rest of his life.

It was August, 1945, just days before atomic bombs would devastate Japan and generate Japan's unconditional surrender. It was still two months before Rosen would celebrate his 21st birthday.

But for Rosen the war was over. He was going home.

Going home. 7th Army Headquarters
Morris Rosen, age 19, on right.
August 1945

The Rest of the Story:

My husband, Morris "Morrie" Rosen, did not complete high school but, with nothing more than his eighth grade education, he passed a college entrance exam and was accepted at Los Angeles City College. Because of his code work at 7th Army Headquarters, he was able to secure a job with the United States Embassy in Paris. He stayed at that post for five years deciphering code.

Following Raymond Deacon's advice, Rosen earned a Bachelor's Degree in English and his Master's Degree in School Administration. He worked as an elementary school teacher and served as an acting elementary school principal while he studied nights to complete his Master's Degree.

Rosen then decided to change careers and switched his focus to the investment business. He became a highly-regarded financial consultant and stock broker. After 23 years in that position, he retired at age 71.

* * *

When Rosen was shot at Anzio in 1944, the War Department sent a telegram to his mother in Pittsburgh stating that he'd been killed in action. The telegram was delivered to her by a local city representative who promised to drive her to the city hall the very next day so she could take the test for her U.S. citizenship. When presiding Judge Musmano learned that Pauline Rosen's son had been killed, he rapped his gavel and declared that she was a citizen, all test questions waived. Three weeks later, the War Department followed up with another telegram stating that Rosen was missing in action. A third telegram announced that he'd been wounded and was recovering in a hospital in Naples.

After the war, Judge Musmano went on to preside over the Nuremberg Trials for war criminals in Germany.

* * *

President Franklin Delano Roosevelt issued a Presidential Unit Citation to the Ninth Division Artillery for their exceptional bravery at the battle of Thala. The entire unit was recognized with this highest honor presented to a unit for unprecedented heroism under enemy fire. Rosen received his medal for this tribute after the war.

* * *

The hat that Rosen had confiscated from the German general in St. Tropez arrived safely in Pittsburgh. Rosen's sister Molly donated it to a War Bond Rally for auction. The general's name had been printed inside the hat, and it raised an astounding $25,000 in cash for the war effort when it was auctioned at the rally.

***

Rosen's brother Hyman Rosen returned safely from Okinawa after serving two and a half years in the 3rd Marine Division.

***

In 1992, we attended a reunion of the Third Infantry Division in San Francisco. One evening the 39th Field Artillery held a dinner for its members. Captain Coates—now General Coates—who'd investigated Lieutenant White's jeep accident attended as an honored guest. General Coates had long since retired and had a hard time remembering the individuals who'd served under his command. Except for Morris Rosen.

General Coates looked at Rosen's name tag and simply stated, "Rosen. You're the one who killed Lieutenant White!"

***

In 1994, we attended a celebration of the 50th Anniversary of the battle of Anzio at the U.S. Military Cemetery at Anzio, Italy. President William Clinton spoke, honoring the Third Division survivors. The program was telecast world-wide.

President Clinton and First Lady Hillary Rodham Clinton hosted a reception for the veterans following the ceremony, and we had the opportunity to shake hands and chat with the Clintons. President Clinton expressed his gratitude to my husband for his service to our country. The first lady whispered to me that she thought my husband was quite good-looking. I agreed.

We also visited hundreds of American graves at Anzio. Subsequent to the armistice, the U.S. government initiated a program to bring soldiers buried in Europe home to their families, but 93,000 American soldiers remain in cemeteries in Europe, mostly in Italy and France.

After the President's reception, the American veterans once again paraded through the streets of Rome, cheered on by thousands of Italian citizens. The veterans walked a little slower, some needed wheelchairs, and many walked with canes, but their spirit and courage still sparkled in their eyes. They were welcomed into Rome with the same jubilation and enthusiasm the Italians had shown 50 years previously in 1944.

* * *

That same summer, we traveled to Germany and visited Bertchesgarten. Hitler's hideaway, the Eagle's Nest, has since been converted into a fine restaurant.

* * *

At Ninth Division reunions, even when Morris Rosen was well into his 60s, 70s, and 80s, the men still referred to him as "The Kid."

* * *

As of this writing the following persons are alive and enjoying life. They are all currently in their 80s:
Morris "Morrie" Rosen, California
Jules "Julie" Posner, California
Julie's wife, Leatrice Posner, California
Staff Sergeant William "Bill" Kunz, Illinois
First Lieutenant William "Rip" Rybka, North Carolina

* * *

When the men of the Third Division meet for their annual reunions, they read a poem that states in part that when they die they know they will all go to heaven because they've already been to hell.

Marion Rosen

Morris Rosen, age 83
World War II Memorial, Washington D.C.
December 2007

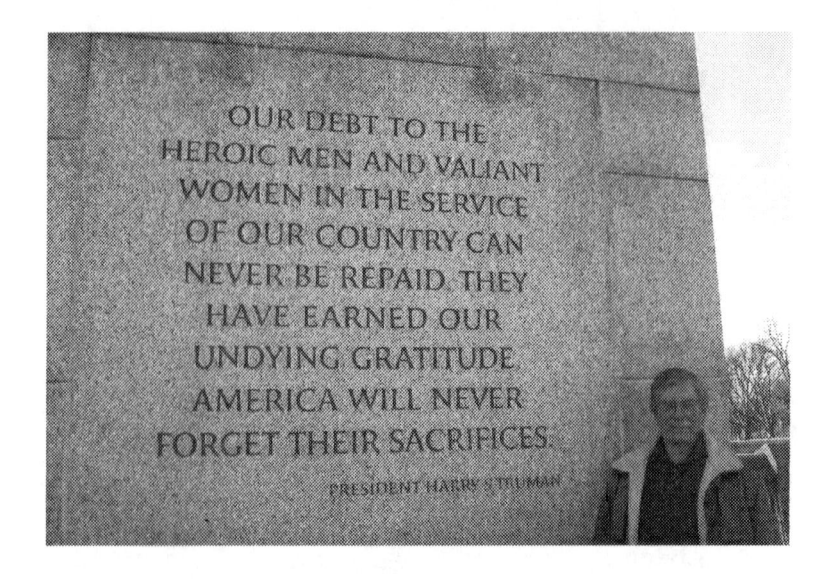

Morris Rosen
World War II Memorial, Washington D.C.
December 2007

Morris Rosen
World War II Memorial, Washington D.C.
December 2007

Left: Morris Rosen, age 84
Right: Julie Posner, age 88
March 2009